Interpretable Machine Learning for Heart Disease Prediction

Lisa Mike

Contents

1 Introduction

The heart is a vital organ primarily responsible for circulating blood throughout the body. Nevertheless, cardiac risks are concerning as they might lead to several health issues. Heart disease, comprising ailments related to the heart, is a distinct medical condition affecting the circulatory system, ranging from arrhythmia to vascular problems [1]. Cardiovascular disease impairs the heart's normal functioning, resulting in the obstruction of blood arteries. This situation increases the risk of stroke, angina, heart attacks, and coronary artery infections, potentially threatening overall health, especially in older people. Healthcare practitioners use a patient's medical history in conjunction with evaluations of blood pressure, cholesterol, and glucose levels to diagnose cardiovascular disease. Advanced diagnostic tools such as ECGs, stress tests, X-rays, echocardiograms, angiography, radionuclide imaging, MRIs, and CT scans help in detecting cardiac diseases [2]. Lowering the risk of heart disease and curbing the increasing mortality rate largely relies on accurate diagnosis and the implementation of appropriate treatments. Beyond the investigations and assessments performed by physicians and healthcare professionals, determining heart disease is a complex and detailed process.

The above-mentioned problems and challenges are reported in this chapter as follows. Section 1.1 specifies the motivation and the problem statement, whereas the research challenges and objectives are mentioned in Sections 1.2 and 1.3, respectively. The proposed contributions are defined in Section 1.4. Finally, the thesis outline and the dissemination of this research study are discussed and summarized in Sections 1.5 and 1.6, respectively.

1.1 Motivations and Problem Statement

Heart disease (HD), referred to as cardiovascular disease (CVD) or coronary artery disease (CAD), is the foremost cause of mortality worldwide and continues to be a significant issue in the medical domain. Cardiovascular diseases have a considerable impact on health and the economy [3]. In today's society, heart disease is the primary cause of death, largely due to sudden strokes and heart attacks (myocardial infarctions) [4]. According to the World Health Organization (WHO), heart attacks and strokes accounted for 32% of all cardiovascular-related deaths in 2019, leading to approximately 17.9 million fatalities worldwide [5]. Current statistics reveal that around 20.5 million individuals succumb to cardiovascular disease each year, with forecasts indicating an increase to 24.2 million by 2030 [6]. Approximately 80% of fatalities attributed to cardiovascular diseases occur in low- and middle-income countries (*LMIC*s), imposing considerable financial strain on their already burdened healthcare systems [7], [8]. In 2016, the American Heart Association (AHA) reported that heart disease impacted 121.5 million American adults and accounted for over 647,000 annual fatalities, establishing it as the foremost cause of mortality in the United States [9]. Data reveal that one in four deaths in the U.S. is due to cardiac conditions. The AHA also indicates that 26% of women face a high risk of mortality within a year after a heart attack, compared to 19% of males [10]. Consequently, early identification of cardiac disease can diminish the likelihood of the condition advancing to a more severe state by facilitating effective treatment. Timely and accurate diagnosis and prognosis of cardiac conditions are crucial for improving patient survival rates. From the Indian viewpoint, cardiovascular diseases, encompassing heart attacks and strokes, are the primary cause of mortality, with incidence rates growing rapidly. Data from India's Ministry of Health and Family Welfare indicates that CVD constitutes 28.1% to 30% of all deaths [11]. In 2023, the Indian Council of Medical Research (*ICMR*) reported that 4.77 million fatalities are ascribed to CVD [12]. Nearly 1 in 4 CVD deaths in India occur in people under 70, which is significantly higher than global averages. The incidence of heart disease in India has nearly doubled over the past 25 years, disproportionately impacting younger demographics. India possesses one of the highest mortality rates from heart disease globally, accompanied by a concerning trend of premature deaths among younger persons. It signifies a combination of lifestyle-associated risk factors and deficiencies within the healthcare system. According to this statistical outcome, precise and consistent prognosis and treatment of cardiac disease are crucial for its prevention, consequently optimizing the utilization of medical resources. Consequently, the prompt identification of cardiovascular illness is crucial to reducing the mortality rate.

Heart disease poses a massive economic burden globally, with costs exceeding $100 billion and projected to surpass $1 trillion by 2035 [13]. In the U.S. alone, annual spending reached over $229 billion (2017–2018) [14], averaging $1 billion daily [15]. In India, heart-related illnesses cost $237 billion between 2005 and 2015, according to WHO estimates [16]. In India, direct treatment expenditures for heart disease include hospitalization, surgical procedures, medications, and diagnostic services. According to a 2023 report by the Public Health Foundation of India, these costs exceed USD 24 billion annually. More than 60% of Indian households encounter catastrophic health expenditures when a family member experiences a cardiac episode. Hence, heart disease in India poses a significant public health and economic challenge, particularly because of its early onset and high treatment costs. Addressing this burden requires comprehensive and multifaceted intervention strategies. Under these circumstances, worldwide standards emphatically advocate for measures designed to avert the advancement of HD. Consequently, reducing the treatment costs for heart disease has become critically important.

Accurate diagnosis and appropriate treatment of heart disease are essential for lowering mortality rates and reducing overall risk. The condition may be diagnosed invasively, which is a costly, time-consuming, and painful process. Consequently, a less expensive, non-invasive cardiac disease diagnosis system is the need of the hour. To meet the above

challenges, a quick and affordable decision support system can be developed by analysing clinical data. These types of systems can help medical professionals to identify an illness early on. Machine learning is playing an increasingly vital role in the early detection of diseases. By identifying patterns within observational data, it enables informed decision-making and accurate predictions from new and unseen data. Many researchers from diverse disciplines have been investigating this issue over the last few decades. Determining the likelihood of a patient receiving a heart disease diagnosis has garnered attention again due to recent advancements in machine learning [17]. One effective approach to optimizing and improving machine learning prediction performance is the use of ensemble learning techniques [18]. An ensemble classifier combines multiple individual classifiers using methods such as stacking, bagging, boosting, or voting to aggregate or average their predictions for improved accuracy. Ensemble classifiers frequently outperform traditional classifiers, according to many researchers, like [19], [20], [21]. In homogeneous ensemble learning, all members use the same base algorithm, though their composition may differ. In contrast, diverse ensembles consist of members with different underlying learning algorithms.
This kind of decision support system can be transformed into a medical chatbot. These types of chatbots may be used by the patient on their own to identify cardiac problems in the early stages. A chatbot can accept some clinical data as input and provide patients with recommendations based on that data. Nonetheless, to guarantee dependability and safety, these medical chatbots need to be subject to the laws. As a result, to reduce safety risks, risk management actions may be implemented. Thus, a decision-support system can address these challenges by efficiently detecting heart disease risk at an early stage, helping reduce mortality.

In general, heart disorders, also known as CVDs, encompass a range of conditions affecting the heart and blood vessels. They are generally classified into five main types: Coronary Heart Disease (CHD)/Coronary Artery Disease (CAD), Congenital Heart Disease, Heart Valve Disease/Rheumatic Heart Disease (RHD), Cerebrovascular Disease, and Abnormal Heart Rhythms (AHR)/Arrhythmias [22]. There are various subtypes of heart disorders, often overlapping with heart disease [23].

- *Coronary Heart Disease (CHD): Damage or blockage of the major blood vessels supplying the heart, often due to plaque build-up or infection [24].*
- *Rheumatic Heart Disease (RHD): Damage to the heart valves and muscle resulting from rheumatic fever, which is triggered by a streptococcal bacterial infection [25].*
- *Cerebrovascular Disease: A disease of the blood vessels supplying the brain [26].*
- *Heart Arrhythmia: Irregular heartbeats [27].*
- *Coronary Artery Disease (CAD)/Ischaemic Heart Disease (IHD): Narrowing or blockage of the coronary arteries due to plaque build-up, leading to reduced blood flow to the heart. [28].*
- *Congestive Heart Failure (CHF) / Heart Failure: A condition where the heart is*

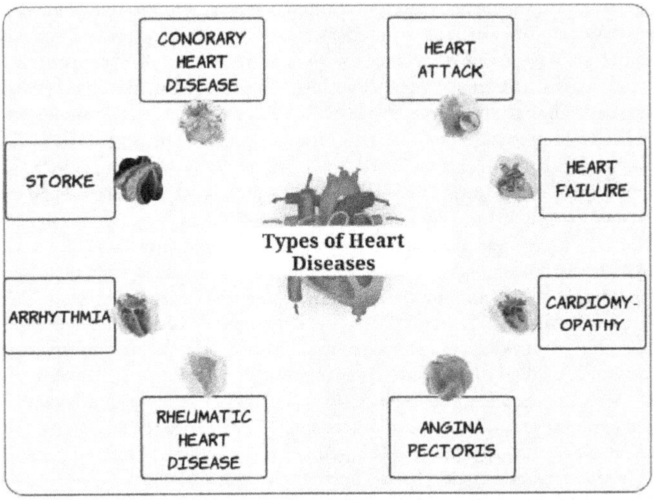

Figure 1.1: The Different Types of Heart Disorders.

unable to pump blood effectively, leading to fluid build-up in the lungs and other tissues. [29].

- *Hypertensive Heart Disease: Heart conditions resulting from prolonged high blood pressure [30].*
- *Inflammatory Heart Disease: Heart conditions caused by bacterial or viral infections that lead to inflammation of the heart tissues [31].*
- *Congenital Heart Disease: Structural abnormalities of the heart present at birth [32].*

Heart attacks and strokes are typically sudden events caused by blockages that restrict blood flow to the heart or brain, often due to fatty deposits in blood vessels. Strokes may also result from brain haemorrhages or blood clots. Other heart diseases include arrhythmias, valve disorders, cardiomyopathies, infections, vascular diseases, and congenital defects [33], as shown in Fig. 1.1.

Among the different types of heart disorders, CHD is the most prevalent and is responsible for the majority of global CVD-related deaths, accounting for four out of every five fatalities [34]. CHD is the predominant type of cardiovascular disease, responsible for

roughly 13% of fatalities in the United States [35]. In India, CHD accounts for 25–30% of all deaths and is estimated to cause 2.5 million per year [36]. Prompt diagnosis of heart disease is essential for mitigating health risks and averting cardiac arrests. A study by the American Heart Association anticipates nearly a 100% rise in CHD cases by 2030 [37]. Accurate diagnosis and timely therapeutic intervention are crucial to preventing severe outcomes, depending on the specific type of heart disease. Different forms of heart disease may manifest through symptoms such as dizziness, syncope, arrhythmia, and shortness of breath. Among these, CHD, also referred to as CAD, is the most fatal and poses significant challenges for prevention, even in otherwise healthy individuals. Among numerous critical diseases, CHD accounts for a substantial proportion of the high mortality rate. This condition demands urgent attention, as arterial blockages can severely restrict blood flow to the heart or brain, potentially leading to heart attacks or strokes. In addition, diseases that predispose individuals to arrhythmias result in abnormal heart rhythms due to underlying damage to cardiac tissue. This mortality rate and the future risk of CHD can be minimized by using a decision-making system early. The advanced machine learning approach based on the ensemble method can be an alternative prediction approach for the early diagnosis of CHD. Also, the deep learning methodology utilising artificial neural networks can be employed to optimise and attain the most accurate performance results.
Prompt and precise detection of cardiovascular illness is crucial for enhancing survival rates. Key risk factors include obesity, ageing, physical inactivity, high blood pressure, high cholesterol, and smoking [38]. Early detection and lifestyle changes, such as increased exercise, quitting smoking, and regular check-ups, can significantly reduce mortality. To diagnose cardiovascular conditions, healthcare providers use various screening methods – blood pressure checks, glucose and cholesterol tests, ECGs, ultrasounds, CT scans, echocardiograms, coronary angiography, calcium scoring, and stress tests. While coronary angiography is highly accurate, it is costly and carries risks, making heart disease diagnosis more complex. Moreover, these screening processes are time-consuming and heavily reliant on manual inputs.
Although heart disease can be deadly, it can be prevented with a healthy lifestyle that encompasses regular exercise, meditation, a balanced diet, and other beneficial practices. Determining the underlying causes of heart disorders is accordingly crucial due to the many risk factors. Accordingly, an effective and targeted treatment strategy can be formulated. Consequently, identifying the underlying causes of heart disorders and developing a reliable system for accurate heart disease diagnosis are critically important. Such a condition cannot be diagnosed using conventional methods; instead, a feature selection-based medical diagnostic system can be established to forecast and assess the illness. Heart disease risk factors can be analyzed by considering the features in Fig. 1.2.

Coronary angiograms, however, are costly and entail considerable risks of complications, complicating the diagnosis of heart disease [39]. Cardiovascular specialists encounter the challenging responsibility of assessing multiple risk factors to produce an appropriate diagnosis. This challenge has driven the development of non-invasive methods for diagnosing heart failure. Presently, the diagnosis of heart disease predominantly depends on clinicians evaluating a patient's medical history, symptoms, and test outcomes. This method achieves

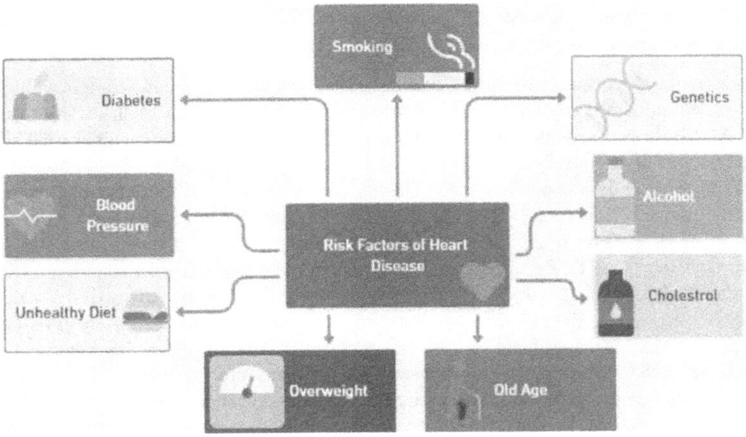

Figure 1.2: The Risk Factors of Heart Disease.

an accuracy of roughly 67% by correlating current symptoms with historical cases [40]. Machine learning is essential for detecting illness risk factors and enhancing predictive systems. By leveraging large datasets, ML can model complex, non-linear relationships to reduce prediction errors [23], [41]. Through pattern analysis, ML can accurately forecast outcomes for new data. Classification, a form of supervised learning, is very efficient in identifying diseases when trained on high-quality data. Prompt and precise prediction of cardiac disease is essential for enhancing survival rates, prompting research aimed at creating decision-support systems that facilitate early detection and cost-effective treatment, particularly in areas of poverty.

An integral component of machine learning and pattern recognition is the feature extraction or selection process. However, because digital medical data is unstructured and constantly grows in bulk, it is very challenging to extract meaningful risk factors for heart disease from electronic diagnostic tests. Using a smart system is one obvious way to reduce computing costs and improve classification efficiency. Feature selection methods allow for this. One of the main issues in data mining and machine learning is finding an appropriate representation of the data from all features. Not every original characteristic works well for problems involving regression or classification. A portion of the features in the dataset's distribution are noisy, superfluous, or unimportant. The performance of classification may be lowered by this feature. The feature selection procedure should be applied to find out the most important factors that contribute to classification or regression issues. These approaches can improve the classification performance and lower the classifier's computing cost. ML and DL are essential for the precise detection and classification of contemporary healthcare issues. Forecasting cardiac disease continues to be a substantial issue in medicine, frequently necessitating much time and expertise. This study aims to create an AI-driven heart disease prediction system utilising sophisticated machine learning and deep learning methodologies to enhance diagnostic accuracy.

Determining the presence of cardiac disease in an individual is frequently complicated and time-consuming for physicians and healthcare practitioners. However, with advancements in AI, ML-based prediction systems offer a promising alternative for the timely and efficient detection of heart disease. Various ML classifiers have been developed and are now widely used for disease prediction. Commonly used supervised ML models are developed using Logistic Regression (LR), Support Vector Machine (SVM), K-Nearest Neighbours (KNN), Naïve Bayes (NB), Linear Discriminant Analysis (LDA), Classification and Regression Tree (CART), Decision Tree (DT), Random Forest (RF), Gradient Boosting (GB), LightGBM (LGBM), CatBoost (CB), Histogram-based Gradient Boosting (HGB), Adaptive Boosting (AB), Extreme Gradient Boosting (XGB), Extra Trees (ET), Multi-layer Perceptrons (MLP), and Artificial Neural Network (ANN). Additionally, advanced ensemble methods such as stacking, bagging, boosting, and voting can further enhance heart disease prediction. Feature selection strategies are utilised to discover and assess the most relevant risk factors influencing heart disease, accordingly enhancing model performance. These selected features are then used to build predictive models for assessing disease risk.

Model effectiveness is typically evaluated using performance metrics such as accuracy (Ac), precision (Pr), recall (Re), F1-score (Fs), Cohen's kappa score (Cks), k-fold cross-validation mean accuracy (Ma), ROC-AUC score (Ra), and standard deviation (Sd). While many existing approaches focus solely on optimizing a single objective, such as accuracy, it is crucial to consider multiple conflicting objectives – like sensitivity, specificity, precision, F1-score, and minimizing false negatives (FN). Consequently, developing an automated and reliable heart disease prediction system is one of the most vital and difficult challenges in healthcare.

1.2 Research Challenges

Developing an efficient heart disease risk prediction model has numerous challenges. Medical datasets frequently exhibit imbalance, featuring a lower incidence of genuine heart disease patients relative to healthy persons. Feature redundancy or irrelevance can diminish model accuracy if not adequately addressed. Deep learning models, despite their potency, frequently exhibit a deficiency in interpretability, complicating their clinical adoption. Ultimately, guaranteeing that models exhibit robust generalization across diverse populations and datasets continues to be a significant issue in practical implementation. Furthermore, although artificial neural networks may identify intricate non-linear patterns, they are frequently regarded as "black-box" models, rendering them challenging to interpret in clinical settings. Addressing these difficulties is essential to ensure the practical application and reliability of the proposed framework.

Consequently, the development of a comprehensive heart disease risk prediction framework that incorporates classical machine learning, ensemble learning, feature selection, and ANNs approaches poses many significant research challenges:

1. **Imbalanced Target Class Distribution:** Medical datasets frequently exhibit a disproportionate abundance of records on non-diseased persons compared to those diagnosed with cardiac disease. This class imbalance may result in biased models that excel in the majority class while inadequately identifying genuine danger cases, thus diminishing clinical value.

2. **Feature Redundancy and Irrelevance:** Raw clinical and demographic data often contain redundant, noisy, or irrelevant features. Inadequate feature selection, such as attributes, can dilute the model's ability to learn meaningful patterns, lead to overfitting, and increase computational cost.

3. **Optimal Feature Selection:** Choosing the appropriate selection of features presents both technical and clinical difficulties. Although statistical and wrapper-based techniques facilitate dimensionality reduction, achieving a balance between accuracy and interpretability is intricate. Feature selection can be compatible with both conventional machine learning models and neural networks.

4. **Model Overfitting and Generalization:** High-capacity models like ANNs and ensemble approaches overfit on little or noisy datasets. These models can be generalize well to unseen patient data for real-world application.

5. **Interpretability of Prediction Models:** Although classical machine learning models offer a degree of interpretability, ensemble methods and ANNs are often black boxes. Clinical decision-making requires both great precision and transparency, as well as faith in the rationale behind predictions.

6. **Dataset Limitations:** Public datasets on cardiac illness, such as UCI Cleveland and Statlog, may exhibit limitations in size, recency, or diversity. This limits the extent of model training and may impact generalization to contemporary, real-world patient demographics. Access to superior, annotated clinical data remains constrained.

7. **Integration of Heterogeneous Learning Methods:** Creating a cohesive framework that harnesses the advantages of classical ML, ensemble learning, and ANNs necessitates meticulous integration. The difficulty resides in determining how to integrate predictions or features from these methods cohesively and efficiently.

8. **Computational Complexity:** Ensemble learning and deep learning models frequently need significant computational resources, particularly during hyperparameter optimization, cross-validation, and feature selection. As the number of data and models escalates, the efficiency of training and evaluation becomes increasingly problematic.

9. **Lack of Standardization in Evaluation:** A universal consensus of the optimal evaluation metric (e.g., accuracy, AUC, F1-score) for heart disease prediction is lacking. Selecting suitable metrics and validation techniques (e.g., k-fold cross-validation, stratified sampling) is essential for equitable performance evaluation.

Overcoming these challenges is difficult for practical and reliable real-world applications.

In summary, the key challenges include achieving high accuracy and interpretability. Also, it involves ensuring data quality, effectively handling class imbalance, identifying optimal risk factors, optimizing ANN models, and integrating multiple predictive approaches.

1.3 Research Objectives

The research aims to effectively address the identified challenges in developing an HD risk prediction framework using classical machine learning, ensemble learning, feature selection, and ANN-based approaches. The research objectives are formulated to align with both technical solutions and practical implications. The primary objective of this study is to design an advanced framework for HD risk prediction by leveraging state-of-the-art machine learning and deep learning techniques. The specific objectives are outlined as follows:

(a) To develop and evaluate state-of-the-art predictive models utilizing classical machine learning, ensemble learning, feature importance, and ANN approaches for precise HD risk assessment.

(b) To address target class data imbalance using resampling techniques such as SMOTE, SMOTETomek, hybrid methods like SMOTEENN, or a novel hybrid sampling method for balanced model training.

(c) To implement sophisticated feature selection methodologies (Boruta or BorutaShap, mutual information gain, recursive feature elimination, Fisher score, chi-square, Lasso, etc.) to remove redundant features and improve model efficacy. Also, integrate interpretable models or explanation techniques through the utilization of XAI methods like SHAP and LIME to enhance transparency and trust in feature importance predictions.

(d) To reduce overfitting and improve generalization, the proposed prediction framework incorporates regularization techniques such as dropout, learning rate adjustment, parameter tuning, ANN model optimization, k-fold cross-validation, and hyperparameter tuning.

(e) To assess model performance thoroughly, utilize several measures like accuracy, precision, recall, F1-score, Cohen-kappa score, standard deviation, ROC-AUC score, k-fold mean accuracy, and rigorous validation methodologies. To develop a cohesive predictive framework that integrates the advantages of many learning methodologies to trade-offs among them, while ensuring computational efficiency.

Developing an alternative decision-making support system can effectively address these challenges. Such a system aims to reduce the mortality rate, minimize treatment costs, and shorten the time required for the early prediction of HD and CHD risk. Also, the risk factors of HD can be assessed and forecast by applying feature selection methods. All the above-mentioned objectives are defined in line with the current technological advancements and challenges.

1.4 Research Contributions

This dissertation aims to develop an HD risk prediction framework using ML classifiers, ensemble methods, feature selection, and deep learning-based neural networks. The proposed framework is aligned with the defined challenges and research objectives. The graphical abstract of the contributions is presented in Fig. 1.3. The effective contributions of this research are highlighted by novelty, impact, and the improvement of the framework and efficiency of the risk prediction model as below:

(a) **Development of a Hybrid Prediction Framework:** To develop an integrated heart disease risk prediction framework that combines classical machine learning, ensemble learning, and optimized hyperparameter tuning techniques. This approach aims to improve diagnostic accuracy, model robustness, and generalization across diverse clinical datasets. In this context, a hyperparameter-tuned dual-stage stacking ensemble method is proposed, following the selection of the best-performing classifiers. The *k-fold cross-validation*, *GridSearchCV*, *RandomizedSearchCV*, and *regularization* techniques are employed to improve model generalization. To further mitigate overfitting and assess generalization, the framework is evaluated on a low-instance dataset, demonstrating stability and robustness.

(b) **CHD risk prediction frameworks based on ensemble learning and the optimized fine-tuned ANN model:** An ensemble-based voting classifier using boosting models is initially proposed for CHD risk prediction. To further improve accuracy, a customized and fine-tuned ANN model is developed. This ANN architecture is optimized using algorithms like Adam, SGD, RMSProp, and AdaDelta, with careful tuning of parameters such as learning rate, epochs, batch size, hidden layers, dropout, neurones per layer, and momentum. Additionally, activation functions like ReLU and LeakyReLU are evaluated to enhance network performance.

(c) **Handling of Class Imbalance:** To address target class data imbalance, resampling strategies such as SMOTE, SMOTETomek, and SMOTEENN are employed to improve model fairness and sensitivity. In addition, a novel two-stage sampling approach is proposed, combining hybrid techniques sequentially to balance class distribution and remove noisy data.

(d) **Integration of Feature Selection Methods and Interpretability using XAI:** To determine heart disease risk factors, an important feature set is derived by utilizing and evaluating advanced feature selection methods, such as BorutaShap, Recursive Feature Elimination (RFE), Mutual Information Gain, Lasso, and Fisher Score. These methods aim to enhance model interpretability, reduce dimensionality, and improve predictive efficacy. Also, the feature importance model outcomes are interpreted by incorporating interpretability techniques, SHAP and LIME, to make the prediction model performance more transparent and clinically acceptable.

(e) **Performance Optimization through Regularization Techniques:** The in-hospital mortality of heart failure patients has been assessed. Risk factors associated with this outcome have been determined using automatic feature selection techniques based on regularization methods to support future heart disease risk prediction. The Lasso (L1) and Ridge (L2) regression methods are tuned by optimizing the regularization hyperparameter alpha (α) for the future risk of heart disease prediction.

(f) **Comparative Analysis of Learning Models:** Finally, for each prediction approach based on the proposed methods, an extensive comparison of traditional ML, ensemble techniques, and the ANN model is conducted across multiple evaluation metrics, highlighting strengths and trade-offs.

The above contributions mitigate key challenges and address the research objectives for heart disease risk prediction models. These contributions are presented step by step across the subsequent chapters, with detailed discussions of each methodology provided in the following sections.

1.5 Thesis Outline

The thesis is organized into seven chapters. The brief descriptions of the chapters are provided as follows:

Chapter 1: Introduction

Chapter 1 primarily focuses on the motivation and problem statements related to the development of heart disease risk prediction frameworks using advanced machine learning and deep learning approaches. Also, the research challenges have been identified in the context of recent technological advancements. Moreover, the objectives of this research study have been determined to mitigate the challenges. To fulfil the objectives, the contribution has been made accordingly by employing the cutting-edge techniques and the state-of-the-art methodologies.

Chapter 2: Background and Related Work

Chapter 2 presents a comprehensive study on various approaches for heart disease prediction, their applications, and performance analysis of the *SOTA* methods. The requisite background study is also reported.

Chapter 3: Dual-Stage Hyperparameter-tuned Ensemble Learning Approach

Chapter 3 proposes an efficient computational risk prediction framework for the HD. It works based on a dual-stage hyperparameter-tuned meta-ensemble stacking approach. To enhance model generalization and combat overfitting, optimization methods – GridSearchCV and RandomizedSearchCV and cross-validation – are employed on two datasets. In addition, advanced sampling techniques are applied to handle the class imbalance problem.

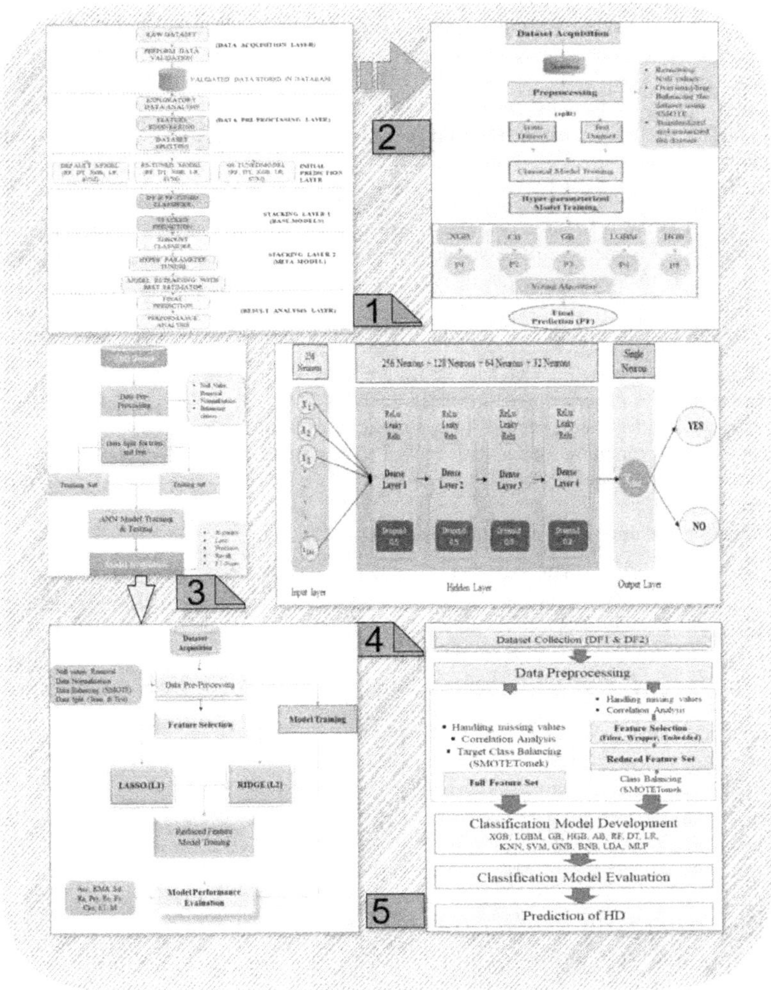

Figure 1.3: Graphical abstract of chapter-wise contributions

Chapter 4: Risk Prediction Framework for Coronary Heart Disease

Chapter 4 presents a prediction framework for the early assessment of the risk of coronary heart disease using a boosting classifier-based voting ensemble learning method. Following this, an alternative deep learning-based ANN approach for better performance was reported.

Chapter 5: Assessment of Risk Factors for Mortality Prediction in Heart Failure Patients

Chapter 5 presents an in-hospital mortality risk prediction model for heart failure patients admitted to the ICU based on the automatic feature selection method of regularization techniques. For the future assessment of heart disease due to heart failure, the risk factors can be determined effectively using regularization methods.

Chapter 6: Interpretable HDP Framework with Feature Selection and XAI

Chapter 6 proposes a comprehensive feature influence heart disease risk factors model based on filter, wrapper, and embedded methods. The risk factors are determined and assessed by considering the real-time hospital dataset for the model generalization, and an advanced sampling technique is applied to address class imbalance challenges. The model's interpretability is facilitated by employing the XAI tools such as SHAP and LIME.

Chapter 7: Conclusion and Future Scope

Finally, *Chapter 7* concludes the thesis with a summary of the entire research work and key findings. Also, it presents the comparative results obtained and also highlights the directions of future scope concerning the other challenges considered in this dissertation.

1.6 Dissemination of this Research

To fulfil the research objectives outlined in the previous section, each objective is addressed individually through publications in reputed journals and conferences. Chapter 3 has been covered by publishing one journal article corresponding to developing a hybrid prediction model for HD. Also, Chapter 4 addressed the CHD risk prediction framework by contributing one conference and one journal article that have already been published. Moreover, one conference paper has been published to fulfil the objective of Chapter 5 by contributing to the risk factor of heart failure patients' in-hospital mortality. Finally, one journal paper has been communicated related to Chapter 6 for determining the risk factor of HD utilizing the feature importance methods. Chapter 2 presents a comprehensive survey of heart disease prediction approaches. It covers recent applications, advanced techniques, commonly used methods and datasets, identifies key challenges, and highlights the existing research gaps. The related contributions have been published in a high-quality Springer Nature journal. The detailed publication is provided below for dissemination.

List of Publications in journals

1. **S. Mondal**, R. Maity, Y. Omo, S. Ghosh, and A. Nag, "An Efficient Computational Risk Prediction Model of Heart Diseases Based on Dual-Stage Stacked Machine Learning Approaches," IEEE Access, vol. 12, pp. 7255-7270, 2024, https://doi.org/10.1109/ACCESS.2024.3350996, https://ieeexplore.ieee.org/document/10382495.

2. **S. Mondal**, R. Maity, A. Nag; "An efficient artificial neural network-based optimization technique for the early prediction of coronary heart disease: comprehensive analysis," Scientific Reports, Nature, 15, 4827 (2025), https://doi.org/10.1038/s41598-025-85765-x, https://www.nature.com/articles/s41598-025-85765-x.

3. **S. Mondal**, R. Maity, A. Nag; "A Comprehensive Survey of Heart Disease Prediction Approaches: Methods, Applications, Performance Analysis, Datasets, Research Challenges, and Future Scopes." Archives of Computational Methods in Engineering (2025), Springer Nature, https://doi.org/10.1007/s11831-025-10438-x, https://link.springer.com/article/10.1007/s11831-025-10438-x.

4. **S. Mondal**, R. Maity, A. Nag; Fetal health risk prediction using ensemble-based machine learning approaches. Knowledge and Information Systems (2025), Springer Nature, https://doi.org/10.1007/s10115-025-02442-1, https://link.springer.com/article/10.1007/s10115-025-02442-1.

5. **S. Mondal**, R. Maity, A. Nag; "An Efficient Feature Influence Heart Disease Prediction Model based on Feature Selection Techniques: A Comprehensive Analysis" (communicated and under review).

List of Publications in Conference

1. **S. Mondal**, R. Maity, Y. R. Singh, S. Ghosh, and A. Nag, "Early Prediction of Coronary Heart Disease using Boosting-based Voting Ensemble Learning," 2022 IEEE Bombay Section Signature Conference (IBSSC), Mumbai, India, 2022, pp. 1-5, https://doi.org/10.1109/IBSSC56953.2022.10037445, https://ieeexplore.ieee.org/document/10037445.

2. **S. Mondal**, R. Maity, and A. Nag, "Heart Failure Patients In-Hospital Mortality Risk Prediction Models Based on Regularization Techniques—Comprehensive Analysis," 2024 IEEE International Conference on Electronics, Computing and Communication Technologies (CONECCT), Bangalore, India, 2024, pp. 1-6, https://doi.org/10.1109/CONECCT62155.2024.10677219, https://ieeexplore.ieee.org/document/10677219.

3. **S. Mondal**, R. Maity, C. Rai, S. Pramanik, and A. Nag, "Lung Cancer Risk Prediction Features Influence Model Based on Machine Learning Techniques," TENCON 2023 - 2023 IEEE Region 10 Conference (TENCON), Chiang Mai, Thailand, 2023, pp. 1339-1344, https://ieeexplore.ieee.org/document/10322343 https://doi.org/10.1109/TENCON58879.2023.10322343.

4. **S. Mondal**, Rai, C., Roy, S., Agarwal, A., Maity, R. (2025). An Intelligence Dual-Stage Heart Arrhythmia Prediction Framework Using Machine Learning Methods. In: Long, N.H., Tavares, J.M.R.S., Pal, S., Son, L.H., Thai Pham, B., Proceedings of the Third International Conference on Intelligent Systems. ICISS 2024. Algorithms for Intelligent Systems. Springer, Singapore, https://doi.org/10.1007/978-981-96-4093-5_38, https://link.springer.com/chapter/10.1007/978-981-96-4093-5_38.

2

Background and Related Work

Cardiovascular disease remains a leading global health challenge, exacerbated by rising disease prevalence, ageing populations, and increased healthcare demands. Traditional diagnostic methods, such as electrocardiograms (ECGs), echocardiograms (ECHO), and coronary angiography (CAG-CT), can be costly, invasive, or unreliable. On the other hand, physician-based diagnosis may be subjective in nature. Consequently, there is a need for accurate, non-invasive, and real-time diagnostic solutions. Machine learning and deep learning can offer transformative tools for developing intelligent healthcare systems that enable early detection, remote monitoring, and effective intervention for CVD. These AI-driven systems support disease diagnosis, classification, prediction, and treatment. As a result, it helps to reduce mortality and healthcare costs. Over the recent decades, ML and DL have played a pivotal role in advancing automated decision-support systems for heart disease prediction and management.

This chapter aims to review the existing methods and technological advancements in heart disease prediction, focusing on state-of-the-art (SOTA) machine learning and deep learning approaches. It evaluates individual and ensemble models, feature importance, and early detection techniques. Additionally, it highlights key challenges and proposes potential solutions. Moreover, it also identifies commonly used datasets and outlines future research directions to support the development of accurate and efficient heart disease prediction models.

The organization of this chapter is as follows: Section 2.1 discusses the objective and contributions. Chapter highlights, article search strategies, and search criteria are discussed in Sections 2.2, 2.3, and 2.4, respectively. Different methods, applications, performance analysis, and challenges with future scope based on machine learning 2.5, ensemble learning 2.6, deep learning 2.7, and feature selection 2.8 are discussed in the next four sections sequentially. Finally, Section 2.9 presents the available open-source datasets, followed by a discussion of performance metrics in Section 2.10. Methods for handling class imbalance are detailed in Section 2.11, and the chapter concludes with a summary of key findings in Section 2.12.

2.1 Objectives and Contributions

The high mortality, treatment costs, and global impact of heart disease underscore the urgent need for advanced predictive methods. This section reviews recent developments in ML and DL for cardiovascular disease prediction, focusing on decision-support systems, feature selection, performance metrics, and publicly available datasets. It also highlights non-invasive diagnostic approaches, categorizes existing methodologies, analyses their effectiveness, and identifies research gaps and future directions.

The main contributions of this chapter are outlined below.

1. To categorize different non-invasive prediction approaches for heart disease decision-support systems. These approaches are based on recent advancements in machine learning classifiers, ensemble learning, feature selection, and deep learning methodologies.
2. To encompass the brief overviews of each approach's current methods, mechanisms, challenges, and their implications for cardiovascular disease.
3. To investigate the recent SOTA applications in this field and summarize the observable performance accuracy concerning the collected datasets and methodology for further improvement.
4. To identify the open challenges of each approach and determine the research gap concerning the recent technological advancement.
5. To identify the available heart disease-related datasets mostly used by the researchers and their risk factors.

2.2 Highlights

This section offers a thorough overview of heart disease prediction (HDP), detailing its distinct objectives and observations. Also, the different approaches of the HDP model are done between machine learning (ML), ensemble learning (EL), feature selection (FS) methods, artificial neural network (ANN) models, and other deep learning (DL) models for the alternative HDP decision-making support system. Furthermore, it offers a detailed explanation of the models and methodologies employed for prediction, as well as the assessment criteria and datasets utilized in their contributions. Ultimately, the prior investigations failed to emphasize the study deficiencies in the previously presented automated strategies for HDP. This study presents recent research gaps in various HDP models along with their related solutions.
The entire literature survey on heart disease prediction and classification using machine learning and deep learning approaches is divided into four categories. The first category includes research articles on classical machine learning classifier-based prediction models, which are used to identify research gaps in the first phase. The second category includes advanced machine learning methods and ensemble learning-based approaches such

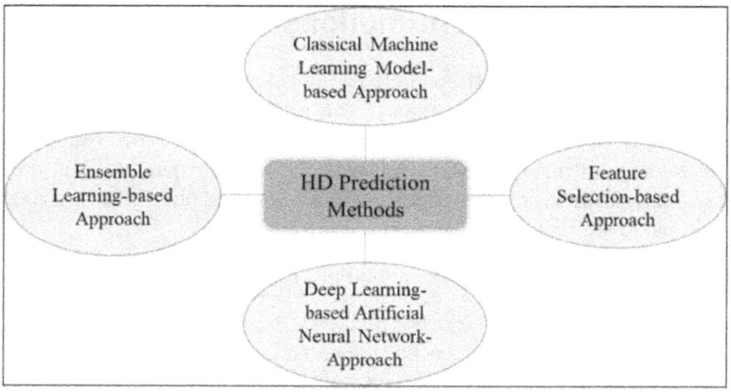

Figure 2.1: The approaches of HD prediction methods are considered in this research.

as stacking, bagging, voting, and boosting techniques, which combine the performance of individual classical classifiers to improve prediction accuracy. The third approach falls into the deep learning approach based on artificial neural networks and their optimization technique-based prediction of heart disease. The risk factors for heart disease prediction using feature importance techniques, known as feature selection-based approaches, are combined into a fourth category, article selection. After conducting a literature review, the research gaps are identified in each phase of the study to define the specific research objective. The following approaches are discussed in the subsection below and pictured in Fig. 2.1.

(a) **Classical Machine Learning Model Approach**

(b) **Ensemble Learning Approach**

(c) **Deep Learning-based ANN Approach**

(d) **Feature Selection Approach**

2.3 Article Search Strategy

The search was undertaken from 2019 to January 2025. The search utilizes the following electronic databases to locate research articles pertinent to ML and DL methodologies for HDP: Google Scholar, Springer, Science Direct, Nature, IEEE Xplore Digital Library, ACM Digital Library, Wiley Online Library, Taylor & Francis Online, and Elsevier. A preliminary investigation is conducted to refine the search string. We examine the collection of previously compiled research articles stored in the database that possess the highest citation counts and are the most relevant. In digital libraries, searches are conducted using carefully selected keywords based on combinations of relevant terms. The selected English-language publications, sourced from reputed journals and conferences, focus on advancements in ML and DL techniques for heart disease prediction. The initial search strategy was determined with the help of different keywords coupled with other keywords, depending on the research objectives, based on the defined approaches outlined in Table 2.1.

Table 2.1: Search Keywords for Heart Disease Prediction Approaches

Level-1 Keywords	Level-2 Keywords
Heart disease prediction/classification/detection/diagnosis	• based on machine learning • based on ensemble learning • based on feature selection methods • based on neural network models • based on deep learning
Cardiovascular disease prediction/classification/detection/diagnosis	• based on machine learning • based on ensemble learning • based on feature selection methods • based on neural network models • based on deep learning
Intelligent system to diagnose heart disease, Decision support system for heart disease diagnosis, Automated heart disease diagnosis.	

This systematic review, conducted through a rigorous methodology, seeks to accomplish three objectives:

- To provide a reference for the current development of the ML and DL techniques applicable to high-dimensional data for the prediction of HD.
- To aid researchers in circumventing redundant efforts to determine the different prediction approaches.
- To facilitate the identification of research gaps in high-dimensional data using ML and DL methodologies and their challenges.

2.4 Article Selection Criteria

This review adopted a comprehensive search approach to identify all relevant literature. Specific keywords and subject headings related to HDP models, ML, DL, feature selection, and ANN were used, as guided by existing studies. To enhance comprehensiveness, both forward and backward citation searches were conducted. Duplicate elimination adhered to a rigorous methodology, integrating automated detection using EndNote and subsequent

manual validation. A keyword-based method was employed to facilitate a thorough and focused literature search. During the selection phase, only those research articles that can address the predetermined research questions were selected for further assessment. The selection criteria were promptly followed by an elimination method to eradicate redundancies and inconsistencies. At this stage, inconsequential research was excluded from consideration following an assessment of the paper's title, abstract, and full text.
Table 2.2 delineates the inclusion and exclusion criteria utilized for the selected literature. Fig. 2.2 illustrates the specific steps of this process, including the quantity of articles assessed at each level. Ultimately, a total of 58 articles were selected for primary research based on the complete text of the articles.

Table 2.2: Articles selection, inclusion, and exclusion criteria considered in this study

Inclusion Criteria (IC)	**Exclusion Criteria (EC)**
IC1: Article published between 2019 and Jan-2025 considering "Title" and "Abstract"	EC1: Exclude non-relevant articles like white papers, MSc. Thesis, Ph.D. dissertation, magazines, and written in other than English languages
IC2: The article is screened by specific "keywords" and "approaches" related to ML, EL, FS, ANN, and DL techniques in HDP	EC2: Articles do not focus on ML, DL, ANN, FS, and EL-related models, methods, and applications.
IC3: Final article categorized based on considered approaches and included only related discussed methods based on defined criteria.	EC3: Studies that do not focus on specific approaches.

2.5 HDP: Classical Machine Learning Model Approach

This section mainly considers the research articles related to conventional machine learning classifiers that are traditionally used for heart disease prediction. The individual ML model's experimental outcomes are analyzed with research articles that consider many well-known classifiers. The diversified machine learning classifiers can be categorized based on their underlying algorithms and approaches. The main categories include tree-based models like Decision Tree (DT), Random Forest (RF), and Extra Trees (ET); boosting-based models such as Adaptive Boosting (AB), Gradient Boosting (GB), eXtreme Gradient Boost (XGB), LightGBM (LGBM), CatBoost (CB), and Histogram-Based Gradient Boosting (HGB); linear-based algorithms like Logistic Regression (LR), Linear Discriminant Analysis (LDA), and Support Vector Machine (SVM) (with linear kernel); neighbour-based models, namely K-Nearest Neighbours (KNN) and Radius Neighbours Classifier (RN); and probabilistic models like Naïve Bayes (NB); and neural network based model like Multi-Layer Perceptrons (MLP), Radial Basis Function Network (RBFN), and ANN.

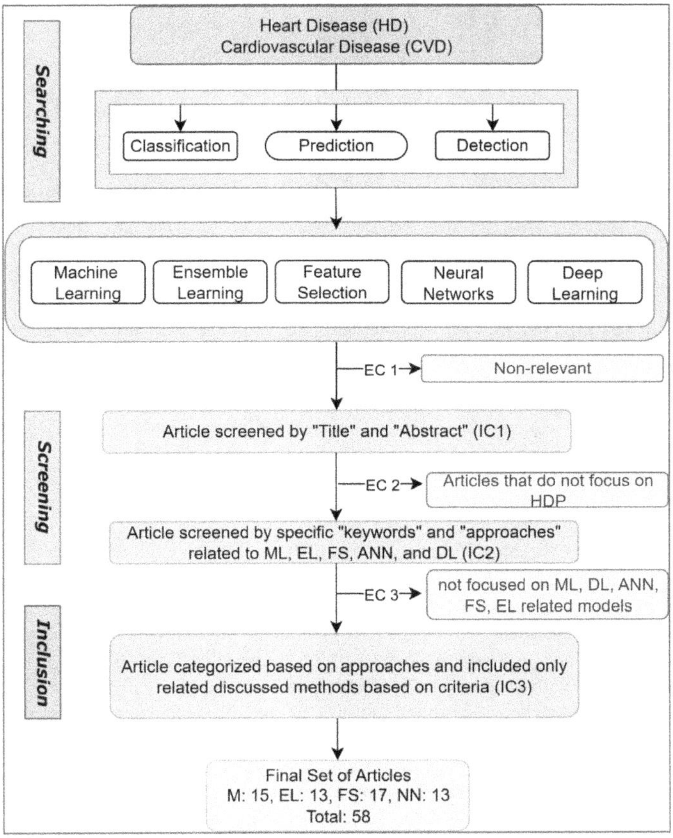

Figure 2.2: Flow diagram of the article search, screening, and selection

The observable classification models with their experimental performance in terms of accuracy are noted in this phase. Recently published journals and conferences from 2019 to 2025 were considered, with article selection based on reputable journals and well-established conference proceedings.
Some of the well-known classifiers are discussed below concerning the heart disease prediction purposes used by many researchers for the decision-making support system.

2.5.1 Decision Tree (DT)

DT is a supervised machine learning algorithm used for classification and regression. It models decisions in a tree-like structure, where internal nodes test attributes, branches represent outcomes, and leaves provide predictions. Built top-down, it recursively selects the best attributes using criteria like information gain, Gini impurity, and entropy. Algorithms such as ID3, C4.5, and CART are commonly used. Decision trees are easy to interpret, handle both numeric and categorical data, and don't require normalization. However, they can overfit and be biased toward attributes with many levels. The mathematical formulas for some of these necessary criteria are as follows in Eqs. 2.1, 2.2, and 2.3:

$$\text{Gini}(D) = 1 - \sum_{i=1}^{n} p_i^2 \quad (2.1)$$

$$H(D) = -\sum_{i=1}^{n} p_i \log(p_i) \quad (2.2)$$

$$IG = H(D) - \sum_{j} \frac{|D_j|}{|D|} H(D_j) \quad (2.3)$$

Where D is the dataset, what n is the number of classes, and what p_i is the proportion of instances in class i. The Gini Index measures the probability of a random sample being incorrectly labelled, while entropy measures the uncertainty in the dataset. High entropy can lead to poor model training, whereas a high Information Gain (IG) and low entropy indicate a model with good accuracy. Decision trees can be efficiently employed to identify cardiac disorders because of their intuitive and interpretable nature for categorization purposes. Splitting criteria such as Gini impurity and information gain enhance feature selection, while pruning mitigates overfitting, consequently boosting generalization. Performance evaluation guarantees reliability in medical diagnosis.

2.5.2 Random Forest (RF)

RF is an ensemble learning method that builds multiple decision trees on random data subsets and aggregates their outputs, typically by majority vote for classification. It offers high accuracy, handles large datasets well, and reduces overfitting compared to single decision trees. However, this comes at the cost of increased complexity and the need for more computational resources, as training and predicting with multiple decision trees require significant processing power. So, RF uses either the Gini Index or the Entropy (IG) to measure the probability of a random sample being mislabelled, defined as 2.1 and 2.2. Also, the IG can determine how much uncertainty is reduced according to 2.3.
These metrics help in refining the decision-making process within each tree, contributing to the overall accuracy of the RF model. It has a wide range of applications, including financial market predictions, such as stock market analysis and risk management; healthcare

for disease diagnosis and medical image analysis; marketing for customer segmentation and churn prediction; and fraud detection to identify fraudulent transactions. Despite its complexity, the RF algorithm is a powerful tool for making reliable predictions in various domains, thanks to its ensemble nature and the strategic use of multiple decision trees. Random Forest is an efficient classifier for heart disease detection because of its capacity to manage non-linearity, mitigate overfitting via bagging, and the interpretability by feature significance.
As a result, it is a popular ensemble learning algorithm that uses multiple decision trees for multi-class classification. It builds trees on random subsets of data and features and aggregates their scores. The importance of each node is measured using the Gini importance formula. This is achieved by assuming two child nodes, thereby forming a binary tree as defined by Eq. 2.4.

$$n_{i_j} = w_j C_j - w_{\text{left}(j)} C_{\text{left}(j)} - w_{\text{right}(j)} C_{\text{right}(j)} \tag{2.4}$$

In this case, n_{i_j} is the importance of node j, w_j indicates a weighted number of samples reaching node j, C_j is the impurity value of node j, $left(j)$ denotes the child node from the left split on node j, and $right(j)$ is the child node from the right split on node j. Then the importance for each node of a decision tree is further computed using the formula 2.5, where fi_i is the importance of the feature i.

$$fi_i = \frac{\sum_{j:\text{node } j \text{ splits on feature } i} n_{i_j}}{\sum_{k \in \text{all nodes}} n_{i_k}} \tag{2.5}$$

After that, it can be standardized with the help of the formula given in 2.6 and brought into a range of values between 0 and 1 with the help of the denominator, i.e., the sum of all attribute importance values.

$$fi_i = \frac{fi_i}{\sum_{j \in \text{all features}} fi_j} \tag{2.6}$$

The last level has the random forest's values, which average the total values by dividing them by the total number of trees T, given as the divisor in 2.7.

$$fi_i = \frac{\sum_{j \in \text{all trees}} \text{norms} fi_{ij}}{T} \tag{2.7}$$

Here, $normsfi_{ij}$ represents the standardized importance of the node i in tree j, and fi_i denotes the final output of the RF. Feature importance is determined by the reduction in node impurity, weighted by the probability of reaching that node – calculated as the ratio of samples at the node to the total number of samples. A higher value signifies greater feature importance.

2.5.3 Support Vector Machine (SVM)

SVM is a supervised learning algorithm that classifies data by constructing an optimal hyperplane to separate classes in an N-dimensional space. Key data points influencing the hyperplane are called support vectors. SVMs are categorized into linear (for linearly separable data) and non-linear types, with linear SVMs aiming to maximize the margin between classes for accurate classification. On the other hand, non-linear SVMs are used when the data is not linearly separable. Such types of nonlinearity may be transformed from a lower dimension to a higher dimension by mapping it with a set of functions known as kernels. This enables the algorithm to create complex boundaries through vector dot products in the transformed space. The mathematical representation of the hyperplane in linear SVM is reported in Eq. 2.8.

$$f(x) = \mathbf{w}^T \cdot \mathbf{x} + b = 0 \tag{2.8}$$

where w is the weight vector, x is the feature vector, and b is the bias term. For non-linear SVM, the hyperplane equation is as follows in 2.9:

$$f(x) = \mathbf{w}^T \cdot \Phi(x) + b = 0 \tag{2.9}$$

where $\Phi(x)$ denotes the mapping function that transforms x into a higher-dimensional space. Its robustness, versatility, and effectiveness in high-dimensional feature spaces mark some of its advantages. However, its complexity, high memory requirements for storing data, and the challenging task of selecting appropriate kernel functions are some of its demerits. SVM is extensively applied in various domains, including text classification for document categorization, image classification for recognizing objects and faces, bioinformatics for classifying proteins and genes, handwriting recognition for identifying handwritten text, and medical diagnosis for classifying diseases based on patient data. Despite its complexities, SVM remains a powerful tool for classification due to its strong theoretical foundation and adaptability to diverse types of data. SVM encounters difficulties in feature selection, imbalanced datasets, non-linearity, computing expense, interpretability, hyperparameter optimization, scaling, and managing noisy data. To optimize the findings, the disparity between the two data points and the hyperplane can be increased. The function utilized for this purpose is known as hinge loss, as detailed below in Eqs. 2.10 and 2.11, where C is the regularization coefficient.

$$L(\mathbf{w}) = \sum_{i=1}^{n} \max\left(0, 1 - y_i\left(\mathbf{w}^T \mathbf{x}_i + b\right)\right) + \lambda \|\mathbf{w}\|_2^2 \tag{2.10}$$

$$\lambda = \frac{1}{C} \tag{2.11}$$

Also, $\lambda \|\mathbf{w}\|_2^2$ is called regularisation, it $L(\mathbf{w})$ denotes the loss function.

2.5.4 Logistic Regression (LR)

This machine learning algorithm is employed for the categorization of data points into certain labels. It is utilized to forecast a new incoming dataset and categorize it according to the established labels. The output obtained falls between the range of 0 and 1, as the specified classes are binary according to Eq. 2.12.

$$h_\theta(X) = \frac{1}{1 + e^{-\theta X}} \tag{2.12}$$

According to the formula, the parameter X represents the input dataset, whereas it θ is the parameter to be trained and optimized for output. To optimize the classification effectively, a loss function is necessary to enhance the prediction, utilizing the log-likelihood function specified as follows in 2.13.

$$J(\theta) = -\frac{1}{m}\sum_{i=1}^{m}\left(y^{(i)}\log(p^{(i)}) + (1 - y^{(i)})\log(1 - p^{(i)})\right) \tag{2.13}$$

In this context, it m represents the number of samples utilized for training the model. Whereas, y^i represents the class of the ith sample and p^i denotes the anticipated value for the ith sample. Also, it $J(\theta)$ represents the quadratic cost function, with lower values signifying a superior model fit to the dataset. The gradient descent algorithm is employed to optimize the loss function towards the global minimum.

2.5.5 Extreme Gradient Boosting (XGB)

XGB is a powerful gradient boosting algorithm known for its speed, accuracy, and efficiency. It builds models sequentially, with each tree correcting errors from the previous ones. With built-in regularization to reduce overfitting, XGB is well-suited for complex tasks like classification, regression, and ranking. The algorithm supports parallel processing for faster computation and high performance, which enhances model generalization. However, it requires careful tuning of hyperparameters and is memory-intensive, with the risk of overfitting if not properly tuned. The final prediction score is derived by summing the individual decision tree scores, represented by equation 2.14:

$$\hat{y}_i = \sum_{k=1}^{K} f_x(x_i), \quad \text{such that } f_x \in \mathcal{F} \tag{2.14}$$

Here, K is the total number of trees over the possible decision tree space F, and small $f(x)$ is the functional space over the data values. XGB is widely used in applications such as image classification for identifying objects like facial recognition, financial modelling for predicting stock prices and credit scoring, medical diagnosis for classifying medical images, patient data for disease detection, and recommendation systems for enhancing content recommendations based on users' behaviours. The mathematical formulation of XGB includes an objective function defined as 2.15:

$$L^{(t)} = \sum_{i=2}^{n} \left[l\left(y^{(i)}, y_i^{(t-1)} + f_t(x_i)\right) + \Omega(f_t) \right] \tag{2.15}$$

Where $L^{(t)}$ is the objective function at the t boosting round, n is the number of samples in the dataset, y^i represents the actual value for the ith sample, $y_i^{(t-1)}$ is the predicted value from the previous round, and $f_t(x_i)$ is the prediction made by the ith tree for the ith sample. The term $l\left(y^{(i)}, y_i^{(t-1)} + f_t(x_i)\right)$ measures the error between the actual and predicted values, while $\Omega(f_t)$ the regularization term prevents the overfitting. This function combines a loss function, which measures the error between actual and predicted values. XGB employs regularization techniques such as *L1 (Lasso)* and *L2 (Ridge)* regression to control overfitting and improve model performance. L1 regularization reduces unnecessary feature coefficients, helping eliminate underfitting, while L2 regularization minimizes the risk of overfitting by penalizing large coefficients with the difference of the coefficient of parameter β_j, which can be expressed mathematically as follows in 2.16 and 2.17:

$$L_1 = \sum_{i=1}^{n} \left(y_i - \sum_{j=1}^{p} x_{ij}\beta_j \right)^2 + \lambda \sum_{j=1}^{p} |\beta_j| \tag{2.16}$$

$$L_2 = \sum_{i=1}^{n} \left(y_i - \sum_{j=1}^{p} x_{ij}\beta_j \right)^2 + \lambda \sum_{j=1}^{p} \beta_j^2 \tag{2.17}$$

Other classifiers include *K-Nearest Neighbours* (*KNN*) and *Naive Bayes* (*NB*). KNN predicts cardiovascular disease based on the majority class among the closest neighbours, using distance metrics like Euclidean distance. Naive Bayes, based on Bayes' Theorem, assumes feature independence and estimates class probabilities given input features, making it efficient for high-dimensional data.

The MLP, a type of ANN, is used for classification and regression tasks. It consists of an input layer, one or more hidden layers, and an output layer, with each node fully connected to the next layer. MLP uses weighted connections and activation functions to process input data, and training is done via back-propagation to minimize prediction error. MLPs can model complex, non-linear relationships and handle large datasets effectively. However, these models may be computationally intensive and prone to overfitting, especially with limited data. Mathematically, the forward propagation in an MLP is expressed as $h = f(\mathbf{w} \cdot \mathbf{x} + b)$, where x represents the input vector, w denotes the weight matrix, b is the bias vector, f stands for the activation function, and h signifies the hidden layer output. This equation illustrates how the inputs are transformed through weighted connections and activation functions to produce the network's output.

2.5.6 SOTA Applications of ML Classifiers in HDP

Machine learning is an effective instrument for forecasting heart disease. It has the potential to improve patient outcomes through its capacity for early identification and tailored treatment. This section presents a comparative analysis of heart disease prediction utilizing ten machine learning classifiers, including NB, SVM, RF, DT, LR, XGB, AB, KNN, MLP, and ANN, among other models. Machine learning classification approaches have been extensively employed for predicting cardiovascular disease across many datasets. This part seeks to discuss the current and prior research on ML classification strategies for prediction and apply the ML classifiers to extract critical features that increase HD prediction.

In [42], Rahul Katarya et al. (2020) proposed a framework using the UCI repository dataset by considering the nine ML classifiers LR, SVM, KNN, NB, DT, RF, ANN, MLP, and DNN for the prediction of HD. After performing data preprocessing techniques, the RF model achieved the highest accuracy of 95.60% compared to others, and the RMSE is much lower, around 0.0439. Finally, the RF model concluded with slow performance and requires high computational power for large datasets. Devansh Shah et al. (2020) [43] proposed a supervised ML classification-based HD prediction model using a UCI repository Cleveland dataset. The four classifiers NB, DT, KNN, and RF were considered to deploy the model after data cleaning and transformation. Among them, the KNN with seven neighbours achieved the highest accuracy of 90.79%, and the lowest accuracy of 80.26% was observed for the DT classifier. In [44], Ilias Tougui et al. (2020) developed a classification model for HD prediction considering six machine learning techniques, LR, SVM, KNN, ANN, NB, and RF, and compared their performance by using six data mining tools. The Cleveland heart disease dataset is used with a ten-fold cross-validation technique, and the combination of the ANN classification model reached the highest accuracy of 85.86% and sensitivity of 83.94%.

In [45], Azizan et al. (2021) proposed a prediction system that used machine learning algorithms to select attributes obtained from the Cleveland dataset. Predictions were made using two machine learning models, ANN and LR. Different sizes of hidden layers and activation functions were used to find the hyperparameters with optimal performance. The ANN resulted in a higher accuracy of 92.31% and an F1-score of 93.2% compared to LR with 90.11% accuracy and an F1-score of 91.26%. In [46], Khurana et al. (2021) implemented six supervised ML classifiers to predict HD using RF, NB, DT, LR, SVM, and KNN models on the collected UCI Cleveland dataset. Among them, RF achieved the best results with an accuracy of 82.81%. The feature selection techniques further improved the classification performance and achieved prediction accuracy up to 83.41%. Jinjri et al. (2021) in [47] compared the five most powerful ML models to classify the cardiovascular disease of a person using the Cardiovascular Disease dataset. The proposed five classifiers were SVM, KNN, LR, DT, and NB for the classification of CVD. The cardiovascular dataset with SVM produced the highest performance accuracy of 72.66% compared to other models. In [48], Bharti et al. (2021) proposed a combination of machine learning and deep learning-based HD model using the UCI Cleveland dataset. Three experimental approaches were conducted using different combinations of data preprocessing techniques,

such as feature selection and outlier detection. These approaches were employed to develop models based on LR, KNN, SVM, RF, DT, and ANN classifiers. It was concluded that the machine learning-based ANN model achieved the highest accuracy of 94.2%.
In [49], Gupta et al. (2022) utilized various classifiers, SVM, LR, DT, KNN, and RF, for predicting the HD in the early stage. Hyperparameter tuning of the classifiers was performed to improve the accuracy. The comparison of the classifiers was reported in this work. It was noted that the LR outperforms the other classifiers with a prediction accuracy of 88.5%. In [50], Trivedi et al. (2022) proposed an ANN-based HD prediction model after analyzing the performance among the other ML models, KNN, SVM, SDG, NB, and LR. The different classification metrics were evaluated to decide on ANN models. The classification accuracy of the ANN model reached 98.3% among others. In [51], Nagavelli et al. (2022), presented a heart disease prediction model (HDPM) that efficiently replaces the use of ECG and MCG-based diagnostic procedures by the clinical expert. Due to the limitations of highly experienced clinical support and time-consuming interpretation of MCG and ECG signals, a clinical decision support system was proposed using three ML models. First, NB with a weighted approach was used for predicting HD. Secondly, two classifiers, SVM and XGB, were used to classify HD after applying outlier detection algorithms using DBSCAN and SMOTE-ENN for balancing training data distribution on the Cleveland dataset. Also, for automatic heart failure identification, the improved SVM (ISVM) based on a duality optimization (DO) scheme was analyzed. Finally, the XGB model exhibited the highest prediction results with an accuracy of 95.9% under experimental conditions. The main purpose of the research was to provide clinicians with tools that predict heart disease at an early stage.
In [52], Ozcan et al. (2023) developed a heart disease prediction model using the CART algorithm, which also extracts decision rules. Using the *Kaggle heart disease dataset*, the model achieved an accuracy of 87.25%. In [53], Bhatt et al. (2023) introduced a k-mode clustering approach with Huang initialization to enhance heart disease classification. Models like RF, DT, XGB, and MLP were evaluated using GridSearchCV with 10-fold cross-validation. It was observed that the MLP achieved the highest accuracy of 87.28%. The study's limitations include the use of a single dataset, exclusion of lifestyle factors, and lack of cluster interpretability. Future work may compare k-mode with other clustering methods and address missing data and outliers.
Ogunpola et al. (2024) [54] addressed the research gap in the existing approaches and developed an advanced predictive model for HD using the two datasets, the UCI Cleveland dataset and the Cardiovascular dataset. After performing several data preprocessing steps during the EDA, the seven machine learning classifiers, including XGB, KNN, LR, SVM, GB, RF, and CNN, were deployed for the early detection of HD. The performance was analyzed by optimizing the XGB model with an accuracy of 98.50% for the cardiovascular disease dataset. In [55], EL-SOFANY et al. (2024) considered multiple machine learning algorithms and feature selection techniques to predict heart disease. The models were tested on both the public UCI Cleveland HD dataset and private datasets. Feature selection methods like *chi-square*, *ANOVA*, and *mutual information* were applied. Ten classifiers, including XGB, AB, and RF, were evaluated. The best results were achieved with XGB and SMOTE on the SF-2 feature subset, with an accuracy of 97.57%, sen-

sitivity of 96.61%, and specificity of 90.48%. This method was later implemented in a mobile app for real-time heart disease prediction. In [56], Pandey et al. (2024) adopted various machine learning classifiers to analyze their effectiveness for heart disease prediction by applying the different sampling techniques like random under-sampling, random over-sampling, cost-sensitive learning, and SMOTE to handle the class imbalance. The four types of sampling techniques were applied to the collected *BRFSS-2021 Heart Disease Health Indicators* Dataset and concluded the performance with random oversampling, with the highest accuracy of 95.11%.

2.5.7 Performance Analysis of ML-based SOTA Methods

A machine learning-based classification model's performance can be analyzed by considering the different metrics – accuracy, precision, recall, F1 score, Cohen's kappa score, and ROC-AUC score. Several studies have observed that the performance of selected classifiers varies when applied to a specific dataset. Depending on the model employed, the highest accuracy is achieved by different classifiers, and the corresponding performance results are summarized in the table below. Table 2.3 presents a summary of the previously reviewed literature, highlighting the reported accuracy values and identifying existing research gaps. It also outlines the study objectives and future scope aimed at addressing the observed limitations. For each SOTA approach, the classifiers employed by different researchers are extracted, and the best-performing models are summarized with respect to the dataset characteristics, including the number of instances (INS) and attributes (ATB).

The comparison analysis of each model shows that the XGB, RF, KNN, and ANN classifier models performed well with an accuracy of above 90%. So, XGB, RF, and the ANN can be the best choices for the further development of the HDP models, considering the classical ML classifiers.

2.5.8 Challenges of ML-based Approach

Based on a comprehensive review of the above approaches, SOTA methods, and the performance of each model, the study identifies the existing open research challenges. Following the analysis of the research gaps, the key challenges are summarized as follows:

1. Among the diversified machine learning classifiers, it is a very challenging task to select the appropriate algorithms for the HDP that can be the most suitable and effective classification model.

2. Most of the researchers have used a specific dataset with varying instances for the deployments of the ML model, which has produced a dataset-centric outcome in terms of accuracy and other performance metrics. The prediction model generalization and overfitting issues need to be handled properly.

3. The data preprocessing steps play a vital role in the machine learning-based disease classification task. Handling target class data imbalances poses significant challenges, as it can result in biased predictions towards a specific class.

Table 2.3: Summary of Recent ML-based HD Prediction Studies

#	Ref	Algorithms Used	Model	Dataset Name	INS	ATB	Ac (%)
1	[42] (2020)	LR, SVM, KNN, NB, DT, RF, ANN, MLP, DNN	RF	Cleveland Heart Dataset [57]	303	14	95.60
2	[43] (2020)	NB, DT, KNN, RF	KNN	Cleveland Heart Dataset [57]	303	14	90.79
3	[44] (2020)	LR, SVM, KNN, ANN, NB, RF	ANN	Cleveland Heart Dataset [57]	303	14	85.86
4	[45] (2021)	ANN, LR	ANN	Cleveland Heart Dataset [57]	303	14	92.31
5	[46] (2021)	NB, DT, LR, RF, SVM, KNN	RF	Cleveland Heart Dataset [57]	303	14	82.81
6	[47] (2021)	SVM, KNN, LR, NB, DT	SVM	Cardiovascular Disease Dataset [58]	70000	12	72.66
7	[48] (2021)	LR, KNN, SVM, RF, DT, ANN	ANN	Cleveland Heart Dataset [57]	303	14	94.20
8	[49] (2022)	SVM, LR, DT, KNN, RF	LR	Cleveland Heart Dataset [57]	303	14	88.50
9	[50] (2022)	KNN, SVM, SDG, NB, LR, ANN	ANN	Heart Disease Dataset (Kaggle) [59]	1025	13	98.30
10	[51] (2022)	NB (weighted), SVM (DO), XGB	XGB	Cleveland Heart Dataset [57]	303	14	95.90
11	[52] (2023)	CART	CART	HD (Comprehensive) [60]	1190	12	87.25
12	[53] (2023)	RF, DT, MLP, XGB with GridSearchCV	MLP	Cardiovascular Disease Dataset [58]	70000	12	87.28
13	[54] (2024)	XGB, KNN, LR, SVM, GB, RF, CNN	XGB	Cleveland Heart Dataset [57]	303	14	98.50
14	[55] (2024)	NB, SVN, XGB, AB, DT, KNN, RF, LR	XGB	Cleveland Heart Dataset [57]	303	14	97.57
15	[56] (2024)	LR, RF, KNN, NB, SVM, ANN, AB, GB, LGBM, XGB	RF	BRFSS-2021 Heart Disease Health Indicators Dataset [61]	202987	22	95.11

4. Each classifier's hyperparameters, along with their optimal estimator values, have the power to alter the performance of the model. As a result, managing the hyperparameters and determining the optimal estimator values is a highly challenging task. So far, the hyperparameter tuning approach with the best estimator value based on ML models has not been tested and considered to justify its significance for HD prediction purposes.

2.5.9 Research Gap of ML-based Approach

By identifying the major challenges of conventional ML-based HDP approaches, contributions can be made by adopting the following suggestions for future scope. The first approach to future scope is determined by a detailed analysis of the SOTA methods and their applications.

1. Diversified ML classifier selection in disease prediction can be addressed by deploying each model individually. Additionally, the researcher can make methodical decisions by measuring performance parameters such as accuracy and combining them with the frequency of use and complexity.

2. To mitigate target class imbalance, techniques such as random under-sampling, random over-sampling, SMOTE, ADASYN, cost-sensitive learning, Tomek Links, SMOTETomek, and SMOTEENN can be applied. These methods help reduce bias and improve model generalization.

3. To address overfitting and enhance generalization, hyperparameter tuning and cross-validation can be applied, particularly for low-resource medical datasets.

4. The widely used hyperparameter tuning methods, RandomizedSearchCV and GridSearchCV, can be applied to optimize the selected models. These methods identify the best estimator values, thereby improving the experimental results.

2.6 HDP: Ensemble Learning Approach

Based on the research challenges, future scopes were identified. An alternative strategy involves leveraging advanced ensemble learning techniques. By combining the predictions of multiple weaker classifiers, ensemble methods can enhance model performance, reduce variance and bias, and improve generalization. Consequently, ensemble-based approaches are well-suited for complex tasks like HDP.

There are mainly three simple methods to perform an ensemble.

(a) **Max Voting:** In this approach, each model in the ensemble casts a vote for a specific class, and the class receiving the highest number of votes is selected as the final prediction. This technique is widely used in classification problems with discrete outputs.

(b) **Averaging:** In this technique, the final prediction is obtained by averaging the outputs of multiple models, making it well-suited for regression tasks.

(c) **Weighted Averaging:** Similar to simple averaging, this method assigns weights to each model's prediction based on its accuracy or another performance metric. The final output is then calculated as a weighted average of all the model predictions.

The advanced ensemble learning methods can be constructed to get better performance by combining the different classifiers' prediction results through different techniques as reported below:

2.6.1 Bagging (Bootstrap Aggregating) EL Method

Bagging trains several instances of the same model on different data subsets created through bootstrap sampling, randomly selecting training samples with replacement. The final output is determined by averaging the predictions for regression tasks or using majority voting for classification. For a particular dataset D with N instances, bagging creates M different datasets $D_1, D_2, \ldots, D_M$ by sampling from D. A base model f_i is trained on each dataset D_i. For a test instance x, the final prediction $\hat{y}$ is as follows in Eq. 2.18:

$$\hat{y} = \frac{1}{M}\sum_{i=1}^{M} f_i(x) \tag{2.18}$$

RF, a popular bagging algorithm, uses decision trees as base models trained on different bootstrap samples. The final prediction is based on the majority vote (classification) or the average (regression), as shown in Fig. 2.3.

2.6.2 Boosting EL Method

Boosting is an iterative ensemble technique where each model is trained to correct the errors of its predecessor by focusing more on misclassified instances. Given a sequence

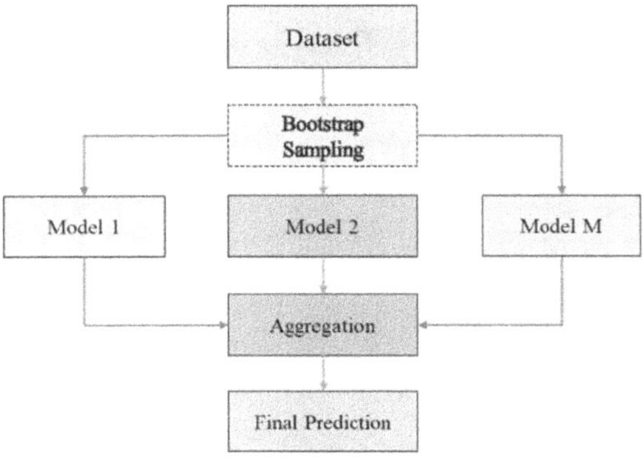

Figure 2.3: The process flow diagram of bagging classifier

of models $f_1, f_2, \ldots, f_M$, each is optimized using a loss function L that highlights prior mistakes. The final prediction $\hat{y}$ for an input x is a weighted sum of all model outputs as follows in Eq. 2.19:

$$\hat{y} = \frac{1}{M} \sum_{i=1}^{M} \alpha_i f_i(x) \tag{2.19}$$

Where α_i the weight for the model is f_i determined based on the model's performance. AB, GB, XGB, LGBM, CB, and HGB are widely used boosting algorithms. These algorithms have shown excellent performance in tasks requiring high accuracy, such as HDP, and perform according to the depicted Fig. 2.4.

2.6.3 Stacking EL Method

Stacking combines multiple models by training a meta-model (or a second-level model) to aggregate the predictions of the base models (first-level models). The meta-model is trained on the outputs of the base models to make a final prediction, leveraging the strengths of different models. Stacking can use any machine learning classifiers for the meta-model, making it highly flexible and powerful in combining diverse models as base models. If they $f_1, f_2, \ldots, f_M$ are the base models and g the meta-model, then for a test instance x, the final prediction $\hat{y}$ can be achieved as follows in Eq. 2.20. This formulation allows the meta-model to optimally combine the strengths of each base model. Stacking can use any machine learning algorithm for the meta-model, making it highly flexible and powerful in combining diverse models' performance according to Fig. 2.5.

$$\hat{y} = g\left(f_1(x), f_2(x), \ldots, f_M(x)\right) \tag{2.20}$$

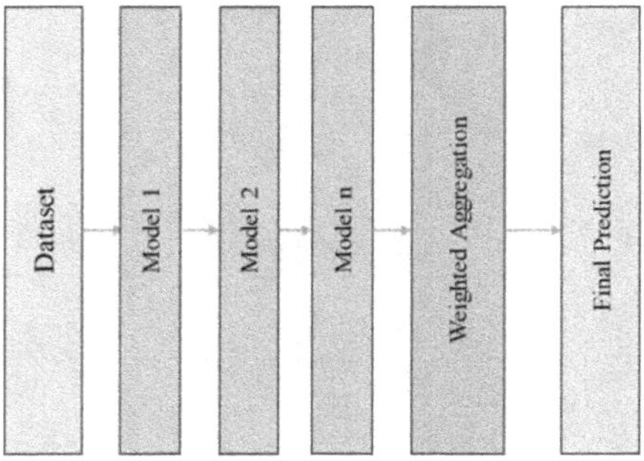

Figure 2.4: The process flow diagram of boosting classifier

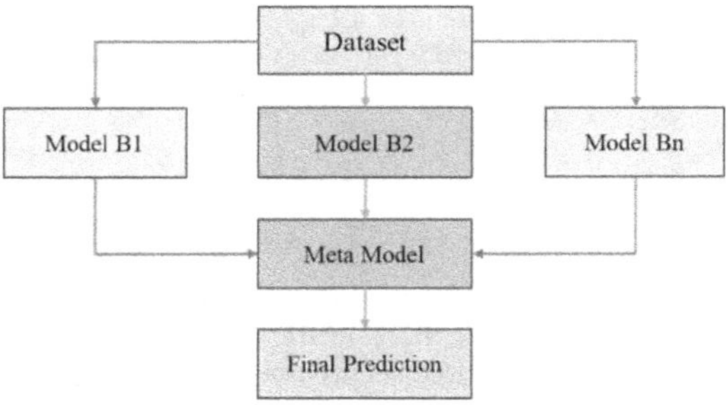

Figure 2.5: The process flow diagram of the stacking classifier

2.6.4 Voting Classifier EL Method

This technique involves multiple models voting for a class label, and the class with the most votes becomes the final prediction. This is like Max Voting but can also use different strategies, such as soft voting, where models vote based on predicted probabilities. In hard voting, each model votes for a class, and the class with the most votes becomes the final prediction. This is straightforward and effective when the individual models are diverse and perform reasonably well. Whereas, in soft voting, each model's predicted probabilities for each class are averaged, and the class with the highest probability is selected. This approach generally performs better than hard voting because it considers the confidence of each model's predictions and when the classifiers are well-calibrated and output meaningful probabilities.

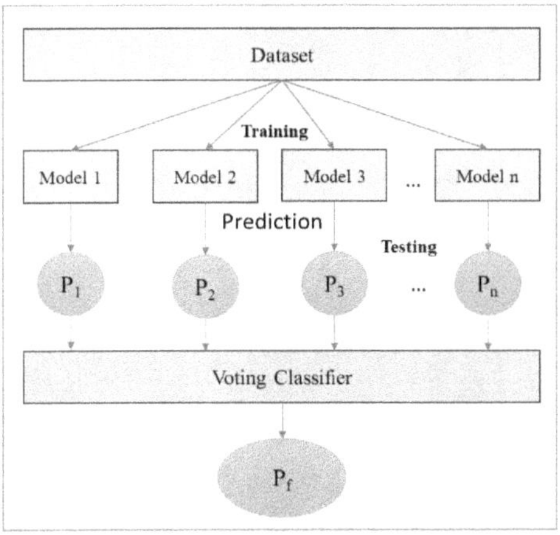

Figure 2.6: The process flow diagram of voting classifier

In hard voting, based on the majority class votes by the individual classifiers, the final prediction is represented as follows 2.21: where $\hat{y}$ is the class predicted by the ith classifiers, n is the total number of classifiers, and the mode function is the majority vote as follows.

$$\hat{y} = \text{mode}(\hat{y}_1, \hat{y}_2, \hat{y}_3, \dots, \hat{y}_n) \tag{2.21}$$

$$\hat{y} = \arg\max_k \left(\frac{1}{n} \sum_{i=1}^{n} P_k^{(i)} \right) \tag{2.22}$$

Also, in soft voting, the final prediction is based on the average of the predicted probabilities for each class, selecting the class with the highest average probability as follows in Eq. 2.22. Where $P_k^{(i)}$ is the probability predicted by the ith classifier for the class k, and $argmax(x_k)$ select the class k with the highest averaged probabilities. The voting classifier process flow is depicted in Fig. 2.6.

To summarize the ensemble learning approaches, there are several techniques to perform the ensemble for combining the individual classifiers' performance. Mainly, the four methods can be performed as follows in Fig. 2.7.

2.6.5 SOTA Applications of Ensemble learning Methods in HDP

Ensemble methods have proven to be effective in predictive modelling. The bagging ensemble method using RF is well-suited for heart disease prediction due to its ability to

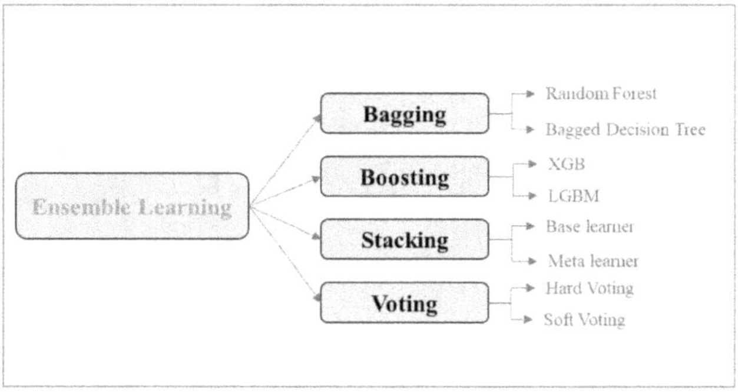

Figure 2.7: The EL methods flow diagram with multiple classifiers

handle large datasets with higher dimensionality. It can reduce overfitting and improve model accuracy by averaging multiple decision trees, each trained on different subsets of the data. Also, boosting like GB is powerful for heart disease prediction, as they sequentially build models that correct the errors of previous models. This results in a highly accurate final model, making it suitable for clinical predictions where precision is crucial. Stacking for heart disease prediction can combine models like LR, DT, and XGB, leveraging their strengths to improve overall prediction accuracy. For example, a model might learn from decision trees to handle non-linear relationships and from logistic regression to manage probabilities. Voting Classifier in medical applications: where multiple models provide diverse insights, a voting classifier can aggregate these insights for more robust predictions. For example, different models might focus on different risk factors, and voting can help combine these perspectives into a comprehensive prediction. An overview of the considered ensemble methods proposed by many researchers is discussed as follows.

Latha et al. (2019) [62] used the Cleveland dataset to predict heart disease risk with base models like NB, RF, BN, C4.5, MLP, and PART. Ensemble methods, including bagging, boosting, stacking, and majority voting, were applied in this study. These approaches achieved accuracy levels of up to 85.48%, with particularly strong performance observed for BN, RF, NB, and MLP under the majority voting scheme. The results show that combining ensemble learning with feature selection enhances early heart disease detection. In [63], Haq et al. (2019) used the Cleveland dataset to apply ML and DL models, including LR, SVM, KNN, NB, ANN, DT, BPNN, and ensemble methods (stacking, boosting, and bagging), for early heart disease detection. SVM achieved 86% accuracy with all features and 88% with selected features, while the ensemble method and BPNN reached 92.3% and 93% accuracy, respectively.

In [64], Mienye et al. (2020) developed an ensemble method using CART and *accuracy-based weighted ageing ensemble* (AB-WAE) for heart disease prediction. By applying a mean-based dataset splitting strategy, multiple CART models were trained to form an ensemble. This ensemble achieved accuracies of 93% on the Cleveland dataset and 91%

on the Framingham dataset, outperforming SVM, RF, LR, LDA, GB, and KNN models. In [65] Yuan et al. (2020) proposed an ensemble model, HGBDTLR (Hybrid Gradient Boosting Decision Tree with Logistic Regression), for large-scale heart disease prediction using the Cleveland dataset. By combining GB, DT, and LR, the model achieved an accuracy of 91.8%, outperforming others.

In [66], Asif et al. (2021) applied multiple ML algorithms to the Cleveland dataset for heart disease prediction. Their proposed ensemble method, combining KNN, XGB, and LR using majority voting, achieved an accuracy of 92%. Shorewala et al. (2021) [67] employed EL techniques, including bagging, boosting, and stacking, for CHD prediction using classifiers such as KNN, LR, NB, RF, SVM, and MLP. The stacking approach combining KNN, RF, and SVM achieved the highest accuracy of 75.1%, while MLP alone reached 73.9%. Bagging improved accuracy by 1.96% over base models, and boosting achieved 73.4% accuracy with the highest AUC of 0.73. Bashir et al. (2021) [68] developed a majority voting-based ensemble approach using four UCI datasets (Cleveland, Hungarian, Long Beach, and Switzerland). Individual classifiers included neural networks, SVM, DT, NB, AutoMLP, and perceptrons. Among five ensemble schemes, the best average accuracy of 83% was achieved using a combination of SVM, NB, and AutoMLP.

Tiwari et al. (2022) [69] presented a novel approach to predicting heart disease using a stacked ensemble classifier. This framework integrates several machine learning algorithms. This includes ETC, RF, and XGB. The model was trained on a comprehensive dataset from IEEE Data Port, incorporating data from various sources like Hungarian, Cleveland, Long Beach VA, and others. Performance was evaluated using ROC, AUC, specificity, F1-score, sensitivity, MCC, and accuracy. The proposed framework achieves an impressive accuracy of 92.34%, outperforming existing models. Alqahtani et al. (2022) [70] described an ensemble learning-based approach based on majority voting to predict cardiovascular disease using a combination of ML and DL algorithms. The study employs six classifiers, including RF, KNN, DT, and XGB, trained on a cardiovascular disease dataset of 70,000 patient records. The stacked ensemble model (XGB, DT, KNN), leveraging RF for feature extraction, achieved the highest accuracy of 88.70%. This method demonstrates a 1.47% improvement over previous state-of-the-art techniques, highlighting its efficacy in early heart disease detection.

Mahesh et al. (2022) [71] presented different combinations of ensemble classifiers to predict cardiac disease. The multiple variances of the decision tree classifiers – CART, alternating decision tree (AltDTree), RF classifier, reduced error pruning tree (RedEPTree), and Naive Bayes (NB) combined with the adaptive boosting (AB) classifiers – were used to construct the ensemble. To handle the imbalanced data, SMOTE was used in the first stage. The combination of heterogeneous (AB) and homogeneous (RF) classifier ensembles achieved the highest accuracy of 95.47%. In [72] Doppala et al. (2022) developed a custom ensemble classifier using NB, RF, SVM, and XGB with tuned parameters. It was trained on three datasets with a 60:40 split. A voting classifier was applied for the final prediction. The proposed model achieved the highest accuracy of 96.75% on the Mendeley dataset, with 88.24% and 93.39% on the other two datasets, respectively.

In [73], Chandrasekhar et al. (2023) used an ensemble classifier technique using the voting method for the prediction of heart disease. Two datasets were used to deploy the individual models of RF, KNN, LR, NB, GB, and AB. Finally, the soft voting technique was considered for a decision support system. After completing data preprocessing and performing hyperparameter tuning for each model using GridSearchCV with five-fold cross-validation, a soft voting ensemble strategy was implemented. The experimental results reached an accuracy of 93.44% and 95% on both datasets, respectively. In [74], Natarajan et al. (2024) proposed an ensemble learning method based on stacking and voting, considering the SVM, NB, and LR as base classifiers. The *Z-Alizadeh Sani* dataset was selected to extract the features by applying the *Firefly algorithm* (*FA*). Following this, the stacking and voting methods were constructed. With feature selection, the stacking method achieved the incremental accuracy from 82.5% to 86.8% compared to voting, which was 83.8%.

2.6.6 Performance Analysis of EL-based SOTA Methods

After reviewing the literature, it was noted that most of the researchers used ensemble learning approaches. The most suitable techniques were listed as stacking, voting, bagging, and boosting. These methods often outperformed the base classifiers' algorithms. It was also observed that different available open-source datasets were used to construct these prediction models. The performances of these models were measured with the help of classification accuracy and other metrics. To identify areas for improvement, the accuracy of the proposed SOTA models using ML and ensemble methods is summarized in Table 2.4.

Typically, ensemble approaches outperform individual models by capturing more complex relationships within the data. They enhance predictive accuracy by combining the predictions of multiple base models rather than relying on a single classifier. Additionally, methods such as bagging and stacking help reduce overfitting by averaging the predictions of multiple models, leading to more stable and reliable results. Ensembles are less susceptible to the idiosyncrasies of the training data, as they integrate many models, resulting in enhanced robustness. However, the difficulties arising from training many models and consolidating their predictions can be computationally intensive, especially for extensive datasets and specific model complexities. The absence of interpretability challenges, particularly with intricate models such as boosting and stacking, is frequently lower than that of individual models. This may pose a considerable disadvantage in a healthcare environment, since comprehending model decisions is essential for patient treatment.

This phase of the research is the continuation of the first approach for the selection of ML classifiers to perform the ensemble methods. The ensemble learning-based cardiovascular, or HDP, models introduced by the researchers can contribute to pinpointing existing research gaps and suggest new directions for experimental enhancement.

Table 2.4: Summary of Ensemble Learning-based HD Prediction Studies

#	Ref	Year	Algorithms Used	Ensemble Method	Dataset Used	INS	ATB	Ac (%)
1	[62]	2019	BN, NB, RF, C4.5, MLP, PART, Ensemble: Boosting, Bagging, Stacking, Voting	Ensemble: NB, BN, RF, MLP with Voting	Cleveland [57]	303	14	85.48
2	[63]	2019	LR, SVM (Linear/RBF), KNN, NB, ANN, DT, Ensemble	Ensemble: Relief-SVM(RBF) + ANN, LR	Cleveland [57]	303	14	92.30
3	[64]	2020	SVM, RF, LR, LDA, GB, KNN, CART	AB-WAE on CART	Cleveland [57]	303	14	93.00
4	[65]	2020	DT, RF, LR, KNN, SVM, AB, GB, HRFLM, HGBDTLR	HGBDTLR	Cleveland [57]	303	14	91.80
5	[66]	2021	KNN, RF, NB, SVM, XGB, LR	Ensemble Voting (KNN, XGB, LR)	Cleveland [57]	303	14	92.00
6	[67]	2021	KNN, RF, LR, NB, SVM, DT, MLP, GNB, Boosting, Bagging, Stacking	Stacking (KNN, RF, SVC)	CVD [58]	70000	12	75.10
7	[68]	2021	NN, SVM, DT, NB, AutoMLP, MLP, Ensemble	Voting (SVM, NB, AutoMLP)	Cleveland [57]	303	14	83.00
8	[69]	2022	CART, AB, SVM, KNN, MLP, SDG, GB, XGB, RF, ETC, Stacking	Stacking (XGB, ETC, RF, GB)	IEEE Comprehensive [60]	1190	12	92.34
9	[70]	2022	RF, DT, KNN, XGB	Stacking Ensemble	CVD [58]	70000	12	88.70
10	[71]	2022	DT (CART, AltDTree, RedEPTree, RF), NB, AB	RF + AB Ensemble	Cleveland [57]	303	14	95.47
11	[72]	2022	DT, NB, RF, SVM, GB, XGB	Voting (NB, RF, SVM, GB)	IEEE [60] Mendeley [75] Cleveland [57]	1190 1000 303	12 13 14	96.75 93.39 88.24
12	[73]	2023	RF, KNN, LR, NB, GB, AB	Soft Voting (6 Models)	Cleveland [57] IEEE [60]	303 1190	14 12	93.44 95.00
13	[74]	2024	SVM, NB, LR	Stacking + Voting	Z-Alizadeh Sani [76]	303	54	86.80

2.6.7 Challenges of EL Approach

This second phase of the HDP approach, based on ensemble learning methods, has numerous challenges due to the diversified classifiers and their different working principles. Ensemble methods can improve generalization and reduce overfitting when base classifiers are carefully selected and effectively combined. The potential challenges that may arise during deployment are outlined below.

1. Due to the complexity of diverse classification models and their varying performance on large datasets, selecting suitable base learners for ensemble optimization is a challenging task.
2. A comprehensive set of ensemble methods, including stacking, voting, and bagging, can be implemented for a heart disease prediction (HDP) framework. These methods can be compared and analyzed to determine their suitability with appropriate justification.
3. Hyperparameter tuning is a key challenge in building effective ensemble models without increasing overfitting or degrading performance. Optimizing ensemble-specific parameters, such as voting weights and bagging thresholds, is particularly complex and computationally intensive.
4. Ensemble models often lack interpretability compared to single classifiers, limiting their suitability for applications requiring transparent decision-making. Additionally, handling class imbalance in ensembles is more complex and typically requires customized strategies such as resampling or cost-sensitive learning.

2.6.8 Research Gap of EL Approach

After reviewing current SOTA applications and research challenges in EL methods, major concerns can be addressed through the following:

1. The selection of diverse classifiers for ensemble learning can be achieved by identifying the best-performing models for heart disease classification based on their classification accuracy.
2. The primary function of bagging, voting, and stacking ensembles is to identify suitable machine learning models as base learners or meta-learners to optimize performance. These challenges can be effectively handled by the integration of machine learning classifiers.
3. The hyperparameters of each model can be adjusted to optimize the learning parameters and derive the most optimal estimator values through hyperparameter tuning methods. The hyperparameter-tuned ensemble model can be deployed in a dual-stage stacking or voting prediction framework for heart disease proposals to improve performance.
4. The interpretability of ensemble models can be enhanced by examining the feature

significance scores generated by ensemble classifiers. The contribution of each feature to the prediction enhances the comprehensibility of the model's behaviour.

2.7 HDP: Deep Learning-based Artificial Neural Networks Approach

After considering the two approaches, particularly the use of diversified ML classifiers for heart disease prediction, alternative decision-making strategies can be adopted. Instead of conventional machine learning-based approaches, there is an alternate method based on advanced machine learning techniques. Specifically, ANNs, inspired by the structure of the human brain, are employed to learn complex patterns in clinical data and accurately determine the target class for HD prediction and classification.
ANNs are extensively used for cardiac disease prediction due to their ability to model complex, nonlinear relationships in medical data. This capability often results in improved predictive accuracy compared to conventional techniques. By utilizing patient data, including clinical history, biomarkers, and imaging results, artificial neural networks can identify nuanced patterns suggestive of cardiac disease. The impetus for employing ANN-based methodologies arises from the escalating global prevalence of cardiovascular disorders and the necessity for precise, early detection. ANN can provide superior predictive accuracy, adaptability, and the capacity to assist healthcare professionals in decision-making. As a result, it can facilitate prompt interventions and mitigate the risks linked to delayed diagnoses.
Before reviewing current ANN applications in heart disease prediction, it is necessary to understand the basic architecture, parameters, optimization techniques, and associated research challenges. In the following, the general structure of an ANN is reported.

2.7.1 General Structure of ANNs

An ANN typically comprises an input layer, one or more hidden layers, and an output layer. The input layer processes data in matrix form, which is passed to hidden layers for further computation. Each neurone uses a summation function followed by an activation function to generate output. The overall ANN structure is illustrated in Fig. 2.8, and the output of each neurone is computed as shown in Eq. 2.23.

$$\sum_{i=1}^{n} w_i x_i + b = w_1 x_1 + w_2 x_2 + w_3 x_3 + \cdots + b \tag{2.23}$$

Where w_i is defined as a weight of every data point, x_i is the input value, and b is called bias, considering n the input length. Also, the output layer achieved the outcomes with the given inputs according to the given Eq. 2.24, in either case.

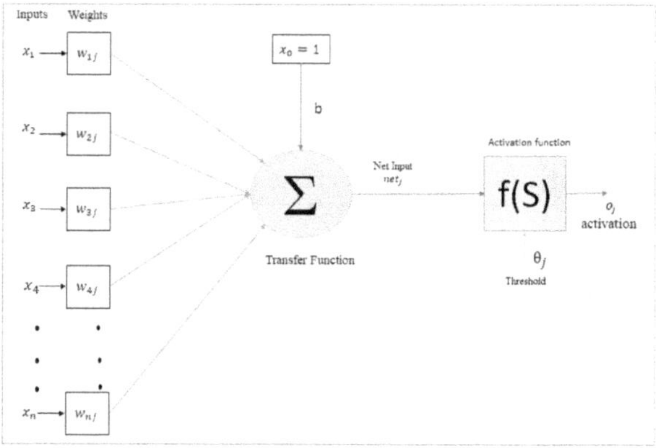

Figure 2.8: The general ANN architecture with activation and summation function

$$f(x) = \begin{cases} 1, & \text{if } \sum w_1 x_1 + b \geq 0 \\ 0, & \text{if } \sum w_1 x_1 + b < 0 \end{cases} \tag{2.24}$$

An ANN is typically made up of several layers of neurones, each performing a simple computation before passing the result on to the next layer. The basic structure includes:

- **Input Layer** – This is where the raw data enters the network. For heart disease prediction, this could include patient demographics, clinical measurements, and medical history. Each neurone in the input layer corresponds to a specific feature from the dataset.
- **Hidden Layers** – Each layer comprises neurones that compute a weighted sum of inputs from the preceding layer, followed by a nonlinear activation function. Hidden layers enable the network to capture complex patterns, with their number and size varying based on the problem's complexity.
- **Output Layer** – The output layer generates the final prediction. In binary classification, it usually has one neurone with a sigmoid activation function. For multi-class tasks, it includes multiple neurones using the Softmax function to output class probabilities.

This layered architecture can allow ANNs to model intricate relationships between inputs and outputs, making them well-suited for predicting outcomes based on complex datasets like those found in medical applications. An ANN consists of layers of neurones that process information, compute a weighted sum of its inputs, and apply an activation function. The network learns by adjusting these weights to minimize prediction error.

2.7.2 Activation Function in ANN

This is the fundamental element that employs a straightforward algorithm to determine the veracity of the answer. This response triggers the activation of a neurone to receive input from the network, which assesses its relevance in predictions through basic mathematical equations. It is utilized to obtain output from various sets of values at a node. A model benefits from analyzing the impact of each value on every label. It also aids in normalizing predictions with non-linear values, meaning that all values not aligned on a straight line can be modified to enhance accuracy. Various types of activation functions found in the literature are listed below.

1. *Linear functions* are employed to forecast values with minimal complexity and need little parameter adjustment concerning the data provided to the neural network. It uses values exclusively ranging from 0 to 1, encompassing both positive and negative indicators.
2. *Non-linear* functions are widely utilized as they adeptly accommodate various datasets and discern predictive patterns. The following are commonly used types of nonlinear activation functions:
   - Sigmoid or logistic function – uses a real data value as input and predicts another value between 0 and 1.
   - ReLU – transforms any negative input into zero on the graph, and that influences the model.
   - Leaky ReLU – is used to solve dying ReLU problems by diverging the value with a very small margin, normally 0.01, which causes the graph to shift and optimize the prediction efficiency.
   - SoftMax – is used to calculate the probability of an event occurring by calculating the chances of each target label over all possible labels.
   - Tanh – that refers directly to the tangent hyperbolic with an output range of -1 and 1.
   - Maxout: a generalized version of RELU and the leaky ReLU function, which works on the principle of a linear function that reiterates the highest of inputs.
   - ELU – uses negative values that acknowledge it to push average element activation closer to zero, and this shift increases the rate of learning by nearing the normal contiguous gradient.

The most used activation functions in ANN within each layer of neurones for getting the output and used to tune the parameters of ANN are discussed below.

1. **Sigmoid Function –** The sigmoid function (σ) is a nonlinear activation function that maps inputs to a range between 0 and 1, making it ideal for binary classification. It's most sensitive in the middle range and is commonly used in logistic regression to activate neurones as follows in Eq. 2.25.

$$\sigma(x) = \frac{1}{1 + e^{-x}} \tag{2.25}$$

2. **ReLU** – Rectified Linear Unit is a widely used non-linear activation function that outputs either the input itself if it is positive or zero otherwise. It is particularly popular in CNNs and MLPs due to its simplicity and effectiveness. Compared to the sigmoid function, ReLU is computationally more efficient and often yields better performance. Its operation is governed by a straightforward equation, as shown in 2.26.

$$f(x) = \max(0, x) \tag{2.26}$$

3. **LeakyReLU** – It is a widely used variant of the ReLU activation function, designed to address some of its limitations. Unlike the standard ReLU, which outputs zero for all negative inputs, Leaky ReLU assigns a small, predefined slope to negative values, preventing the issue of inactive neurones. This slope coefficient is set before training and remains constant, rather than being learnt during the training process. Leaky ReLU is especially useful in scenarios where gradient updates are infrequent, such as in training generative models or dealing with the "dying ReLU" problem. Its behaviour is defined by the following formula: 2.27.

$$f(x) = \max(0.01, x) \tag{2.27}$$

4. **SoftMax** – It is a unique approach to solving problems by estimating our outputs within a range of (0,1) and determining every output in a manner that their sum is 1. The output achieved in this is a probability distribution. It is normally used in the final layer to train a cross-entropy model that gives a non-linear version of multi-class logistic regression. The formula 2.28 used for finding the probability distribution is given as follows, where Z is the vector of inputs.

$$\sigma(z)_j = \frac{e^{z_j}}{\sum_{k=1}^{K} e^{z_k}}, \quad j = 1, \ldots, K \tag{2.28}$$

2.7.3 Optimization Techniques in ANNs

It is a strategy employed to train the machine repeatedly, facilitating the assessment of both functions' maxima and minima. This is accomplished through the comparison of outcomes obtained from the model with various parameter tunings. The outcome can be significantly enhanced by precisely calibrating the hyperparameters to optimal accuracy. This aids in reducing the errors in a model's predictions while simultaneously ensuring the model's fit to the problem is maintained. This method is known as backpropagation, which is essential when utilizing ANN. Various methods exist to attain this efficiency, and a few are outlined here.

1. **SGD (Stochastic Gradient Descent):** It is an optimization technique that randomly selects small data batches to compute gradients in each iteration. It adjusts model parameters iteratively for each sample to minimize the cost function, making it efficient for large-scale problems. The goal is to reduce the cost function and find an optimal solution using repeated parameter updates by Eq. 2.29.

$$\theta = \theta - \eta \cdot \nabla_\theta J(\theta; x^{(i)}; y^{(i)}) \tag{2.29}$$

   - θ = Gradient of cost function
   - $J(\theta)$ = Parameterized objective function
   - $x^{(i)}$ = Training examples
   - $y^{(i)}$ = Labels or Outcomes
   - $\nabla_\theta J(\theta)$ = Gradient of the objective function
   - η = Learning rate

2. **RMSProp (Root Mean Squared Propagation):** It is an advanced optimization algorithm that enhances traditional gradient descent by adapting learning rates for each parameter. It does this by maintaining an exponentially decaying average of past squared gradients, which helps dampen oscillations and stabilize learning, especially in deep networks. This allows for faster convergence and better performance on non-stationary objectives, even when using smaller mini-batches. Unlike AdaGrad, which rapidly reduces learning rates and can slow down training, RMSProp avoids this issue by continuously updating its memory of past gradients. It also draws from RPProp by adjusting learning based on the consistency of error direction. While RMSProp significantly boosts training efficiency and stability, it still requires manual selection of the learning rate, which can impact its overall effectiveness if not properly tuned. Eq. 2.30 defines a value function, denoted by $v(w, t)$ 'for a system in a state of w at a time t.

$$v(w, t) := \gamma v(w, t-1) + (1-\gamma)\,(\nabla Q_i(w))^2 \tag{2.30}$$

   Where γ is a discount factor ($0 < \gamma \leq 1$) that balances the immediate reward with the expected future rewards. A higher discount rate γ gives more weight to future rewards. $v(w, t-1)$ represents the value of the system being in state w at the previous time step $(t-1)$. $(1-\gamma)$: This weighs the importance of the immediate reward compared to future rewards and $(1-\gamma)$ balances the contribution of the squared term. Also, $\nabla Q(w)$: this is a state-value function, which assigns a value to each state w. The exact definition ∇Q depends on the specific problem you are trying to solve. Here, it $\nabla Q(w)$ is squared. The weights are updated by the following Eq. 2.31.

$$w := w - \frac{\eta}{\sqrt{v(w,t)}} \nabla Q_i(w) \tag{2.31}$$

3. **AdaDelta:** This is a well-known SGD technique that fundamentally incorporates adaptive learning rates in each dimension, addressing two significant concerns. The difficulties involve the ongoing degradation of the learning rate during training, as well as the manual selection of the entire problem. It is a robust variation of the AdaGrad method, recognized for its ability to adjust to prior gradients and modify the learning rate accordingly. AdaDelta employs a gradient window to adjust the learning rate. Consequently, it improves optimization efficiency and enhances overall model accuracy. It also does not necessitate the constancy of the learning rate hyperparameter during problem resolution. To address these issues, two formulas, Eqs. 2.32 and 2.33 are reported below for the cost function.

$$\eta'_t = \frac{\eta}{\sqrt{\alpha_t + \varepsilon}} \tag{2.32}$$

$$\alpha_t = \sum_{i=1}^{t} \left(\frac{\partial L}{\partial w_{t-1}} \right)^2 \tag{2.33}$$

- t = Time step (iteration)
- α = Sum of squared gradients
- η = learning rate

AdaDelta uses $s_{(dw_t)}$ in place of α, ε is a small positive constant calculated as follows: 2.34.

$$s_{dw_t} = \beta \cdot s_{dw_{t-1}} + (1 - \beta) \left(\frac{\partial L}{\partial w_{t-1}} \right)^2 \tag{2.34}$$

4. **Adam (Adaptive Moment Estimation):** It is a modern optimization algorithm widely used in deep learning. Building upon the foundation of traditional Stochastic Gradient Descent (SGD), Adam introduces an efficient approach to iteratively update network weights using training data. Unlike standard SGD, it does not rely on a fixed learning rate throughout training. Instead, it adapts the learning rate by incorporating ideas from two other optimizers: AdaGrad and RMSProp. This allows Adam to achieve more accurate results with faster convergence. Due to its low memory usage and strong performance across a wide range of problems, Adam is especially favoured in deep learning applications. Moreover, it is user-friendly, as its default parameter settings often yield excellent results without extensive tuning. The formulas used for calculating the results and updating the weights are given below as 2.35, 2.36, and 2.37.

$$w_{t+1} = w_t - \hat{m}_t\left(\frac{\alpha}{\sqrt{\hat{v}_t} + \varepsilon}\right) \tag{2.35}$$

$$\hat{m}_t = \frac{m_t}{1 - \beta_1^t} \tag{2.36}$$

$$\hat{v}_t = \frac{v_t}{1 - \beta_2^t} \tag{2.37}$$

- $\hat{v}_t, \hat{m}_t$: Bias-corrected weight parameters
- m_t, v_t: Normal weight parameters
- ε: Small positive constant
- β_1, β_2: Decay rates of mean and variance of the gradient
- α: Step size parameter (learning rate)

2.7.4 Learning Rate in ANN

Learning rate is a critical hyperparameter in ANN that controls the speed at which the model's weights are updated during training. A proper understanding and tuning of the learning rate are essential for the successful training of a neural network. The learning rate is represented as η in the gradient descent algorithm, where it determines the step size for updating the weights. The update rule for a weight w in a neural network is given by the formula 2.38.

$$w_{t+1} = w_t - \eta\frac{\partial L}{\partial w_t} \tag{2.38}$$

Here:

- w_t is the weight at a time step t.
- η is the learning rate.
- $\frac{\partial L}{\partial w_t}$ is the gradient of the loss function L with respect to the weight of w_t.

A small learning rate can make the training process slow, while a large learning rate might cause the model to converge quickly to a suboptimal solution or even diverge. So, choosing the optimal learning rate is a challenging task for the neural network optimization corresponding to a specific problem. Practical considerations for the learning rate are considered as follows.

- **Choosing the Learning Rate:** Practitioners often start with a moderate learning rate (e.g., 0.01) and then adjust based on the performance during training. Techniques such as learning rate annealing or using adaptive learning rate algorithms

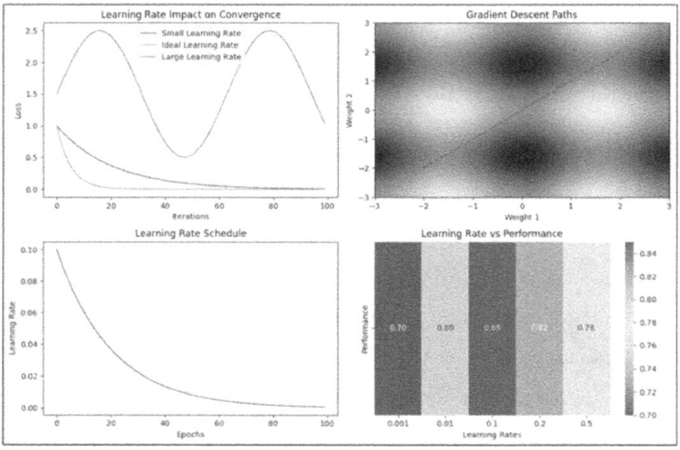

Figure 2.9: The different scenarios of the learning rate concerning epochs, loss, varying performances

like AdaGrad, RMSProp, or Adam can be employed to optimize the training process.

- **Learning Rate Decay:** To avoid overshooting as the model approaches the optimal solution, the learning rate is often reduced gradually using a decay schedule over epochs. This reduction helps the model to fine-tune the weights and settle into a better minimum. This prevents overshooting the ideal solution and enhances convergence by allowing more precise weight adjustments in later training stages, as a result improving model stability and performance.

The practical relationship of learning rate concerning model losses, number of epochs, the convergence, and the model performances varies, as depicted in Fig. 2.9.

2.7.5 SOTA Application of DL-Based ANNs approach in HDP

This section highlights the application of ANNs for heart disease classification and prediction, including models enhanced with Genetic Algorithms (GA), Particle Swarm Optimization (PSO), and other hybrid approaches proposed in the literature.

Shahid et al. (2020) [77] proposed a hybrid model combining Emotional Neural Networks (EmNNs) with Particle Swarm Optimization (PSO) for Coronary Artery Disease (CAD) diagnosis. Using four feature selection methods, the model achieved 88.34% accuracy, 92.37% precision, 91.85% sensitivity, and a 92.12% F1-score on the Z-Alizadeh Sani dataset, outperforming the PSO-ANFIS model (70% accuracy) and PSO-ENN with all features (86.33% accuracy). In the article [78], Aniruddha Dutta et al. (2020) proposed a CNN-based model for CHD prediction using clinical data and LASSO-based feature selection with majority voting to address multicollinearity. The CNN includes dense layers with 64 and 512 neurones (ReLU activation), followed by a SoftMax layer for classification. The model achieved 82.3% overall accuracy, 77% for CHD presence, 81.8% for absence, and a balanced accuracy of 79.5%, outperforming SVM and RF in handling class imbalance. In the article [79],Ibomoiye Domor Mienye et al. (2020) reported an improved sparse autoencoder (SAE) optimized with Adam and combined with ANN for heart disease prediction. Batch normalization was applied to reduce overfitting. The model outperformed ANN, KNN, CART, and other standard methods, achieving 90% accuracy on test data. In [80], Masih et al. (2020) developed an MLP-based deep learning model using Framingham Heart Study data for CHD prediction. Initially, the model achieved 92.87% accuracy but only 50% sensitivity. After applying feature selection and preprocessing, accuracy improved to 96.50% with over 91% sensitivity. This highlights the importance of data preprocessing and the effectiveness of MLP in enhancing predictive performance over traditional methods.

Nandy et al. (2021) [81] proposed an intelligent healthcare framework based on the Swarm-ANN technique for cardiovascular heart disease prediction. It uses a swarm-based approach to optimize the weights in a three-layer ANN. The Swarm-ANN method incorporates two phases of weight modification, leveraging back-propagation and a novel heuristic-based adjustment. The technique achieves a high prediction accuracy of 95.78% on a benchmark healthcare dataset, outperforming the traditional learning models. In [82], Priya R. L. et al. (2021) proposed an early CHD prediction model using genetic algorithms for feature selection and hyperparameter optimization. Using the Framingham dataset, the dataset size was reduced by 20% without compromising predictive accuracy. The TPOT classifier improved computational efficiency. A hyperparameter-tuned RF achieved 90.7% accuracy, which is comparable to the 91.6% obtained without feature selection. These results demonstrate the effectiveness of genetic algorithms and optimization techniques. In [83], Akella et al. (2021) applied six traditional ML algorithms to predict HD using the Cleveland dataset. Four models achieved 85% accuracy, while ANN outperformed them with 93.03% accuracy. A 93.80% sensitivity, 89.84% F1 score, and AUC scores ranging from 0.79 to 0.88 were also noted during the experimental study.

Moreover, in conjunction with the ANN, the other deep learning methods based on CNN, Deep CNN, Sparse Autoencoder (SAE), and attention mechanisms are also proposed by some researchers. The collective research on cardiovascular disease prediction highlights the advancements in ML and DL techniques for early diagnosis. In [84], a deep convolutional neural network (DCNN) trained on the UCI heart disease dataset, comprising 1025 patients and 14 attributes, was reported. The feature vector passed through the DCNN as an input and achieved a validation accuracy of 91.7% through image classification. This study emphasizes the efficacy of DCNN in medical diagnostics. In addition, Rahman et al. [85] proposed a novel transformer architecture that leverages self-attention mechanisms for predicting CVD risk. The model was tested on the Cleveland dataset, resulting in an accuracy of 96.51%. This model not only predicts CVD with high precision but also offers interpretability by focusing on essential features through self-attention mechanisms. In [86], researchers focused on feature augmentation by combining CNNs with Sparse Autoencoders (SAEs) to enhance data features for better classification accuracy. This approach was evaluated on heart disease datasets and achieved an accuracy of 90.09%. It outperformed existing methods by 4.4%, demonstrating the strong potential of advanced deep learning techniques for improving early detection of cardiovascular diseases. In [87] Bhavekar et al. (2022) proposed a hybrid deep learning method based on an RNN combined with LSTM. The experimental results indicate strong performance across different cross-validation settings. Using the sigmoid activation function with 15-fold cross-validation, the model achieved an average classification accuracy of 95.10% on the UCI Cleveland dataset. Hassan et al. (2023) [88] proposed a novel approach for HD prediction, combining a pre-trained DNN for feature extraction, PCA for dimensionality reduction, and LR for prediction. The proposed model underwent testing through various experiments using the Cleveland dataset, achieving a classification accuracy of 93.33%. In [89] Dileep et al. (2023) proposed a cluster-based bi-directional long-short term memory (C-BiLSTM) for heart disease prediction. To improve the classification accuracy, the UCI heart disease dataset, along with the real-time dataset were used. The duplicate data was removed by the K-Means clustering algorithm. Thereafter, the prediction was made by using the C-BiLSTM. Conventional classification algorithms, including Regression Tree, SVM, LR, KNN, Gated Recurrent Unit (GRU), and Ensemble, were compared with C-BiLSTM findings, achieving an accuracy of 94.78% with the UCI dataset and 92.84% with the real-time dataset. Collectively, these studies demonstrate the use of diverse datasets and advanced techniques such as DCNNs, transformers, and feature augmentation.

These approaches contribute to significant improvements in the accuracy and effectiveness of HDP models, reinforcing their potential for real-time healthcare applications.

2.7.6 Performance Analysis of DL-based ANN SOTA Methods

Various research has been undertaken to forecast disease occurrence with ANN in conjunction with MLP, PSO, GA, SAE, and ENN, as found in the literature. However, it seems that they did not employ data preparation procedures that could enhance the accuracy of the HDP model. Nevertheless, the study endeavours to forecast CHD via data preprocessing approaches. This demonstrates better performance in comparison to results obtained without such techniques. Numerous learning methodologies exist for prediction. However, ANN demonstrates greater efficiency relative to traditional classification algorithm methodologies. The primary advantages of the ANN technique encompass its efficacy in addressing challenging and complicated issues. Moreover, several applications of ANNs have been examined in the literature study, substantiating the generality and efficacy of the ANN learning framework. Consequently, it exhibits much superior learning efficiency compared to alternative classification methods. Table 2.5 presents the number of experiments performed on several widely used classification datasets, combined with additional techniques aimed at improving classification performance, with an emphasis on accuracy.

According to the performance analysis, the DL-based methods, ANN alone and combined

Table 2.5: Summary of DL-based ANN approach HD Prediction Studies

#	Ref	Year	Algorithm(s) Used	Best Models	Dataset Used	INS	ATB	Ac (%)
1	[77]	2020	Fisher Score, Relief-F, MRMR, Emotional Neural Network (ENN), PSO, ANFIS	PSO-ENN	Z-AS CAD [76]	303	54	86.33
2	[78]	2020	Lasso, Majority Voting followed by CNN	MLP	NHANES	37079	NA	82.30
3	[79]	2020	ANN based on Sparse Autoencoder (SAE)	ANN-SAE	FHS [90]	4238	15	90.00
4	[80]	2020	MLP	MLP	FHS [90]	4238	15	92.87
5	[81]	2021	Swarm-Artificial Neural Network (Swarm-ANN)	Swarm-ANN	Cleveland [57]	303	14	95.78
6	[82]	2021	GA with DT, RF, NB, LR, KNN, XGB, AB, TPOT	GA-RF	FHS [90]	4238	15	91.60
7	[83]	2021	LR, DT, RF, SVM, KNN, ANN	ANN	Cleveland [57]	303	14	93.03
8	[84]	2022	Deep convolutional neural network (DCNN)	DCNN	UCI HD [91]	1025	14	91.70
9	[87]	2022	RNN with LSTM	RNN, LSTM	Cleveland [57]	303	14	95.10
10	[86]	2023	CNNs with Sparse Autoencoder (SAE)	CNN	IEEE Data Port [60]	1190	12	90.09
11	[88]	2023	Deep Neural Network (DNN) with PCA and LR	DNN	Cleveland [57]	303	14	93.33
12	[89]	2023	Cluster-based bi-directional LSTM (C-BiLSTM), K-Means	C-BiLSTM	Cleveland [57] Real-time	303	14	94.78 92.84
13	[85]	2024	Self-Attention-based Transformer Model	Transformer Model	CVD [58] Cleveland [57]	70000 303	12 14	95.20 96.50

with Swarm optimization was performed well compared to other methods. So, the ANN-based approach is the alternate method in conjunction with the proper optimization techniques, which can produce the optimal performance. Moreover, optimizing the hyper-parameters of the ANN model, such as the learning rate, batch size, number of epochs, activation functions, and choice of optimizer, remains a challenging task for developing an efficient heart disease prediction model.

2.7.7 Challenges of ANN-based Approaches

The third phase of research challenges is formulated after briefing the deep learning-based, mainly ANN, approaches for the HDP current methods, technological advancements, and SOTA applications concerning the recent developments in this field. Many challenges can be addressed by the development of tailor-made ANN frameworks, considering their tuning parameters like batch size, learning rate, activation functions, optimizers, number of hidden layers, neurones per layer, momentum, and others. During model deployment, the following challenges can be addressed:

1. The intricate architecture of the ANN model integrates multiple sequential, fully connected dense layers as hidden layers. Determining the optimal number of dense layers for developing a customized, task-specific neural network therefore remains a significant challenge.

2. Parameter tuning is essential for determining the output of each neurone in a dense layer, and choosing the right activation function is a critical part of this process in an ANN model.

3. Optimizing ANN prediction errors through effective backpropagation requires the selection of a suitable optimizer. Choosing the most appropriate optimizer from the available options remains a key challenge, as improper selection can degrade performance or increase the risk of overfitting.

4. The learning rate is a key hyperparameter in an ANN model that regulates how quickly the model's weights are adjusted during training. Properly tuning and selecting the optimal learning rate is crucial for effectively training a neural network.

5. The existing literature lacks studies that focus on optimizing neural network architectures using different optimizers. In particular, limited attention has been given to tuning key parameters such as the learning rate, weights, number of neurones per layer, and the number of hidden layers to minimize the network's loss function.

2.7.8 Research Gap of DL-Based Approaches

After reviewing current SOTA applications and research challenges in deep learning–based ANN approaches, we felt that the major concerns can be addressed through the following proposals. Key considerations include improving model generalization through a tailored ANN framework. It also involves effectively controlling overfitting and addressing target class imbalance by applying recent techniques or proposing a hybrid sampling strategy. The appropriate optimization technique can also be selected, and parameters tuned accordingly.

1. To examine and evaluate the tailored ANN architecture employing various optimization strategies and activation functions inside dense layers for the development of a decision-making support system regarding the future risk of HD.

2. A fine-tuned, customized ANN architecture can be developed and evaluated using various optimization techniques such as Adam, AdaDelta, SGD, and RMSProp. Additionally, the impact of different activation functions like ReLU and LeakyReLU in the dense layers can be compared to enhance neurone performance and overall model effectiveness.

3. Furthermore, refining the optimal values of tuning parameters such as learning rate,

epochs, batch size, number of hidden layers, neurones per layer, weights, and momentum can significantly improve the efficiency of the prediction model. This improvement is reflected in higher validation accuracy, reduced loss, and enhanced performance across other evaluation metrics.

4. Additionally, to address class imbalance and reduce biased predictions, techniques like SMOTE, SMOTETomek, SMOTEENN, and two-stage sampling can be applied to balance the target classes in highly skewed datasets.

2.8 HDP: Feature Selection-Based Approach

This concluding part of the literature review highlights the role of feature selection methods in heart disease and CVD prediction. Between 2019 and 2025, research has focused on identifying relevant risk factors using feature selection and feature importance techniques. Since not all features in large datasets are useful, eliminating redundant or irrelevant data is essential to improve model performance and reduce computational complexity. Feature selection addresses the "curse of dimensionality" by identifying a minimal yet meaningful subset of inputs, thereby enhancing prediction accuracy and efficiency.

Despite the availability of various algorithms, limited attention has been given to comparing the effectiveness of different feature selection strategies, filter, wrapper, and embedded methods, within heart disease prediction models. This motivates the need for a comparative study to evaluate their impact on classification performance. Major risk factors for heart disease include poor diet, ageing, smoking, high blood pressure, alcohol use, and inactivity. While preventable through lifestyle changes, accurately identifying these causes is vital for early diagnosis. Traditional methods fall short, underscoring the need for a feature selection-based diagnostic system to effectively predict and manage heart disease.

Feature selection is vital in machine learning and pattern recognition, especially for handling large, unstructured medical data. Extracting meaningful risk factors from such data is challenging, but feature selection reduces computational cost and improves classification efficiency. Not all features contribute equally; some may be noisy, redundant, or irrelevant—potentially degrading model performance. Thus, selecting the most relevant features enhances both accuracy and efficiency. Various feature selection techniques exist, and the choice depends on the problem's specific goals. An overview of these methods is illustrated in Fig. 2.10.

2.8.1 Filter Methods

Filter methods are a category of feature selection techniques that operate by choosing features according to specific criteria before constructing the model. Due to the absence of direct testing of the subset features with a model, they are computationally efficient and adaptable for any machine learning technique. Filter methods serve as an effective preliminary approach for reducing the feature set to the most pertinent and predictive variables. During the preprocessing phase, filter-based techniques are employed irrespective

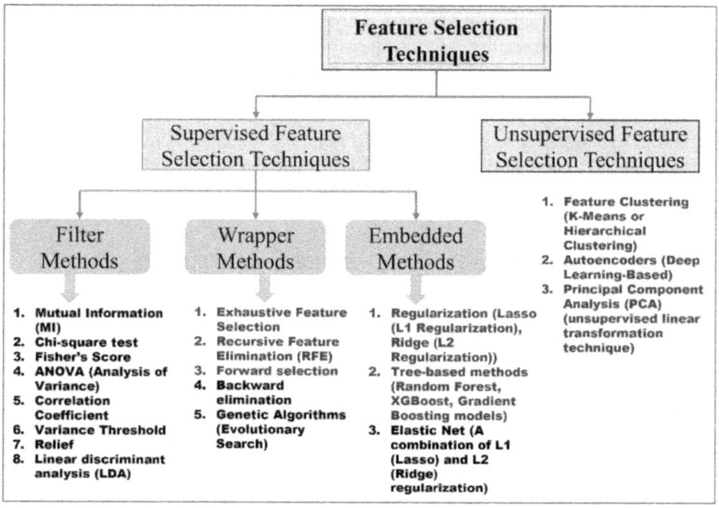

Figure 2.10: The different approaches of the feature selection methods

of the learning algorithm in use. This method calculates the score with statistical measures contingent upon the class label for each attribute. Subsequently, a predetermined quantity of relevant features is chosen by further organizing all attributes according to these evaluations. Various feature selection criteria, including correlation coefficients (Pearson, Spearman, and Kendall Tau), relief, chi-square, information gain, and Fisher score, can be employed inside the filter process. The general workflow diagram of the filter method is depicted in Fig. 2.11.

Pearson's Correlation coefficient

This method is used as a measure for quantifying linear dependence between two continuous variables, as a feature X and the target variable of Y. The Pearson correlation coefficient (r) between the two attributes is calculated by the formula 2.39 below in between -1 and 1. Such that r represents the correlation coefficient, x_i is the value of the attributes X, $\bar{x}$ denotes the mean of the attribute's values X, y_i indicates the values of the target class Y and $\bar{y}$ is the mean of the Y values.

$$r = \frac{\sum(x_i - \bar{x})(y_i - \bar{y})}{\sqrt{\sum(x_i - \bar{x})^2 \sum(y_i - \bar{y})^2}} \tag{2.39}$$

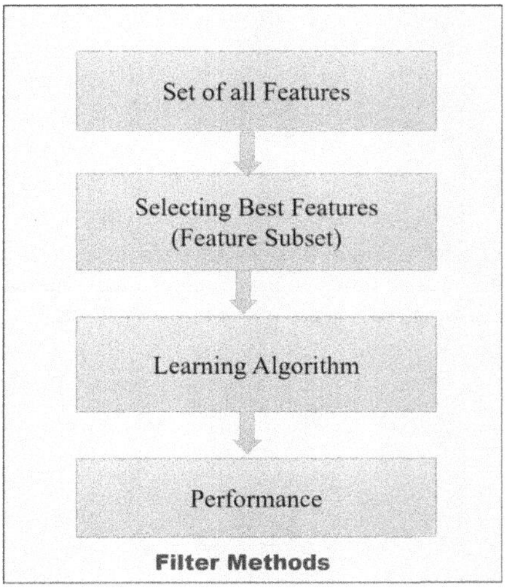

Figure 2.11: Filter method workflow diagram

Linear discriminant analysis (LDA)

LDA is a supervised dimensionality reduction and feature selection method mainly used for classification tasks. Unlike the unsupervised PCA, LDA focuses on maximizing class separability by identifying a linear combination of features that best distinguishes two or more categories of a target variable.

Analysis of Variance (ANOVA)

This statistical technique is used to assess whether the means of two or more groups differ significantly. Commonly applied in feature selection, it helps determine if a feature shows significant variation across target classes in classification tasks. Similar to LDA, it differs in that it involves one or more categorical independent variables and one continuous dependent variable. It offers a statistical test to evaluate whether the group means are equal.

Chi-Square

The chi-square test assesses the association between categorical variables by comparing their frequency distributions. It calculates the chi-square value between each feature and the target to identify the most relevant ones. A higher χ^2 score indicates a stronger dependency on the target, making the feature more valuable for classification. The test uses observed (O) and expected (E) frequencies to determine this relationship, as shown in Eq.

2.40.

$$\chi^2 = \sum \frac{(O_i - E_i)^2}{E_i} \tag{2.40}$$

Variance Threshold

Variance Threshold is used to remove low-variance features, which are often uninformative. It assumes that features with very little variation do not contribute significantly to the model. The variance of a feature X is calculated using the formulas 2.41 and 2.42:

$$\mu = \frac{1}{N} \sum_{i=1}^{N} x_i \tag{2.41}$$

$$\sigma^2 = \sqrt{\frac{1}{N} \sum_{i=1}^{N} (x_i - \mu)^2} \tag{2.42}$$

Where, x_i is the instance values of an attribute, x_{mean} or μ is it the mean value of the training samples and σ the standard deviation of the x attributes. A feature with low variance (e.g., all values are nearly identical) can have a small σ^2, meaning it does not provide much useful information.

Mutual Information (MI)

The MI is a statistical measure that evaluates the level of interdependence or uncertainty reduction between two random variables of a dataset. A feature's correlation with the target variable is measured with the help of it. To interpret the gain values, a non-negative value between two random variables indicates the degree of dependence between them. Higher values reflect stronger dependence, while a value of zero indicates that the two random variables are independent. The mutual information scores determine the relationship between the features and the target. The features are ranked according to the MI scores in descending order. The high-scoring feature is considered to be more important. Computationally, the mutual information between two random variables, X and Y, is expressed as follows in Eq. 2.43:

$$I(X;Y) = \sum_{x \in X} \sum_{y \in Y} P(x,y) \log\left(\frac{P(x,y)}{P(x)P(y)}\right) \tag{2.43}$$

Where $I(X;Y)$ is the mutual information for X and Y, $P(x,y)$ is the joint probability of X and Y. $P(x)$ and $P(y)$ is the marginal probability of X and Y.

Relief Algorithm

Relief is a filter-based feature selection technique that assigns weights to features based on their ability to differentiate between nearby instances of different classes. It effectively handles noisy, redundant, and irrelevant features across binary, multi-class, and continuous data. However, it can be computationally intensive and less effective on large, imbalanced datasets. Feature weights are updated using the following Equation 2.44:

$$W(f) = W(f) - \frac{(X_i[f] - H_i[f])^2}{N} + \frac{(X_i[f] - M_i[f])^2}{N} \tag{2.44}$$

For a randomly selected sample X_i from the dataset, where $W(f)$ is the weight of feature f. $X_i[f]$ denotes the value of the feature f in sample X_i. $H_i[f]$ is the value of the feature f in the nearest hit. $M_i[f]$ is the value of the feature in the f nearest miss, and N is the total number of samples.

Fisher Score

Fisher Score is a supervised filter-based method that ranks features based on their class-separating ability. It evaluates each feature independently using Fisher's criterion, where higher scores indicate stronger discrimination. Though effective, this independent evaluation can lead to a suboptimal feature set. It is commonly used in classification tasks to identify the most informative features. Mathematically, the Fisher Score for a feature x_i is calculated as in the following Eq. 2.45:

$$S(x_i) = \frac{\sum n_j(\mu_{ij} - \mu_i)^2}{\sum n_j \cdot \rho_{ij}^2} \tag{2.45}$$

Where μ_{ij} and ρ_{ij} are the mean and the variance of the ith feature in thej^{th} class, respectively, n_j is the number of instances in the jth class, and μ_i is the mean of the ith feature.

2.8.2 Wrapper Methods

Wrapper methods identify the most appropriate features for a specific dataset by utilizing a designated learning method. The prediction accuracy of the learning algorithm dictates the selection of features. Subsequently, characteristics are added to or eliminated from the subset based on the model's accuracy. This procedure continues iterating until the optimal subset is identified. The complexity of these approaches may be significant if the dataset possesses numerous dimensions. Examples of interdependent wrapper-based feature selection methods include exhaustive feature selection, recursive feature elimination, forward feature selection, Boruta, and reverse feature elimination. Wrapper approaches may incur high computational costs due to the necessity of training several models. Yet, they frequently produce superior outcomes compared to filter methods. The working principle of the wrapper methods is represented through a diagram in Fig. 2.12.

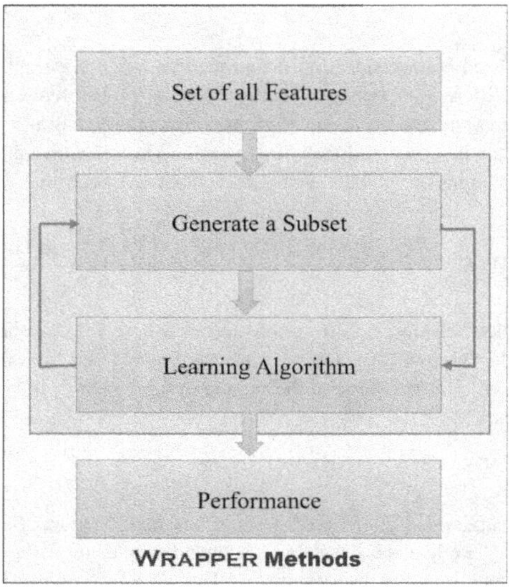

Figure 2.12: Wrapper methods working principle diagram

Forward Selection

Forward selection, or forward search, is an iterative procedure that commences with an empty feature set. Following each iteration, a feature is incrementally added, and its performance is assessed to determine if there is an enhancement in efficacy. The process persists until the incorporation of an additional variable or feature fails to enhance the model's performance. This method is computationally efficient relative to exhaustive search and can readily identify an ideal feature subset with fewer features. However, this method has certain limitations due to its greedy search strategy. As a result, it may fail to identify the globally optimal feature subset and can be sensitive to noise and feature correlations within the data.

Backward Elimination

Backward elimination is an iterative method that contrasts with forward selection. This technique initiates the process by evaluating all qualities and eliminating the least significant one. The elimination procedure persists until the removal of features ceases to enhance the model's performance. This strategy effectively eliminates irrelevant characteristics, mitigates overfitting, and is more straightforward than an exhaustive search. It is resource-intensive for large datasets and may eliminate important features if the selection process is not properly calibrated.

Recursive Feature Elimination (RFE)

Recursive feature elimination is a greedy optimization technique that chooses features by repeatedly shrinking the set of candidates to isolate the most informative ones. It repeatedly builds models and, at each step, keeps either the best-performing or worst-performing features. It develops the subsequent model utilizing the remaining features until all features are depleted. It subsequently prioritizes the traits according to the sequence of their removal. An estimator is trained with each feature set, and the significance of each feature is assessed using *coef_attribute* or *feature_importances_attribute*. It can manage high-dimensional datasets and discern the most significant aspects more effectively than alternative methods. However, these approaches may be computationally intensive. Effectively manages interactions among features and is well suited for complex datasets. However, RFE can mitigate the risk of overfitting by selecting the most significant characteristics. Nonetheless, the elimination of critical traits may result in underfitting. In summary, RFE is an effective method for automated feature selection in machine learning. It functions effectively with models that yield feature significance scores, including linear regression, SVMs, and tree-based models. While such models are computationally intensive, it ensures a reduced set of features without compromising accuracy. The optimal feature subset that enhances the model's performance is the final feature subset, FS^*, obtained using RFE as per the below Eq.2.46.

$$FS^* = \underset{FS_i}{\operatorname{argmax}}\, M(FS_i) \tag{2.46}$$

Where M represents the intended number of features retained post-RFE procedure, FS_i denotes the set of features at iteration i, and $M(FS_i)$ indicates the model's efficacy when trained on the subset FS_i.

Exhaustive Feature Selection

Exhaustive feature selection methodology is regarded as a brute force method for assessing feature subsets. It generates all potential subsets, constructs a learning algorithm for each, and identifies the subset with the optimal model performance. In contrast to greedy methods such as forward selection or backward elimination, which incrementally make decisions, exhaustive search evaluates every conceivable combination of attributes. This method ensures the identification of the ideal subset. However, it is computationally intensive due to the exponential growth of feature subsets. Exhaustive feature selection ensures the optimal feature subset. Nonetheless, it is computationally intensive and only practical for limited feature sets. For large values of n, alternate techniques such as Recursive Feature Elimination (RFE) or Forward Selection are considered as potential members. The optimal feature subset S^* is derived by formula 2.47:

$$S^* = \underset{S \in X}{\operatorname{argmax}}\, f(S) \quad \text{where} \quad |\mathcal{P}(X)| = 2^n - 1 \tag{2.47}$$

Where, $P(X)$ denotes the power set $X = \{x_1, x_2, \ldots, x_n\}$, and $f(S)$ indicates model performance (S).

In conclusion, wrapper-based feature selection approaches are effective instruments for determining the most pertinent characteristics of a machine learning model. They provide excellent precision, although this is achieved at the expense of computing efficiency. They are optimally designed for small-to medium-sized datasets where enhancement of performance is paramount.

2.8.3 Embedded Methods

Embedded approaches amalgamate the benefits of wrapper and filter methodologies. It is executed via algorithms that employ their feature selection strategies. The selection procedure in embedded techniques is integrated into the training of the prediction model. The training procedure of the classifier algorithm involves identifying an optimal selection of characteristics. Consequently, a singular machine learning model is employed to choose features in embedded approaches. The model's training duration corresponds to its computational expense. A standard embedded feature selection method involves training a machine learning model, assessing the importance of features, and selecting the top-ranking predictor variables. The working methods of the embedded technique are depicted in Fig. 2.13. In comparison to wrapper approaches, these tactics use less computational power. Algorithms such as Lasso Regression, Ridge Regression, Elastic Net, Decision Trees, Random Forests, and Gradient Boosting methods (XGB and LGBM) play a significant role in the development of embedded feature selection techniques. Nonetheless, formulating an explicit mathematical model for an embedded feature selection–based classifier can be challenging.

Regularization is a method employed to mitigate overfitting by imposing a penalty on the model's complexity. It aids in diminishing variance, enhancing generalization, and stabilizing training. Regression methods that incorporate built-in penalization mechanisms to reduce overfitting include Lasso and Ridge regression. These techniques are among the most commonly used approaches in regularized modeling. Lasso regression applies $L1$ regularization, imposing a penalty equivalent to the absolute values of the coefficients' magnitudes to the loss function (L). Ridge regression employs $L2$ regularization, which penalizes the square of the coefficient magnitudes. Lasso regularization for linear models and feature importance based on information gained in decision trees are the most prevalent embedding approaches.

$$Costfunction(L1) = \beta = \sum_{i=1}^{M} \left(y_i - \sum_{j=1}^{p} \left(w_j x_{ij} \right) \right)^2 + \lambda \sum_{j=1}^{n} \left| w_j \right| \tag{2.48}$$

$$Costfunction(L2) = \beta = \sum_{i=1}^{M} \left(y_i - \sum_{j=1}^{p} \left(w_j x_{ij} \right) \right)^2 + \lambda \sum_{j=1}^{n} w_j^2 \tag{2.49}$$

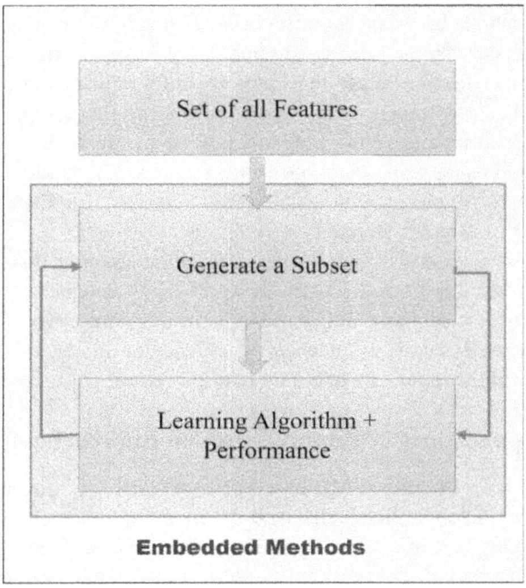

Figure 2.13: Embedded methods working principle diagram

$$Cost function(L1 + L2) = \beta = \sum_{i=1}^{M} \left(y_i - \sum_{j=1}^{p} \left(w_j x_{ij} \right) \right)^2 + \lambda_1 \sum_{j=1}^{n} |w_j| + \lambda_2 \sum_{j=1}^{n} w_j^2 \quad (2.50)$$

The above formulae, 2.48 and 2.49 for $L1$ and $L2$ regularization have some very important variables that are to be considered for evaluating the cost function, such as the weights of the features considered. The y_i in the given formula defines the actual value, and the $\hat{y}_i$ is the predicted output, whereas w_j is the coefficient weight of each feature, while x_{ij} is the feature. The λ value is the regularization parameter that controls feature elimination. $L1$ regularization reduces certain coefficients to zero, as a result eliminating unimportant features. $L2$ regularization reduces feature coefficients without eliminating them, aiding in the prevention of overfitting, although it does not facilitate feature selection as Lasso does. The Elastic Net Regression model integrates both $L1$ and $L2$ regularization techniques. This indicates the incorporation of both the absolute norm and the squared measure of the weights. It utilizes an additional hyperparameter that controls the relative contribution of $L1$ and $L2$ regularization, enabling a balanced combination of sparsity and coefficient shrinkage. This model is advantageous when features exhibit a strong correlation. The parameter λ_1 governs Lasso, which eliminates features, while λ_2 regulating Ridge, which mitigates overfitting, according to Eq. 2.50.
Tree-based models such as DT, RF, and GB inherently provide feature selection capabil-

ities. They rank features based on their importance in splitting decision nodes, allowing the most relevant features to be selected automatically during training. DT partitions data at nodes according to feature values that optimize information gain or reduce impurity. Features that significantly influence these splits are deemed more important. Also, RF and GB sequentially construct trees, enhancing predictions incrementally. Feature relevance is commonly evaluated using gain, which measures how much a feature improves a split. It is also assessed by the frequency with which a feature is used in splits and by cover, which reflects the number of samples affected by a split
Feature selection is an essential component of machine learning that entails identifying the most pertinent features from a dataset. It significantly enhances model performance, mitigates overfitting, accelerates training and inference, and improves interpretability. The objective of feature selection is to enhance the efficacy of an ML model by diminishing the dimensionality of the input data and eliminating irrelevant or redundant features.

2.8.4 SOTA Applications of Feature Selection Approaches in HDP

Numerous studies have developed ML-based decision support systems for heart disease prediction. Despite challenges like high data dimensionality, ML techniques such as SVM, ANN, DT, LR, XGB, GB, and RF have shown effectiveness. Feature selection plays a key role by identifying the most relevant features, enhancing prediction accuracy, and reducing the risk of medical errors. This section reviews the ML models with/without feature selection for predicting heart disease.

In [92], Pooja Rani et al. (2021) proposed a hybrid decision support system for heart disease prediction using the Cleveland dataset. They handled missing values with MICE and applied GA with RFE for feature selection. Among different classifiers (SVM, NB, LR, RF, AB), the RF-based classifier achieved the highest accuracy of 86.6%. In [93], Gokulnath et al. (2019) proposed a GA-based feature selection method with SVM for heart disease prediction using the Cleveland dataset. The GA–SVM model achieved an accuracy of 88.34%. It outperformed Relief, CFS, IG, and Chi-Squared feature selection methods. These results highlight the effectiveness of genetic algorithms in selecting relevant features and enhancing SVM performance. Noroozi et al. (2023) [94] analyzed the impact of sixteen feature selection methods categorized into filter, wrapper, and evolutionary on the performance of seven machine learning algorithms for heart disease prediction using the Cleveland Heart Disease dataset. The key classification algorithms evaluated in the study included SVM, RF, and Bayes Net. The results showed that filter-based feature selection methods, particularly SVM combined with CFS, IG, and symmetrical uncertainty, achieved the highest accuracy of 85.5%. While some techniques improved model performance, others, such as MLP and RF, exhibited reduced accuracy after feature selection. The dataset comprised 297 records with 13 features.
Pathan et al. [95], analyzed the effect of feature selection on heart disease prediction using CVD and Framingham datasets. Using ANOVA-F, key features like age, hypertension, and glucose were selected. Models trained on reduced features (SVM, LR, DT, RF, NB, MLP) achieved better accuracy (0.75 for CVD, 0.71 for Framingham) with lower computational cost, proving feature selection's effectiveness. In [96], G. Manikandan et al. (2024) ap-

plied the Boruta feature selection algorithm to improve heart disease prediction using the Cleveland dataset. Boruta identified six key features, enhancing the performance of LR, DT, and SVM classifiers. LR achieved the highest accuracy of 88.52%, followed by SVM at 83.61%, highlighting Boruta's effectiveness in refining model performance. In [97], Gárate-Escamila (2020) investigated heart disease prediction using ML techniques on UCI datasets. Feature selection via chi-square and PCA was applied to enhance performance. Among six classifiers tested, random forests combined with chi-square and PCA yielded the highest accuracies: 98.7% (Cleveland), 99.0% (Hungarian), and 99.4% (combined). The study highlights PCA's role in improving prediction by emphasizing relevant features. Dissanayake et al. (2021) [98] analyzed the effectiveness of ten feature selection methods on heart disease prediction using the Cleveland dataset. Combined with six classifiers, the study revealed that backward feature elimination paired with a decision tree yielded the best results, achieving 88.52% accuracy, 91.30% precision, 80.76% sensitivity, and an F1-score of 85.71%. In [99] Hasan et al. (2020) conducted a comparative study of feature selection algorithms for cardiovascular disease prediction using a two-stage approach. Initially, filter, wrapper, and embedded methods were applied separately, followed by combining key features based on a Boolean "True" condition. Among various classifiers tested, XGBoost with wrapper-based feature selection achieved the highest accuracy of 73.74% on a dataset of 70,000 patient records, outperforming models like RF, SVC, KNN, NB, and ANN. Yar Muhammad et al. (2020) in [100] explored early heart disease detection using ten ML algorithms, including DT, RF, and SVM, along with feature selection techniques like FCBF, mRMR, LASSO, and Relief to eliminate irrelevant features. Using the Cleveland and Hungarian datasets, the Extra Tree (ET) classifier paired with Relief achieved the highest accuracy of 94.41%, outperforming earlier models and providing clinically relevant insights. Also, in [101], V. Jothi Prakash et al. (2021) proposed a GA-LDA-based feature selection method combined with a hybrid ensemble model for CVD prediction. Using Statlog, SPECTF, and NHANES datasets with SVM, neural networks, and decision trees, the approach achieved accuracies of 93.65%, 82.81%, and 84.95%, respectively, demonstrating its effectiveness in enhancing prediction performance. In addition to the above articles, Robinson Spencer et al. (2020) [102] explored HDP using a combined dataset of 720 instances with four feature selection methods (Chi-squared, PCA, ReliefF, and Symmetrical Uncertainty) and eight classifiers. The best result, 85% accuracy, was achieved by combining chi-squared with the Bayes Net algorithm, identifying CP, exang, and oldpeak as key predictors. Nagarajan et al. (2022) [103] proposed a hybrid *genetic-based crow search algorithm* (GCSA) with deep convolutional neural networks (DCNN) for heart disease prediction. GCSA optimized feature selection, while DCNN enhanced classification using SVM, Naive Bayes, RF, and DT. Tested on ten datasets, it achieved 88.30% accuracy on Statlog, outperforming models like DT and Artificial Crow Colony algorithms.

Aggrawal et al. (2020) [104] proposed a sequential feature selection-based death event detection during the heart disease treatment. The features were extracted for classification. Several machine learning classifiers - LDA, RF, DT, SVM, KNN, and GB were used. An accuracy of 86.67% was obtained using SFS combined with RF. In [105] El-Sofany et al. (2024) used three feature selection methods: chi-square, ANOVA, and information gain to extract three feature sets. After that, ten classification models were deployed on the Cleveland and private hospital datasets. The combined dataset, along with ANOVA, the XGBoost algorithm performed optimally and achieved an accuracy of 97.57% on feature subset SF2. Mahalingam P. R. et al. (2024) in [106] proposed a customized ANN-based prediction pipeline (IPANN) combined with the effect of the feature selection MIST-CC along with the regularization STIR, named ClasifyIT. The performance increased by considering the Cleveland dataset after sequential implications. The prediction accuracy reached 87.16%. Finally, the proposed pipeline was deployed in a cloud architecture using the concept of federated learning and optimized to support IoT-enabled devices. Biswas et al. (2023) [107] built a potential early-stage heart disease prediction model using the significant features by applying chi-square, ANOVA, and mutual information feature selection methods as SF1, SF2, and SF3. Six ML classifiers, KNN, LR, SVM, RF, NB, and DT, were used for the most suitable models and feature set. Finally, the RF model with the SF3 feature set provided the best accuracy of 94.51% on the UCI Cleveland dataset. In [108] Al-Alshaikh et al. (2024) proposed an HD prediction model based on the derived features from the combination of genetic algorithms and RFE. The multilayer deep convolutional neural network (MLDCNN) was used for classification by adopting the concept of the adaptive elephant herd optimization method (AEHOM) and reached the highest accuracy of 95.5% on the most commonly used UCI Cleveland dataset.

2.8.5 Performance Analysis of SOTA Methods

Feature selection method development is a crucial and challenging task for better prediction model performance in heart disease. It is observed that variations of feature selection techniques can produce different combinations of feature importance. The selected machine learning classifiers can be combined with the reduced feature set to predict heart disease. The performance varies depending on the feature set and its interaction with the ML model. Also, the diversified dataset produces varying performance accuracy. This section summarizes the various feature selection methods and the performance of multiple machine learning models on the available datasets, considering the accuracy values presented in Table 2.6. The performance analysis identifies future research gaps and guides the adoption of appropriate strategies to streamline the prediction process. The main objective of this part is to summarize the available approaches with their proposed prediction model performance accuracy and to find out the available datasets.

The performance comparison of the FS methods by considering the metric accuracy of each method shows that the filter methods with chi-square and ANOVA with the RF and XGB models have produced better accuracy. Also, combined feature selection methods with GA-RFE in conjunction with the DCNN achieved better performance. So, the individual and the sequential implications of feature selection methods can be a better option for the HDP models based on the feature selection approach.

2.8.6 Research Challenges of FS-based HDP Approaches

The last stage of the research challenge concerning HDP approaches based on feature selection is determined after a rigorous literature review and the current methods. Due to the multiple varieties of feature selection methods, deriving the important feature sets by applying the specific technique is a very vital task. Also, the selection of the most appropriate ML classifiers for the final prediction without compromising the performance and the interpretability of the driving risk factors for HD is a challenging step. Some of the major concerns are summarized below for further research in this study.

1. Heart disease datasets often contain numerous clinical, biochemical, genetic, and imaging-based features. Due to the high-dimensional data complexity, many of which have numerous features, but some of which may be redundant or irrelevant, it is very challenging to identify the most relevant ones.

2. Among the diversified feature selection approaches like filter, wrapper, embedded, and evolutionary methods, it is required to choose the correct method for dimension reduction and consequently derive the proper feature set. Otherwise, inappropriate feature space can lead to overfitting and reduced model generalizability.

3. Traditional feature selection techniques struggle to capture complex, non-linear interactions between risk factors. Also, heart disease is influenced by non-linear interactions between multiple factors (e.g., age, lifestyle, genetics, and environmental influences). So, there is a need to choose the correct non-linear feature selection technique to handle these phenomena.

4. Heart disease datasets often have an over-representation of non-disease cases compared to disease cases, leading to biased feature selection that may ignore important features related to rare cases. Also, combining features from different sources (e.g., clinical data, genetic markers, imaging) leads to incomplete or noisy patient records, which remains a challenge that can affect the feature selection.

5. Different studies use different feature selection methods, making direct comparison more difficult. Also, combining filter, wrapper, and embedded methods for optimal feature selection is under-explored. So, the lack of standardization and the limited integration of hybrid models is a challenging task.

6. Many feature selection techniques optimize predictive accuracy but do not ensure clinical interpretability. Clinicians need to understand why specific features are chosen for decision-making. So, clinical adaptability is a highly required interpretable feature selection method for the heart disease decision-making system.

#	Ref.	Year	Algorithms Used	Best Model	Dataset	INS	ATB	Ac (%)
1	[92]	2021	GA, RFE, RF, SVM, NB, LR, AB	GA-RFE-RF	Cleveland [57] Z-AS CAD [58]	303 303	1454	86.60
2	[93]	2019	GA, Relief, CFS, Info Gain, Chi-Squared, SVM, KNN, J48, MLP	GA-SVM	Cleveland [57]	303	14	88.34
3	[94]	2023	Filter, Wrapper, Evolutionary methods; classifiers: Bayes net, Naïve Bayes, MLM, SVM, logit boost, j48, RF	SVM+CFS/Info Gain/Symmetrical uncertainty	Cleveland [57]	303	14	85.50
4	[95]	2022	ANOVA-F, SVM, LR, DT, RF, NB, MLP	MLP SVM	FHS [90] CVD [75]	423870000	1512	71.0075.00
5	[96]	2024	Boruta, LR, DT, SVM	Boruta-LR	Cleveland [57]	303	14	88.52
6	[97]	2020	Chi-square, PCA, LR, DT, RF	CHI-PCA-RF	Cleveland [57]	303	14	98.70
7	[98]	2021	ANOVA, Chi-square, Lasso, mutual info, ReliefF, backward feature elimination, Ridge, DT, RF, LR, KNN, SVM, NB	backward feature elimination-DT	Cleveland [57]	303	14	88.52
8	[99]	2020	Chi-square, Pearson, RFE, LASSO, RF, KNN, SVM, NB, XGB, ANN	RFE-XGB	CVD [75]	70000	12	73.74
9	[100]	2020	FCBF, mRMR, LASSO, Relief, DT, RF, SVM, ETC	Relief-ETC	Cleveland [57]	303	14	94.41
10	[101]	2021	GA, LDA, SVM, NN, DT, Ensemble	GA-LDA-Ensemble	Statlog [109] SPECTF Heart [110]	270 267	1344	93.6584.95

#	Ref.	Year	Algorithms Used	Best Model	Dataset	INS	ATB	Ac (%)
11	[102]	2020	Chi-squared, PCA, ReliefF, SU, BN, LR, RF	Chi-squared with BN	Cleveland, LB-VA, Hungarian, Switzerland [59]	1025	13	85.00
12	[103]	2022	GCSA + DCNN, NB, RF, DT, SVM	GCSA-SVM	Statlog [109]	270	13	88.30
13	[104]	2020	SFS, LDA, RF, DT, SVM, KNN, GB	SFS-RF	Heart Failure [111]	299	13	86.67
14	[105]	2024	Chi-square, ANOVA, info gain, NB, SVM, voting, XGB, AdaBoost, bagging, DT, KNN, RF, LR	ANOVA-XGB	Cleveland [57] Private dataset	303	14	97.57
15	[106]	2024	ANN pipeline, MIST-CC + STIR (ClasifyIT)	sequential implications of all models	Cleveland [57]	303	14	87.16
16	[107]	2023	Chi-square, ANOVA, mutual info, KNN, LR, SVM, RF, NB, DT	RF model with SF3	Cleveland [57]	303	14	94.51
17	[108]	2024	GA, RFE, MLDCNN, AE-HOM	GA-RFE-MLDCNN	Cleveland [57]	303	14	95.50

Table 2.6: The Related Study of Feature Selection Approaches ML Algorithms in Heart Disease Prediction

2.8.7 Research Gap of FS Approaches in HDP

After reviewing current methods, SOTA applications, and identified challenges, future scopes can be formulated accordingly. This study adopts some of the proposals on the feature selection-based HDP approaches and addresses the concerns, like comprehensive feature selection methods analysis, ML models' suitability, features' interpretability, feature balancing, and model generalizability.

1. To address high-dimensional data complexity, different feature selection methods can be constructed to derive the most important features for each dataset. Finally, their findings can be compared to extract the most relevant feature set for heart disease.
2. Multiple feature selection techniques (filter, wrapper, embedded) can also be combined to leverage their strengths. Evolutionary and metaheuristic algorithms can be the other options to leverage the individual selection method to be promising; these approaches need more benchmarking against traditional methods.
3. To overcome the curse of dimensionality, the regularization-based method is a way that can automatically shrink less important feature weights to zero using L1 regularization or L2 regularization (Lasso/Ridge Regression). Also, using the k-fold cross-validation method can control while selecting features prevents overfitting.
4. To ensure clinically interpretable feature selection, XAI techniques such as SHAP and LIME can be applied to highlight feature importance in complex models.
5. Non-linear feature relationships can be effectively addressed using non-linear feature selection methods. These include tree-based approaches such as RF and XGB, as well as deep learning–based techniques like autoencoders and attention mechanisms.
6. To address target class and feature imbalance, sampling techniques such as SMOTE, SMOTETomek, SMOTEENN, ADASYN, ensemble approaches, or cost-sensitive learning (e.g., weighted loss functions) can be applied. Heterogeneous data sources can be managed through multi-modal data fusion techniques, such as integrating CNNs for images with tabular ML for lab results.

2.9 Open-Source Heart Disease Datasets

Researchers have proposed various state-of-the-art (SOTA) approaches for heart disease prediction using publicly available clinical datasets from online repositories. Among these, the Cleveland Heart Disease dataset from the UCI Machine Learning Repository is the most commonly used. Although it contains 76 attributes across 303 instances, only 14 (13 predictors and 1 target) are typically used for model development. A summary of key open-source heart disease datasets and their respective sources is presented in Table 2.7.

2.9.1 Cleveland, Hungarian, Switzerland, and Long Beach VA Datasets

All four datasets, available in the UCI Repository, contain 76 features, including both continuous and categorical variables. However, researchers commonly use only 14 attributes, 13 predictive and 1 target variable indicating disease presence. The target value ranges from 0 (no disease) to 1-4 (varying severity levels). All datasets include missing values, with the Cleveland dataset being the most widely used in heart disease research [57].

2.9.2 Statlog Dataset

This dataset contains 13 predictive features, with one feature denoting the presence or absence of heart disease. The collection has 270 cases. The presence of cardiac disease is denoted by 1, whereas its absence is shown by 0. This dataset, the Statlog Dataset, contains no missing values [109].

2.9.3 Z-Alizadeh Sani Dataset

This dataset has records of 303 individuals. The dataset has 54 predictive characteristics categorized into four groups: ECG, demographic, symptom and examination, and laboratory. An individual is categorized as either a normal or a CAD patient based on these prognostic factors. This dataset has no missing values [76].

2.9.4 SPECTF Heart Disease Dataset

This dataset has characteristics derived from cardiac SPECT (single photon emission computed tomography) pictures. The dataset comprises a total of 44 variables utilized for diagnosing heart disease. This dataset has records of 267 individuals. This dataset can be accessed in the UCI repository (SPECTF Heart) [110]. Each patient is categorized as either normal or aberrant.

2.9.5 Heart Disease Dataset (IEEE Comprehensive)

This heart disease dataset is generated by amalgamating five well-known heart disease datasets that were previously available independently but not integrated. This dataset amalgamates five heart datasets over 11 shared features, rendering it the most extensive heart disease dataset currently accessible for research purposes. The five datasets utilized for its curation are Cleveland, Hungarian, Switzerland, Long Beach VA, and Statlog (Heart) Data Set. This dataset comprises 1190 instances and 11 characteristics. The datasets were aggregated to facilitate research on heart disease or CAD-related machine learning and data mining methods to enhance clinical diagnosis and early treatment available in IEEE Data Port [60].

2.9.6 Cardiovascular Disease (Mendeley) Dataset

Additionally, another dataset is accessible at the Mendeley Data portal, like the IEEE Data Port, with around 1000 cases and 12 associated attributes about an individual's risk of heart disease. There is only one extra feature, termed "number of major vessels". This heart disease dataset was obtained from a multi-speciality hospital in India. It encompasses over 14 prevalent characteristics, rendering it one of the most comprehensive heart disease datasets available for research purposes. This dataset comprises 1000 participants with 12 attributes. This dataset can facilitate the development of early-stage cardiac disease detection and the creation of predictive machine learning models [75].

2.9.7 Framingham Heart Disease (FHS) Dataset

The Framingham dataset, available on Kaggle [90], contains 4,240 records and 15 features representing demographic, behavioural, and medical risk factors. Its goal is to predict a patient's 10-year risk of developing coronary heart disease (CHD). Some feature values are missing, and the data originates from an ongoing cardiovascular study in Framingham, Massachusetts.

Table 2.7: Heart Disease Datasets Overview

#	Dataset	# Features	# Instances	# No Risk (0)	# Risk (1)
1.	Cleveland	76 (14)	303	164	139
2.	Hungarian	76 (14)	294	188	106
3.	Switzerland	76 (14)	123	8	115
4.	Long Beach	76 (14)	200	51	149
5.	Statlog	76 (14)	270	150	120
6.	Z-Alizadeh Sani	54 (14)	303	87	216
7.	Heart Disease Dataset (IEEE)	11	1190	561	629
8.	Cardiovascular Disease (Mendeley)	12	1000	420	580
9.	Framingham Heart Study (FHS)	15	4240	3596	644
10.	SPECTF Heart	44	267	55	212

2.10 Performance Measurement Metrics

In heart disease risk prediction, it is essential to thoroughly assess the efficacy of predictive models to guarantee precise, reliable, and clinically pertinent results. Performance evaluation measures offer quantifiable insights into a model's efficacy in differentiating between healthy persons and those at risk of heart disease. These measurements are crucial for informing clinical decision-making and enhancing patient care. This section examines the prevalent performance measures utilized in heart disease prediction and categorization models.

The various performance metrics are utilized to evaluate the predictive efficacy and clinical reliability of heart disease risk prediction models. In healthcare, the selection of suitable evaluation measures is essential to balance the trade-offs between accurately identifying at-risk patients (sensitivity) and preventing wasteful interventions for healthy persons (specificity). The subsequent subsections elaborate on these indicators comprehensively. This section examines diverse performance indicators, such as accuracy (Ac), precision (Pr), recall (Re), specificity, F1-score (Fs), and confusion matrix (CM), among others. Also, the evaluation of the model includes k-fold mean accuracy (Ma), Cohen's Kappa score (Cks), model standard deviation (Sd), and ROC-AUC scores (Ra).

2.10.1 Confusion Matrix (CM)

Machine learning-based heart disease classification models are evaluated using a confusion matrix, which compares actual and predicted classes in a binary scenario (presence or absence of disease). It helps identify correct and incorrect predictions, especially in imbalanced datasets. The matrix includes True Positives (TP) – correctly predicted positives, True Negatives (TN) – correctly predicted negatives, False Positives (FP) – negatives wrongly predicted as positives (Type I error), and False Negatives (FN) – positives wrongly predicted as negatives (Type II error). This aids in understanding and improving model performance. The binary classification model's confusion matrix is shown in Table 2.8.

Table 2.8: Confusion Matrix for Heart Disease Prediction

Actual Target Level	**Prediction Target Level**	
	HD = 1 (Positive)	**Normal = 0 (Negative)**
HD = 1 (True)	True Positive (TP)	False Negative (FN) Type II Error
Normal = 0 (False)	False Positive (FP) Type I Error	True Negative (TN)

2.10.2 Accuracy (Ac)

Accuracy is a crucial parameter for assessing the performance of a classification model and is derived from the CM. It quantifies the overall ratio of accurate predictions generated by the model and how frequently the model's predictions align with the actual class labels. In the context of heart disease prediction, high accuracy indicates that most individuals, regardless of their heart disease status, are accurately categorized. Nevertheless, accuracy may be misleading in the presence of class imbalance; for instance, if most dataset samples are healthy, a model could achieve high accuracy by predicting "healthy" for all instances. The accuracy is calculated according to the given formulas 2.51 and 2.52.

$$Accuracy = \frac{(Number\ of\ correct\ prediction)}{(Total\ number\ of\ predictions)} \tag{2.51}$$

$$Accuracy = \frac{(TP + TN)}{(TP + FP + FN + TN)} \tag{2.52}$$

2.10.3 Precision (Pr)

Precision, also known as positive predictive value, is an important metric that measures how accurately a classification model identifies true positive cases. In the context of heart disease prediction, it represents the proportion of patients correctly predicted to have the disease out of all those labelled as positive by the model. A high precision score means that most individuals flagged as at risk genuinely have the condition, helping to minimize false positives and avoid unnecessary tests or treatments for healthy individuals. Also, it is evaluated according to Eq. 2.53.

$$Precision = \frac{TP}{(TP + FP)} \tag{2.53}$$

2.10.4 Recall/Sensitivity (Pr)

Recall assesses the model's efficacy in identifying all genuine positive cases, specifically people who genuinely have heart disease. In medical applications such as heart disease prediction, recall is essential, as overlooking actual cases (false negatives) can significantly impact patient health. High recall indicates that the model identifies the majority of people who genuinely have heart disease. It guarantees a reduced number of missed patients (low false negatives). In this case, high recall indicates that the model identifies the majority of people who genuinely have heart disease. It guarantees a reduced number of missed patients (low FN). The recall is derived from the CM as follows: Eq. 2.54.

$$Recall = \frac{TP}{TP + FN} \tag{2.54}$$

2.10.5 Specificity (Sp)

Specificity is a crucial parameter that assesses a model's efficacy in identifying true negative cases. The statement addresses the inquiry regarding the number of genuinely healthy patients (lacking cardiac disease) that the model accurately classified as normal. In the context of heart disease risk prediction, high specificity indicates that the model reduces false positives (FP). Specificity is especially advantageous when the expense of false positives (unneeded therapies, further testing) is significant. It is essential to remember that while documenting positive cases, healthy patients should not be unnecessarily worried. The formula 2.55 represent the specificity of an ML model classification.

$$Specificity = \frac{TN}{TN + FP} \tag{2.55}$$

2.10.6 F1-Score (Fs)

The F1-score combines precision and recall into a single metric, making it useful when balancing false positives and false negatives. As the harmonic mean of precision and recall, it ranges from 0 to 1, with 1 representing ideal performance. A high F1 score reflects a model's strong balance between accuracy and completeness in predictions, as in Eq. 2.56.

$$F1\_Score = 2 \times \frac{\text{Precision} \times \text{Recall}}{\text{Precision} + \text{Recall}} \tag{2.56}$$

2.10.7 Standard Deviation (Sd)

Standard Deviation (SD) quantifies the degree of variation or dispersion within a set of predictive outcomes. It indicates the extent to which the performance parameter (such as accuracy, precision, etc.) fluctuates throughout numerous iterations of your model. If your model's accuracy (or any other measure) fluctuates significantly across runs, it indicates that the model's performance is less reliable (high standard deviation). A low standard deviation indicates that the model exhibits consistent performance throughout various iterations, demonstrating robust stability. Identifies the discrepancies in the projected values and quantifies the variance between the erroneous and the actual score to be forecasted. A lower standard deviation indicates a more stable model, as in Eq. 2.57.

$$Sd = \sqrt{\frac{1}{n-1}\sum_{i=1}^{n}(x_i - \bar{x})^2} \tag{2.57}$$

where:

- n: Number of repeated runs or experiments.
- x_i: Performance metric value from the ith run.

- $\bar{x}$: Mean of the performance metric across runs.

$$\bar{x} = \mu = \frac{1}{n}\sum_{i=1}^{n} x_i$$

2.10.8 Cohen's Kappa Score (Cks)

Cohen's Kappa estimates the degree of consistency between two evaluators (or a model and the actual data) who categorize objects into distinct, non-overlapping classifications. It adjusts for coincidental agreement. In classification tasks, it is more reliable than mere accuracy, particularly when addressing imbalanced datasets. This statistic assesses the model's reliability and validity, reflecting the agreement between the two raters about the prediction model.

In the context of heart disease risk prediction models, high accuracy may be misleading when applied to an imbalanced dataset (e.g., a significantly greater number of patients without heart disease compared to those with it). The Cohen-Kappa score accounts for agreement that may occur just by coincidence.

In medical applications, such as forecasting cardiovascular disease, false positives and false negatives yield major implications. The Cohen-Kappa statistic indicates if the predictions of the model outperform random chance. A low κ value, despite excellent accuracy, indicates a potential issue that the model may not be genuinely applicable in real clinical environments. The mathematical formula is derived as follows: 2.58.

$$Kappa = \kappa = \frac{p_o - p_e}{1 - p_e} \tag{2.58}$$

where:

- p_o: is the observed agreement (accuracy).

$$p_o = \frac{TP + TN}{TP + TN + FP + FN}$$

- p_e: is the expected agreement by chance.

$$p_e = \frac{(TP + FP)(TP + FN) + (FN + TN)(FP + TN)}{(TP + TN + FP + FN)^2}$$

2.10.9 ROC-AUC Score (Ra)

The Receiver Operating Characteristic (ROC) curve plots True Positive Rate (TPR) against False Positive Rate (FPR) across various thresholds. The Area Under the Curve (AUC-ROC) measures the model's ability to distinguish between classes, with higher AUC values indicating better performance. It is especially effective for evaluating models on imbalanced datasets, as it captures the trade-off between sensitivity and false positives across all thresholds. The ROC curve is generated by adjusting the threshold employed by the model to categorise probability as positive or negative. Every point on the ROC curve signifies a distinct threshold. The AUC (area under the curve) encapsulates the complete ROC curve into a singular metric. AUC-ROC assesses the model's capacity to detect heart disease patients across various decision thresholds. It is especially advantageous when seeking to equilibrate sensitivity (recall) in identifying all heart disease instances with specificity in minimizing false positives among healthy individuals. A higher AUC indicates that the model more effectively differentiates between healthy and at-risk patients. The following Eqs. 2.59 and 2.60 uses to derive the ROC-AUC score from the CM.

$$TPR = \frac{TP}{TP + FN} \tag{2.59}$$

$$FPR = \frac{FP}{FP + TN} \tag{2.60}$$

2.10.10 Mean Accuracy (Ma)

K-fold cross-validation is a reliable method for assessing the efficacy of machine learning models. It facilitates the model's ability to generalize effectively to novel data by employing various segments of the dataset for training and testing throughout several iterations. This is a model validation technique that assesses the performance of the heart disease prediction model using unseen data, particularly beneficial for small to medium-sized datasets to mitigate overfitting concerns. The performance metrics are averaged from the values predicted by the model, utilizing various k split datasets for training and testing. The approach divides the dataset into k equal segments (folds) for training purposes. For each fold k, designate the fold k as the validation set and utilize the remaining $k-1$ folds as the training set. Subsequently, the model is trained and assessed for each fold, culminating in the documentation of the accuracy (or any other measure) for each of the k folds. The mean accuracy is derived from the following Eq. 2.61.

$$MeanAccuracy = \frac{1}{K}\sum_{i=1}^{K} \text{Accuracy}_i \tag{2.61}$$

where:

- K = total number of folds
- Accuracy_i = accuracy score on the i-th fold

2.10.11 Binary/Categorical Cross Entropy (BCE/CCE)

Cross-entropy, referred to as logarithmic loss or log loss function, is a widely utilised loss function in deep learning for optimising and assessing the efficacy of a classification model. Binary cross-entropy, often known as log loss, is a loss function employed in binary classification tasks. It measures the disparity between the actual class labels

(0 or 1) and the anticipated probabilities generated by the model. A lower binary cross-entropy value indicates a closer alignment between the model's predictions and the true labels. Binary cross-entropy quantifies the divergence between actual labels and expected probability. When the projected probability p_i closely aligns with the actual label y_i, the BCE value is minimal, signifying an accurate prediction. Conversely, when the anticipated likelihood greatly diverges from the actual label, the BCE value is elevated, signifying a subpar prediction. The logarithmic element of the BCE function imposes a greater penalty on erroneous forecasts than accurate ones.

Binary cross-entropy acts like the loss function for training neural networks in binary classification problems. In a deep learning framework for heart disease risk prediction, binary cross-entropy facilitates the model in adjusting its weights to reduce the discrepancy between actual and anticipated labels. In this case, the ANN models employ a sigmoid activation function in the output layer. BCE is especially advantageous in situations with imbalanced datasets, when one class predominates greatly. Concentrating on probability predictions enables the model to provide precise forecasts despite class imbalance. Categorical cross-entropy, commonly referred to as softmax loss, employs a softmax activation in conjunction with cross-entropy loss for multiclass classification models. The BCE and CCE are calculated by the following two formulas, 2.62 and 2.63.

$$BCE = -\frac{1}{N}\sum_{i=1}^{N}\left[y_i \cdot \log(\hat{y}_i) + (1 - y_i) \cdot \log(1 - \hat{y}_i)\right] \tag{2.62}$$

$$CCE = -\frac{1}{N}\sum_{i=1}^{N}\sum_{c=1}^{C} y_{i,c} \cdot \log(\hat{y}_{i,c}) \tag{2.63}$$

where:

- N = no. of samples
- y_i = true label (0 or 1) for sample i
- $\hat{y}_i$ = predicted probability of heart disease (class 1) for sample i
- C = number of classes
- $y_{i,c}$ = true label (1 if sample i belongs to class c, else 0)
- $\hat{y}_{i,c}$ = predicted probability that sample i belongs to class c

In summary, the performance measurement metrics, which include accuracy, precision, recall, specificity, F1-score, standard deviation, Cohen-Kappa score, ROC-AUC, K-fold mean accuracy, and binary cross-entropy or categorical cross-entropy, provide comprehensive evaluation tools for assessing the efficacy of heart disease prediction frameworks. Adequate comprehension and analysis of these indicators guarantee dependable, generalizable, and resilient models, facilitating enhanced decision-making for heart disease risk evaluation.

2.11 Handling Class Imbalance

Class imbalance is a prevalent challenge in heart disease prediction. Heart disease prediction generally entails datasets in which healthy samples (normal) surpass instances of the disease (positive heart disease), resulting in class imbalance. If not adequately addressed, classifiers often exhibit bias towards the majority class, compromising the identification of heart disease cases, which are the primary focus of clinical concern. To tackle this issue, researchers have investigated several sampling methodologies. These include *oversampling, undersampling, and hybrid strategies* aimed at improving minority class representation and achieving more reliable predictions. This section examines these strategies, their mathematical principles, and their application in predicting cardiovascular risk.

2.11.1 SMOTE (Synthetic Minority Oversampling Technique)

SMOTE is an over-sampling method commonly employed to rectify class imbalance by generating synthetic instances of the minority class instead of replicating existing samples. SMOTE produces synthetic instances for the minority class (heart disease cases) by interpolating between existing minority samples and their nearest neighbours. It enhances the model's ability to discern the decision boundary between classes by augmenting the minority class within feature space. The synthetic sample $\mathbf{x}_{\text{new}}$ is created by linearly interpolating between an existing minority sample $\mathbf{x}$ and one of its k-nearest neighbors $\mathbf{x}_{\text{nn}}$. The mathematical formula is as follows in Eq. 2.64.

$$\mathbf{x}_{\text{new}} = \mathbf{x} + \delta \cdot (\mathbf{x}_{\text{nn}} - \mathbf{x}) \tag{2.64}$$

where:

- $\mathbf{x}$ is the original minority class sample.
- $\mathbf{x}_{\text{nn}}$ is one of the k-nearest neighbors of $\mathbf{x}$.
- δ is a random number from a uniform distribution that generates a point along the line segment between x and x_{nn} Uniform$(0, 1)$.

Justification: In heart disease datasets, minority classes frequently denote patients with circumstances such as pathological cases. Employing SMOTE improves the model's understanding of the minority class feature space, thereby increasing sensitivity and reducing false negatives. By generating synthetic samples rather than duplicating existing ones, SMOTE helps prevent overfitting to minority instances and enhances model robustness in clinical applications.

Clinical data frequently contain noisy or marginal situations. SMOTE facilitates the creation of varied minority class instances within the decision zone, prompting the classifier to establish a broader border for heart disease prediction. Nonetheless, SMOTE may provide overlapping (noisy) samples adjacent to the majority class boundary, thus impairing performance in certain situations.

2.11.2 ADASYN (Adaptive Synthetic Sampling)

ADASYN is a sophisticated oversampling method aimed at addressing imbalanced datasets. It dynamically generates synthetic samples in regions of the feature space where the minority class is under-represented or more difficult for the model to learn. In contrast to SMOTE, which generates synthetic samples uniformly across all minority class instances, ADASYN focuses on more challenging samples. It produces additional synthetic data for minority class instances that lie near class boundaries or in sparsely populated regions of the feature space. This "adaptive" feature enhances the classifier's efficacy in difficult-to-choose regions. For each minority instance x_i, the number of synthetic samples is calculated as follows in Eq. 2.65.

$$G_i = \frac{d_i}{\sum_{j=1}^{n_{\text{minority}}} d_j} \cdot G \tag{2.65}$$

where:

- d_i: number of majority class neighbours of x_i (local density measure).
- G: total number of synthetic samples to generate.

Justification: In heart disease datasets, ADASYN focuses on oversampling more in borderline/difficult regions, like patients with borderline cholesterol levels, making the model more sensitive to clinically ambiguous cases. ADASYN is an adaptive over-sampling method that produces synthetic samples primarily in locations where the minority class is more challenging to learn, specifically in areas with a higher local density of majority class instances. Additional synthetic samples are generated in challenging regions, enhancing classifier sensitivity in certain areas. Conversely, in regions that are easier to learn and where the minority class is already well represented, ADASYN generates fewer synthetic samples, thereby reducing redundancy and preserving data quality.

2.11.3 Tomek Links

Tomek Links is a data cleansing method employed for under-sampling the majority class and enhancing the separation of class boundaries. For two given samples, x_i and x_j, both belong to different classes, one in the majority and the other in the minority, if they are each other's nearest neighbours, then they (x_i, x_j) form a Tomek Link. Formally it is represented as follows in Eq. 2.66.

$$d(x_i, x_j) = \min \{d(x_i, x_k) \mid x_k \in \mathcal{D}\} \quad \text{and} \quad d(x_j, x_i) = \min \left\{d(x_j, x_k) \mid x_k \in \mathcal{D}\right\} \tag{2.66}$$

where:

- $d(x_i, x_j)$ is the distance (commonly Euclidean).

- $\mathcal{D}$ is the dataset.

The Tomek Links can be formed accordingly between (x_i, x_j) as using the formula 2.67:

$$C(x_i) \neq C(x_j) \quad \text{and} \quad N(x_i) = x_j \quad \text{and} \quad N(x_j) = x_i \tag{2.67}$$

- $C(x)$ denote the class of instance x.
- $N(x)$ denote the nearest neighbor of x.

After that, it can remove the majority class instance of the Tomek Link pair or remove both instances to further clean the decision boundary.

Justification: In heart disease prediction datasets, the majority class samples (healthy persons) significantly outnumber the minority class (disease cases). Tomek Links eliminates borderline majority samples, consequently diminishing overlapping zones. The result is that the Cleaner class borders diminish misclassification risk, consequently reducing false positives (incorrectly identifying healthy individuals as diseased) and false negatives (overlooking actual illness cases). This preprocessing step improves overall model generalization, particularly when applied prior to advanced oversampling techniques such as SMOTE.

2.11.4 SMOTETomek

SMOTETomek is a hybrid sampling method that integrates two effective ways to tackle class imbalance in datasets, applying SMOTE and Tomek Link in two phases: In the 1st phase, SMOTE produces synthetic instances for the minority class to balance the class distribution. Finally, applying Tomek Links, it eliminates borderlines and potentially loud majority-class instances that are in proximity to the minority class. SMOTETomek combines the strengths of both SMOTE and Tomek Links. It balances the dataset by generating synthetic minority class samples while removing borderline majority class instances. This integration reduces noise and improves class separation, leading to more reliable classification performance.

Justification: The dual-action of SMOTETomek renders it especially useful for imbalanced datasets, such as those found in heart disease risk prediction. SMOTETomek enhances recall in heart disease detection by balancing data and eliminating ambiguous instances, consequently minimizing the likelihood of undiagnosed cases. Additionally, it can improve the model's generalization by mitigating the influence of noisy majority occurrences. In clinical decision-making, the consequences of missing a heart disease diagnosis are substantial. By improving class balance and decision boundary clarity, SMOTETomek becomes a well-suited and effective choice for heart disease prediction frameworks.

2.11.5 SMOTEENN

SMOTEENN is a hybrid data balancing method that integrates both SMOTE and Edited Nearest Neighbours (ENN) undersampling. This combination addresses two primary concerns: Insufficient representation of the minority class, such as cases of heart disease. The existence of noisy or ambiguous majority samples that confound the classifier. SMOTE is initially employed to augment the minority class. Subsequently, Edited Nearest Neighbour (ENN) is utilized to eliminate noisy samples by discarding instances whose class label deviates from the majority label of their k-nearest neighbours. For each instance x_i in the dataset: Identify its k nearest neighbours, commonly $k = 3$. If the majority of its neighbours belong to a different class, the instance x_i is removed using Eqs. 2.68 and 2.69.

$$N_k(x_i) : \{\text{k nearest neighbors of } x_i\} \tag{2.68}$$

$$\text{If: } C(x_i) \neq \text{majority class in } N_k(x_i) \tag{2.69}$$

Justification: In datasets for heart disease prediction, the minority class (instances of heart illness) is limited, yet essential. Noisy majority instances (healthy cases resembling ill cases) might mislead classifiers. SMOTE balances the dataset by generating synthetic minority class samples, thereby improving model sensitivity and recall in heart disease detection. Edited Nearest Neighbours (ENN) further removes noisy samples, sharpens decision boundaries, and reduces false positive predictions. This combined effect enhances both recall (identifying actual disease cases) and precision (preventing the misclassification of healthy individuals as diseased), as a result augmenting the model's robustness in clinical risk prediction tasks.

In conclusion, this section examined diverse strategies for addressing data imbalance, including SMOTE, ADASYN, Tomek Links, SMOTETomek, and SMOTEENN. In the context of heart disease prediction, these methods address the critical problem of class imbalance that often biases classifiers toward the majority class. At the same time, these methods ensure improved recognition of the minority class, which represents true disease cases and is central to clinical diagnosis. Also, these methods improve prediction accuracy and model reliability by effectively synthesizing minority samples, eliminating noisy instances, and balancing the data distribution. Ultimately, employing approaches such as SMOTE, SMOTETomek, and SMOTEENN enhances sensitivity (recall) while simultaneously augmenting overall predictive efficacy without impacting data integrity. Their applications are especially significant for clinical datasets where timely and precise prediction of minority disease cases is essential.

2.12 Summary and Key Findings

This chapter presented a thorough investigation of heart disease prediction frameworks through the analysis of conventional ML classifiers, EL methods, ANNs, and FS strategies. The procedures, applications, datasets, and performance measures were examined, with emphasis on merits, limitations, and challenges. Ensemble methods, including bagging, boosting, stacking, and voting, exhibited enhancements in generalization, whilst ANNs and DL models provided sophisticated learning skills but encountered issues related to

interpretability. Feature selection techniques facilitated dimensionality reduction and improved performance.
Classical ML models (**Approach 1**), such as LR, DT, SVM, RF, KNN, XGB, and others, have repeatedly demonstrated strong baseline performance in predicting cardiac disease, especially within structured clinical datasets. Nevertheless, they frequently encountered difficulties associated with overfitting and generalization in imbalanced or high-dimensional datasets.
Also, in the investigation of ensemble learning methodologies (**Approach 2**), strategies such as bagging, boosting, stacking, and voting markedly improved prediction accuracy and stability by leveraging multiple base learners. Random Forest (bagging) and XGB (boosting) have consistently demonstrated superior performance in many trials. Notwithstanding these advancements, ensemble models encountered difficulties in interpretability and computational expense, requiring meticulous trade-offs in clinical applications.
The segment on artificial neural networks (**Approach 3**) addressed the adaptability of deep learning frameworks in modelling intricate, non-linear associations within cardiovascular data. Research employing multilayer perceptrons (MLPs), convolutional neural networks (CNNs), and recurrent neural networks (RNNs) demonstrated enhanced prediction efficacy compared to conventional models. These methodologies often require extensive hyperparameter tuning and careful optimization of ANN architectures. It also involves selecting suitable optimizers and activation functions, addressing challenges related to overfitting and generalization, and managing class imbalance. In addition, many approaches exhibit limited transparency in decision-making, which can hinder clinical interpretability.
Finally, the feature selection strategies (**Approach 4**) were demonstrated to significantly improve prediction accuracy and interpretability. Filter, wrapper, and embedding approaches, in conjunction with sophisticated tools such as Boruta and SHAP-based feature selection, facilitated the elimination of unnecessary features, resulting in enhanced generalization and model simplicity. Research indicates that proficient feature selection enhances predictive accuracy and elucidates critical clinical indicators of heart disease.

The chapter concludes by highlighting key research gaps and future directions. Specifically, there is a pressing need for hybrid frameworks that integrate multiple base learners into ensembles, combine feature selection with deep learning architectures, and employ more advanced interpretability tools for complex models. Furthermore, underexplored areas such as deep feature selection and multi-modal data integration present significant opportunities to advance heart disease prediction. These insights lay the foundation for the subsequent chapters. These chapters address the identified gaps by proposing an innovative hybrid predictive framework that integrates ensemble learning, advanced feature selection, and explainable AI. This framework advances the development of more accurate, efficient, and clinically interpretable cardiovascular risk prediction models.

This chapter's research contributions have been published in a peer-reviewed (Archives of Computational Methods in Engineering, Springer), high-quality review journal [112]. This is a comprehensive survey of HDP approaches, confirming its originality, novelty, and significant importance in the HD risk prediction framework design for the decision support system.

3

Dual-Stage Hyperparameter-tuned Ensemble Learning Approach

The precise and prompt forecasting of heart disease (HD) risk is essential for efficient clinical intervention and preventive therapy. Despite the efficacy of individual ML and ensemble classifiers, challenges such as overfitting, limited generalization, and class imbalance continue to compromise prediction reliability in clinical healthcare data. This chapter presents an advanced computational framework for predicting heart disease risk, aligning with the first research objective of this thesis. It solves existing constraints via a dual-stage hyperparameter-tuned meta-ensemble stacking methodology. The proposed method utilizes the predictive capabilities of ensemble learning to improve model resilience, optimize predictive performance, and enhance generalization. This system combines the strengths of various classifiers using a stacking method while optimizing each component's hyperparameter utilizing GridSearchCV and RandomizedSearchCV methods.

This framework is designed using five machine learning classifiers: LR, SVM, DT, RF, and XGB, chosen for their shown efficiency and prevalence in the literature. The selection of these models is driven by their synergistic advantages: linear models for clarity, tree-based models for managing non-linearity and feature interactions, and ensemble approaches for revealing deep interactions. The proposed stacking ensemble architecture combines optimized RF and DT classifiers as base learners, with a hyperparameter-tuned XGB model performing as the meta learner. This combination is chosen because XGB demonstrated higher performance compared to the five baseline models in initial trials. Furthermore, to rectify an inherent class imbalance in the datasets and guarantee uniform model performance across all classes, a sophisticated sampling technique, SMOTETomek, is incorporated into the data processing pipeline.

The framework's efficiency is assessed employing two extensive benchmark datasets: the *IEEE comprehensive heart disease dataset*, comprising 1190 examples, and the *Mendeley CVD dataset*, having 1000 instances, each with 12 clinically significant features. This ensures a thorough assessment of the model's effectiveness across diverse data situations, providing insights into its adaptability and generalizability. To improve predictive performance and reduce overfitting, advanced hyperparameter tuning methods, GridSearchCV and RandomizedSearchCV, are employed with cross-validation-based assessment.

This chapter is organized initially by defining the motivations and the objectives in Section 3.1, aligned with the first research objective of this thesis. The corresponding contributions are stated in the next section, 3.2. Also, it provides a comprehensive overview of the datasets, preprocessing strategies, selected machine learning models, hyperparameter tuning techniques, and the architecture of the proposed stacking ensemble framework in Section 3.3. Moreover, it methodically outlines the conceptual foundations, methodological factors, implementation procedures, and evaluation strategies employed to determine the efficacy of the framework in predicting heart disease risk. Furthermore, experimental results and rigorous performance analysis validate the effectiveness and interpretability of the proposed approach, which is presented in Sections 3.4 and 3.5, addressing key challenges highlighted in the previous chapters. Finally, the chapter summary with key findings is summarised in Section 3.6.

3.1 Motivations and Objectives

Cardiovascular disease continues to be a primary cause of illness and death worldwide. Timely intervention and treatment planning necessitate early detection and accurate risk assessment. In the age of data-driven healthcare, various ML methodologies have been introduced to forecast cardiac disease utilizing structured clinical data. Nonetheless, numerous significant problems continue to restrict the practical implementation and dependability of these models. A primary difficulty highlighted in the preceding chapter is that individual ML models frequently struggle to generalize effectively across diverse datasets. Models such as LR, SVM, DT, RF, and XGB exhibit considerable performance variability contingent upon data attributes, including feature interactions, noise, and imbalance.

Furthermore, the class imbalance is an ongoing issue in clinical datasets, characterized by a much greater number of non-heart disease occurrences (majority class) compared to heart disease instances (minority class). This disparity results in biased learning, causing models to preferentially represent the majority class, consequently lowering recall and F1-score for the minority class, which is crucial in medical diagnoses. A significant constraint is model overfitting and insufficient generalization, particularly when models are trained on limited or imbalanced datasets. Conventional ML models, if not properly optimized, often acquire misleading patterns, resulting in elevated training accuracy but poor results in real-world applications.

To address these concerns, ensemble learning approaches, especially stacking, provide a robust solution to these problems. Stacking integrates several base learners and inputs their predictions into a superior meta-learner. This utilizes the diversity of multiple models, collecting varied data patterns while mitigating the risk of overfitting. The efficacy of a stacking ensemble is significantly influenced by appropriate hyperparameter optimization and the selection of base and meta learners.

The prime research objectives of this chapter are as follows:

- To integrate the advantages of multiple classifiers with a base as well as a meta-learner of an ensemble method.

- To develop a framework based on a dual-stage hyperparameter-tuned stacking ensemble, optimized by tuning methods like GridSearchCV and RandomizedSearchCV to enhance model performance.
- To utilize the cross-validation and optimization method to guarantee resilience across datasets, combat overfitting, and generalization.
- Advanced resampling methodologies, such as SMOTETomek, are employed to address class imbalance efficiently.
- To validate generalizability and robustness across two real-world datasets.

The selection of ML models and methodologies is based on a comprehensive literature assessment; the first two approaches, as mentioned in Chapter 2, Sections 2.5 and 2.6. It reveals a unique research potential for creating a more generalized, precise, and interpretable heart disease risk prediction system.

3.2 Research Contributions

The *first objective* of this research study is formulated through the extensive literature survey related to the classical ML classifiers and the ensemble learning approaches that are considered for the prediction of HP. This chapter discusses challenges associated with varied ML model selection, overfitting, generalization, and class imbalance in HDP by introducing a robust, optimized ensemble-based prediction framework. The principal contributions are as follows:

- **Model Selection Based on Literature Evidence:** The selection of commonly utilized and high-performing conventional ML classifiers, including XGB, LR, RF, DT, and SVM, is made for initial deployment. Their performance comparison is predicated on their accuracy and prominence in existing heart disease research.
- **Dual-Stage Hyperparameter-Tuned Stacking Framework:** A novel two-stage stacking ensemble prediction framework is introduced. It utilizes hyperparameter-optimized RF and DT models as base learners, alongside an optimized XGB model as the meta-learner to improve predictive accuracy and generalizability.
- **Model Optimization via Hyperparameter Tuning:** To obtain optimal predictive performance, two systematic hyperparameter optimization methods, GridSearchCV and RandomizedSearchCV, are employed for each base model and meta-learner. These methods determine the most effective estimator configurations.
- **Prevention of Overfitting and Generalization Error:** The k-fold cross-validation method is employed to ensure performance stability across different data partitions during the modelling phase. Additionally, standard deviation analysis is also conducted to reduce overfitting and underfitting and to validate model performance.
- **Handling Data Imbalance with Advanced Sampling:** To resolve class imbalance in datasets, sophisticated hybrid sampling methods like SMOTETomek are

employed during the preprocessing stage. It facilitates enhanced recognition of the minority class and overall model resilience.

- **Comprehensive Evaluation:** Thorough assessment employing various measures, accuracy, precision, recall, F1-score, ROC-AUC, Cohen's kappa, standard deviation, and cross-validation mean accuracy on two datasets.

This chapter study has been published in a peer-reviewed journal [113], confirming its originality, novelty, and practical importance in the clinical HD risk prediction framework.

3.3 Proposed Methodology: Datasets and Preprocessing

The workflow diagram of the proposed framework for HD risk prediction is shown in Fig. 3.1. The layer structure one through five includes the detailed insight presentation: dataset collection, exploratory data analysis (EDA), preprocessing, dataset splitting, model training with default and hyperparameter customization, and, finally, the presented stacking model.

3.3.1 Dataset Collection and Description

The dataset used in this research is gathered via IEEE Data Port, an open-source web platform [60]. This has been linked to five additional datasets that came from various origins: the Statlog dataset, the Hungarian dataset, the Cleveland dataset, the Switzerland dataset, and the Long Beach dataset. The combined dataset (DF-1), which has been gathered from the five datasets mentioned above, includes 1190 instances, a total of 11 significant features, and a binary target outcome (HD: 1, Normal: 0) that indicates if a person has a heart risk. Additionally, DF-2, another dataset like the IEEE Data Port but with fewer instances of roughly 1000 records and 12 associated features indicating an individual's risk of heart disease, is gathered from the Mendeley Data Portal [75]. There is only one more feature, "number of major vessels". The performance of the deployed model with comparable features but more varied database variance is validated using the DF-2. Table 3.1 below provides the collected IEEE comprehensive HD dataset descriptions along with the corresponding instances. Also, Table 3.2 summarizes an in-depth investigation of the features of two datasets, including their definitions, data types, and the quantity of null values observed during the EDA pipeline.
The motivation is to use this study to utilize two datasets to validate the effectiveness of the proposed model and to examine its generalization capability by identifying any signs of overfitting or underfitting.

3.3.2 Data Preprocessing

In machine learning models, data preprocessing, also known as feature engineering, is a crucial technique for preparing raw data so that it may be used for model training and testing. To attain the objective of obtaining an improved outcome, the features are redesigned and made simpler. To adequately train the dataset, several preprocessing procedures are

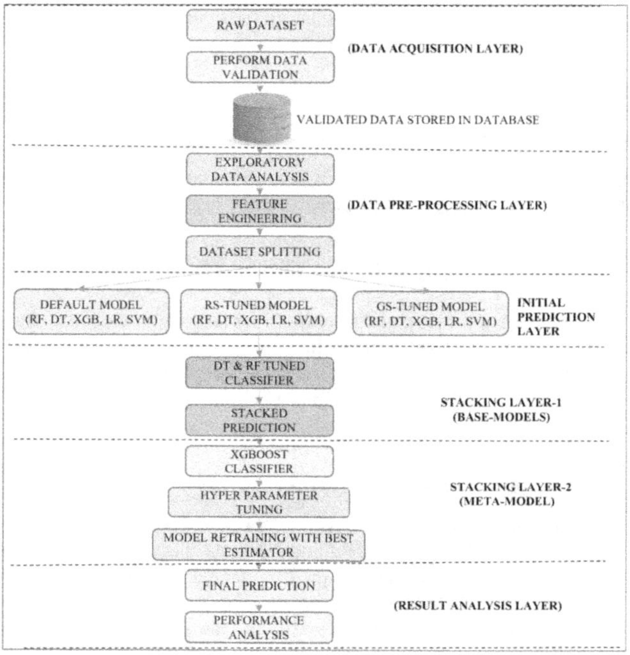

Figure 3.1: The workflow diagram of the proposed framework of the boosting-based meta-ensemble stacked model

Dataset Origin	**# Instances**
Statlog (Heart) Dataset	270
Switzerland Dataset	123
Hungarian Dataset	294
Cleveland Dataset	303
Long Beach VA Dataset	200
Total	**1190**

Table 3.1: Summary of Collected IEEE Comprehensive HD Dataset

implemented. Because each feature in the two datasets, DF-1 and DF-2, had identical properties, the same preprocessing procedures are used on both. EDA revealed two extra

#	Feature Name	Data Types Numerical (N) Categorical (C)	DF-1 # NULL	DF-2 # NULL	Description
1	Age	N	0	0	Age of patients in years (20 to 80)
2	Sex	C	0	0	Gender: male (1) and female (0)
3	Chest pain type	C	0	0	1 = typical angina, 2 = atypical angina, 3 = non-anginal pain, 4 = asymptomatic
4	Resting BP	N	1	0	Resting blood pressure level
5	Cholesterol	N	172	53	Concentration of cholesterol
6	Fasting blood sugar	C	0	0	1 if fasting blood sugar > 120 mg/dl, else 0
7	Resting ECG	C	0	0	0 = normal, 1 = abnormal ECG result at rest
8	Max heart rate	N	0	0	Maximum recorded heart rate
9	Exercise Angina	C	0	0	0 = no angina, 1 = angina induced by exercise
10	Old Peak	N	0	0	ST depression induced by exercise relative to rest
11	ST slope	C	0	0	0 = Normal, 1 = Unsloping, 2 = Flat, 3 = Down sloping
12	Target	C	0	0	Heart disease status: 1 = HD, 0 = Normal

Table 3.2: Feature summary with data types and missing values in DF-1 and DF-2

columns in DF-2 ("patientid" and "noofmajorvessels"), which are dropped as redundant without affecting model performance. The acquired datasets are preprocessed using several techniques to prepare them for model training and testing.

Handling Null/Missing Values

In the dataset, null values stand in for missing or absurd values. EDA revealed 172 null values in "cholesterol" (DF-1) and 53 in "serumcholesterol" (DF-2). Accordingly, the tailored imputation technique is used to fill such null values. In DF-1, the invalid 'Resting BP' value (0) is corrected using median-based customized imputation to preserve dataset originality.

In these two datasets, let $X = \{x_1, x_2, \ldots, x_n\}$ be the values of a feature (e.g., cholesterol), where some values may be missing (*NaN*). Let $\tilde{x} = \text{median}(X_{\text{observed}})$ denote the median of all non-missing values in X. Then, the imputed value x_i^* for each $x_i \in X$ is defined as follows in equation 3.1:

$$x_i^* = \begin{cases} x_i, & \text{if } x_i \neq \text{NaN} \\ \tilde{x}, & \text{if } x_i = \text{NaN} \end{cases} \tag{3.1}$$

Feature Correlation Heat Map

Finding a feature correlation heat map involves determining the relationship between two or more variables. In this instance, determining how the features match the target variable is necessary to use highly correlated features for training. The dataset's correlation feature heat map makes this task simple. The heat map is generated using the Pearson correlation coefficient among the features and the target variable as follows: Let the dataset have p features $\{X_1, X_2, \ldots, X_p\}$. The Pearson correlation coefficient between two features X_i and X_j is computed as in equation 3.2:

$$\rho_{ij} = \frac{\sum_{k=1}^{n}(x_{ki} - \bar{x}_i)(x_{kj} - \bar{x}_j)}{\sqrt{\sum_{k=1}^{n}(x_{ki} - \bar{x}_i)^2} \cdot \sqrt{\sum_{k=1}^{n}(x_{kj} - \bar{x}_j)^2}} \tag{3.2}$$

where:

- x_{ki} is the kth observation of feature X_i.
- $\bar{x}_i$ is the mean of feature X_i.
- $\rho_{ij} \in [-1, 1]$ indicates the linear correlation between X_i and X_j.
- The complete correlation matrix $\mathbf{R} \in \mathbb{R}^{p \times p}$ is constructed by computing ρ_{ij} for all $i, j \in \{1, \ldots, p\}$.

The resulting correlation matrix is:

$$\mathbf{R} = \begin{bmatrix} 1 & \rho_{12} & \cdots & \rho_{1p} \\ \rho_{21} & 1 & \cdots & \rho_{2p} \\ \vdots & \vdots & \ddots & \vdots \\ \rho_{p1} & \rho_{p2} & \cdots & 1 \end{bmatrix}$$

In Fig. 3.2, the DF-1 and DF-2 heat maps in which the displayed cool and dark shades, respectively, indicate the features' negative and positive correlations with the target features.

Feature Density Distribution

Feature density is a useful tool for determining the distribution of features across a dataset and identifying outliers, whether they are present or not. A histogram illustrates the probability distribution of each feature. The features are dense, and most of the values are thought to be non-zero. Consequently, the dense feature vectors are manageable for the ML classifiers. Given the modest size of each feature space value, features ought to be crucial for HD prediction. In the histogram, it is observed that all feature values are numerical (either integers or floats), and some of them are categorical values with labels. So, there is no need to apply any kind of encoding techniques to convert them into numerical values. The feature density curves of all the features for both DF-1 and DF-2 are derived. However, for authenticity, only the DF-1 density curves are given below in Fig. 3.3.

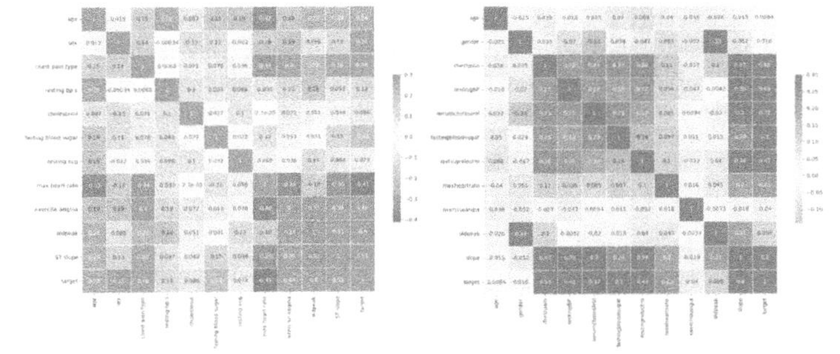

(a) Correlation heat map of DF-1 (b) Correlation heat map of DF-2

Figure 3.2: The Correlation heat map of DF-1 and DF-2 before sampling

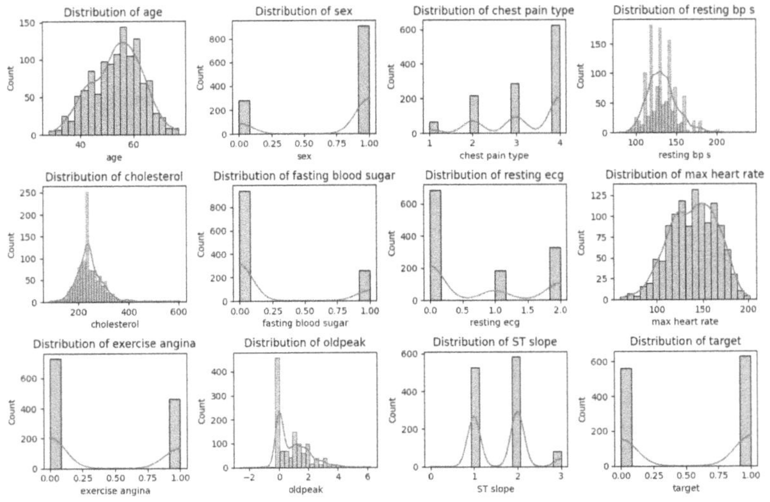

Figure 3.3: The feature density distribution of DF-1

Normalization or Feature Scaling

Feature scaling or normalization is a useful technique for eliminating outliers from each feature in a dataset. In general, it entails lowering the values of all features except the goal outcome to the same scale between 0 and 1. To standardize and scalarize the ranges of values in the DF-1 and DF-2 datasets, the Scikit Learn *StandardScaler* module is used.

The following formula 3.3 is used to generate the scaled values between 0 and 1, resulting in a normalized distribution with zero mean and unit variance. This normalization is particularly beneficial for machine learning classifiers that are sensitive to the scale of input features, as it ensures balanced feature contributions and stable model training.

$$x' = \frac{x - \mu}{\sigma} \tag{3.3}$$

- x = original feature value
- μ = mean of the feature
- σ = standard deviation of the feature
- x' = standardized (normalized) value

Target class Data Imbalance

The EDA of the datasets revealed that the objective variable is nearly balanced in DF-1 but imbalanced in DF-2. As a result, oversampling approaches are applied to achieve target class balance. But it is not desirable to construct synthetic values for the target column in disease prediction with a low-instance dataset, since this could lead to biases in the predictions made by the machine learning models. But, in this case, the minority class (HD) is smaller than the majority class, so it is a better choice to apply the sampling method. To prevent bias toward the majority class, the hybrid SMOTETomek method, combining SMOTE for oversampling and Tomek Links for noise reduction, is applied. Table 3.3 illustrates the class distribution of DF-1 and DF-2 before and after applying the SMOTETomek method. Also, the distribution of classes in DF-1 and DF-2 with the effect of sampling is depicted in Fig. 3.4 and Fig. 3.5.

Target	Without Sampling		Sampling (SMOTETomek)	
	# DF-1	# DF-2	# DF-1	# DF-2
HD: 1	629	580	616	572
Normal: 0	561	420	616	572
Total	1190	1000	1232	1144

Table 3.3: Class Distribution Before and After Applying SMOTETomek Sampling

3.3.3 Validation Methods

Since there are fewer examples in the dataset, the next step is to determine how many instances can be used as training data for the models. As a result, before training, the datasets are appropriately partitioned using k-fold cross-validation, which divides the data into train and test subsets at suitable split points. This is mostly used to calculate the

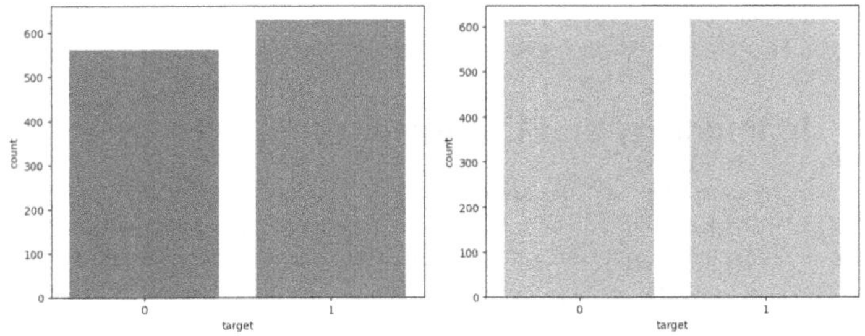

(a) Class Distribution of DF-1 before Sampling

(b) Class Distribution of DF-1 after Sampling

Figure 3.4: The class distribution of DF-1 before and after applying SMOTETomek

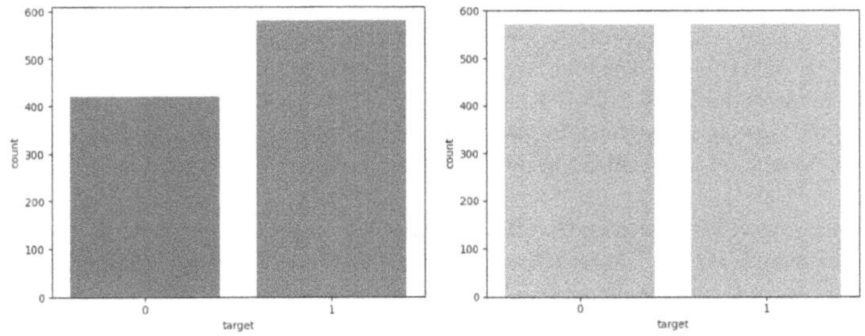

(a) Class Distribution of DF-2 before Sampling

(b) Class Distribution of DF-2 after Sampling

Figure 3.5: The class distribution of DF-2 before and after applying SMOTETomek

prediction model skill that can be tested each time on hypothetical data. The various k-reference values are utilized to determine the precise k-fold value to expand the model's prediction. Before each model deployment, the appropriate value of k is selected to trade off the bias-variance of the deployed models as well as the gathered data taken into consideration.

The two different model validation techniques used in this work are k-fold validation and hold-out validation. 90% of the data instances are used to train the various models in the hold-out strategy, while the remaining 10% are used in each example to assess the performance of the prediction model. The k-fold validation process divides the dataset into k sections. Using $(k-1)$ groups for model training and one group for model testing, the classification performance is evaluated over k iterations. Each cycle uses the other groups for training and selects one group for testing. Averaging the predicted outcomes across k rounds yields the classifier's performance. To obtain more accurate findings with a reduced likelihood of overfitting the deployed models, the 10-fold cross-validation is employed.

3.4 Methodology and Experimental Results

The subsequent methodology for deploying the HD risk prediction model involves using two datasets, DF-1 and DF-2. These datasets are now prepared for deployment following the use of necessary preprocessing procedures. The selection of the initial ML classifier and correctly training the models came next. For this purpose, the five well-known machine learning models - LR, SVM, DT, RF, and XGB are chosen. In the literature, these models are predominantly employed by researchers to estimate HD risk with greater precision and accuracy.

This section describes the proposed framework for predicting the risk of heart disease, which is based on a dual-stage ensemble stacking method. The original and SMOTETomek-balanced datasets are first deployed to the default parameter settings of five standard machine learning models: LR, SVM, DT, RF, and XGB. After that, the hyperparameter tuning is employed with GridSearchCV and RandomizedSearchCV on each model to improve prediction performance. The final two-stage stacking ensemble is formed by selecting the top three tuned models – XGB, RF, and DT – based on evaluation metrics. In this framework, XGB serves as the meta-learner, while RF and DT are used as base learners. Both the benchmark datasets utilized in this study are consistently subjected to this methodology.

The Mendeley CVD dataset and the IEEE HD dataset are the two benchmark datasets used to assess the framework using k-fold cross-validation. To make sure the framework can be applied to actual medical diagnosis situations, the performance is evaluated using a variety of metrics like Ac, Ma, Pr, Re, Fs, Cks, and Ra. The standard deviation (Sd) for each model is also computed using the accuracy metric. The experimental results for the baseline model training, the hyperparameter configurations, and the final proposed two-stage tuned stacking models are reported in the following sections.

3.4.1 Experimental Setup

The architecture defines the best configurable experimental simulation platform, which is replicated programmatically to deploy the models and find the experimental results. An *Intel(R) Core(TM) i5-1334U CPU @ 1.30 GHz PC running Python 3.7 and Jupyter Notebook 6.5.2* simulates the initial EDA and data preparation experiment. Additionally, by integrating the *GPU T4* into the *Google Collaboratory Compute Engine backend using the Python 3* simulation environment, the significant resource dependency is satisfied. An *i5 processor, an Nvidia GeForce RTX GPU, and the Windows 11 operating system* are used to meet the high computational needs for the hyperparameter search of the models utilizing GridSearchCV and RandomizedSearchCV. Normal computation is carried out in the CPU setup. Additionally, for improved performance, the bagging, voting, and stacking ensemble learning techniques are emulated on a GPU system using a Python programming language environment.

3.4.2 Default Model Deployment

In this first deployment stage, five popular machine learning classifiers are trained and evaluated using their default parameters by mentioning as *random_state: '0'*. To create baseline performance measurements and determine the effect of class imbalance, the models are tested on both the original and SMOTETomek-balanced datasets. The detailed analysis of the above-mentioned default models' experimental results under test conditions with default parameters set is noted in Table 3.4 of DF-1 and DF-2. Also, after applying the sampling method SMOTETomek to balance the target class with the same conditions on the datasets DF-1 and DF-2, the effect on performance is depicted in Table 3.5.

Model	Ac (Ma)	Pr	Re	Fs	Cks	Sd	Ra
DF-1							
RF	96.64	0.95	0.98	0.97	0.93	1.37	0.97
XGB	96.64	0.95	0.98	0.97	0.93	1.13	0.97
DT	95.80	0.95	0.97	0.96	0.92	1.94	0.96
SVM	88.24	0.86	0.94	0.89	0.76	0.35	0.88
LR	84.87	0.86	0.86	0.86	0.70	1.34	0.85
DF-2							
RF	96.00	0.97	0.97	0.97	0.92	0.89	0.96
XGB	95.00	0.95	0.97	0.96	0.90	1.05	0.95
DT	95.00	0.96	0.95	0.96	0.90	1.13	0.95
LR	93.00	0.95	0.93	0.94	0.86	0.57	0.93
SVM	93.00	0.95	0.93	0.94	0.86	1.29	0.93

Table 3.4: The experimental results of deployed models for DF-1 and DF-2

3.4.3 Hyperparameter-Tuned Model Deployment

Thereafter, the *RandomizedSearchCV (RS-CV)* and *GridSearchCV (GS-CV)* are used to optimize hyperparameters for each of the five classifiers to improve model accuracy and generalization. To identify the best combinations, these methods methodically investigate parameter spaces. To assess the improved performance of the adjusted models, they are subsequently redeployed on both datasets. An optimization technique called Randomized Search (RS) finds the best estimators' values of the associated parameters from the models by randomly combining various hyperparameters with the relevant training parameters of a model. All five models are trained using RS-CV, and after using those parameters to carry out the tuning procedure, the optimal parameter values are identified. To improve the results under the test conditions, the models are trained once again using the optimal

Model	Ac (Ma)	Pr	Re	Fs	Cks	Sd	Ra
			SMOTETomek-DF-1				
RF	96.87	0.98	0.95	0.97	0.94	4.06	0.97
XGB	96.71	0.97	0.94	0.95	0.94	4.34	0.97
DT	96.34	0.95	0.94	0.93	0.93	3.22	0.97
SVM	87.10	0.87	0.87	0.87	0.74	3.73	0.87
LR	83.06	0.90	0.74	0.81	0.66	4.42	0.83
			SMOTETomek-DF-2				
RF	99.13	0.98	1.00	0.99	0.98	0.50	0.99
XGB	99.13	0.98	1.00	0.99	0.98	0.64	0.99
DT	98.26	0.97	1.00	0.98	0.97	0.48	0.98
LR	98.26	0.98	0.98	0.98	0.97	0.82	0.98
SVM	97.39	0.98	0.97	0.97	0.95	1.13	0.97

Table 3.5: The experimental results of SMOTETomek with the default parameter of deployed models for DF-1 and DF-2

parameter values. Table 3.6 below lists the results of the 10-fold cross-validation of RS-CV models on both DF-1 and DF-2 in the testing environment.

Another hyper-parameter tuning technique, called *Grid Search (GS)*, looks through every conceivable combination of the best parameter values from the supplied list of parameters. The ideal parameters with optimal estimator values for each model are identified using GS-CV. Again, selected models are then trained using those optimal parameters. The outcomes of the model's execution after it is tested using the 10-fold CV test dataset are reported in Table 3.7.

The primary challenge encountered during the Grid Search Cross-Validation (GS-CV) process lies in selecting appropriate model parameters, as GS evaluates all possible parameter combinations. This exhaustive search significantly increases computational time; therefore, restricting the search space to a small set of the most influential parameters is often more practical and can still yield optimal performance. Additionally, GS-CV requires substantial computational resources to execute efficiently. These challenges were addressed by allocating sufficient system resources during parameter optimization. However, a comparison of the experimental results obtained from the default models, Random Search Cross-Validation (RS-CV), and GS-CV revealed that performance improvements were not consistently satisfactory across all classifiers. Due to the inherent characteristics of linear models (LR and SVM), only the tree-based and the boosting models outperformed them in terms of performance accuracy. The identical experimental setup is used for both datasets to assess the experimental outcomes. To generalize the proposed model across datasets, the same hyperparameter and estimator values for each ML classifier are also considered for deployment under the same experimental setup.

It is observed that in both datasets, after performing RS-CV and GS-CV, considering the applied SMOTETomek to balance the target class, the models like RF, XGB, and DT produce good outcomes compared to linear models like SVM and LR. The deployed models' ROC-AUC curves of the RS-CV and GS-CV concerning datasets DF-1 and DF-2 are derived and are depicted in Figs. 3.6 and 3.7.

Model (RS-CV)	Ac (Ma)	Pr	Re	Fs	Cks	Sd	Ra
DF-1							
RF-RS	97.58	0.98	0.97	0.98	0.95	3.93	0.98
XGB-RS	96.97	0.98	0.97	0.96	0.94	4.72	0.96
DT-RS	96.64	0.98	0.96	0.97	0.94	3.55	0.97
SVC-RS	91.39	0.98	0.98	0.98	0.97	4.49	0.98
LR-RS	83.06	0.90	0.74	0.81	0.66	4.70	0.83
DF-2							
RF-RS	99.13	0.98	1.00	0.99	0.98	0.78	0.99
XGB-RS	99.13	0.98	1.00	0.99	0.98	0.97	0.99
DT-RS	98.65	0.98	0.98	0.98	0.96	1.33	0.99
SVC-RS	97.39	0.98	0.97	0.97	0.95	1.26	0.97
LR-RS	97.39	0.97	0.98	0.97	0.95	1.25	0.97

Table 3.6: The experimental results of the different metrics of the deployed models with RS-CV for DF-1 and DF-2

Further model deployment is decided based on the performance outcomes of the RS-CV and the GS-CV employed models. The difficult task is choosing the models among them to determine how the ensemble methods based on stacking can be deployed going forward. The top-performing classifiers are selected from the three deployment strategy types mentioned above. The comparative results of the RS-CV and GS-CV classifiers, along with the accuracy of the models using a standalone classifier with default parameter values, are graphically represented for the DF-1 and DF-2 in Figs. 3.8 and 3.9. The randomized search CV model performs better than the others, as can be seen in the diagram.

3.4.4 Stacking Ensemble Model Deployment

At this stage of model deployment, outcomes from individual models are found inadequate and varying in nature after thorough examination. A two-stage stacking ensemble strategy is employed to combine the strengths of individual classifiers. In general, the various

Model (GS-CV)	Ac (Ma)	Pr	Re	Fs	Cks	Sd	Ra
DF-1							
RF-GS	96.97	0.98	0.95	0.97	0.94	4.22	0.97
XGB-GS	96.97	0.97	0.95	0.96	0.92	4.86	0.97
DT-GS	96.44	0.97	0.95	0.97	0.92	4.59	0.97
SVC-GS	91.39	0.98	0.98	0.98	0.97	4.49	0.98
LR-GS	83.87	0.90	0.76	0.82	0.68	4.94	0.84
DF-2							
XGB-GS	99.13	0.98	1.00	0.99	0.98	1.24	0.99
RF-GS	99.13	0.98	1.00	0.99	0.98	0.64	0.99
DT-GS	98.26	0.98	0.98	0.98	0.97	1.26	0.98
LR-GS	98.26	0.98	0.98	0.98	0.97	1.31	0.98
SVC-GS	97.39	0.98	0.97	0.97	0.95	1.46	0.97

Table 3.7: The experimental results of the different metrics of the deployed models with GS-CV for DF-1 and DF-2

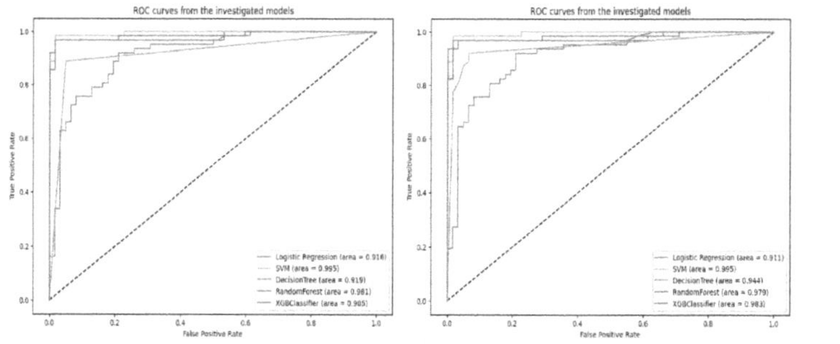

(a) The ROC-AUC curve of DF-1 with RS-CV

(b) The ROC-AUC curve of DF-1 with GS-CV

Figure 3.6: The ROC-AUC curve of DF-1 after applying RS-CV and GS-CV

heterogeneous weak learners are layered as a base prediction, while strong learners are typically pushed as meta-predictors, yielding significantly superior outcomes. The accuracy comparisons among the standalone models, RF, DT, and XGB, provided the best outcomes for the RS-CV model, according to an analysis of the model findings from the tables and graphs of both RS-CV and GS-CV. These three are used to construct the two-stage stack-

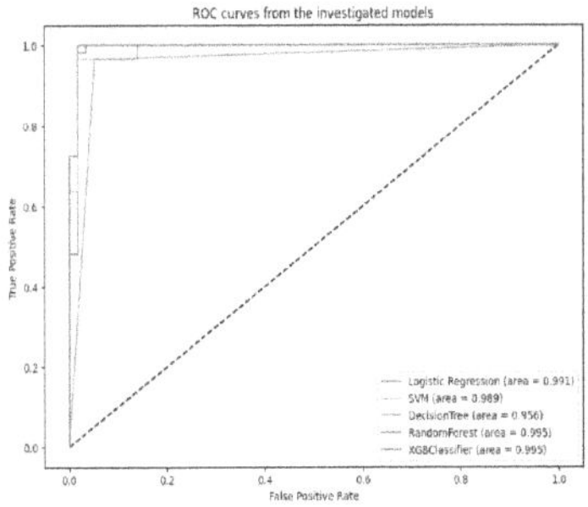

(a) The ROC-AUC curve of DF-2 with RS-CV

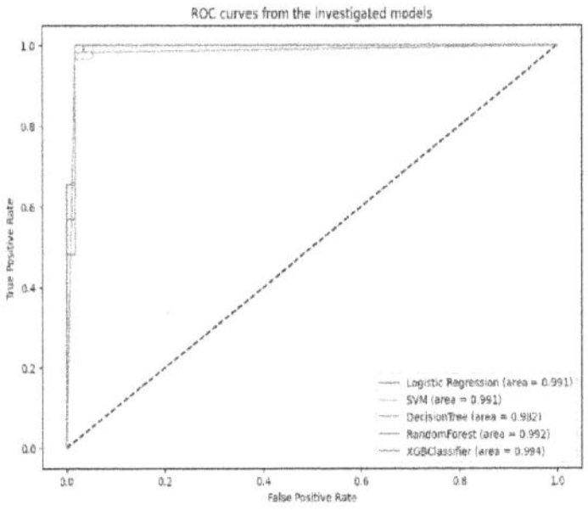

(b) The ROC-AUC curve of DF-2 with GS-CV

Figure 3.7: The ROC-AUC curve of DF-2 after applying RS-CV and GS-CV

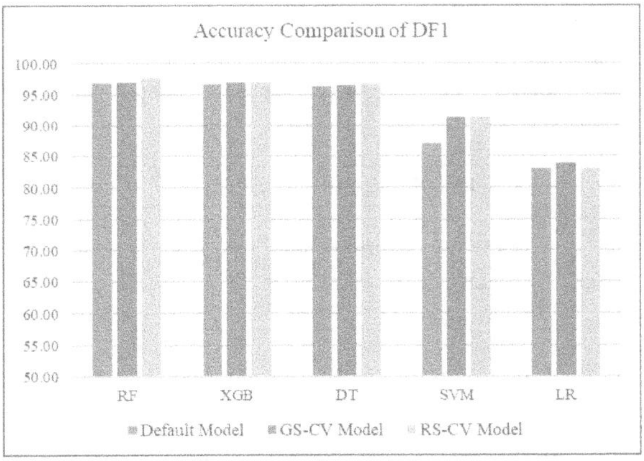

Figure 3.8: Comparative accuracy of the deployed models for DF-1

ing framework with hyperparameter-tuned models, though determining which can serve as base-level or meta-learners posed challenges. After testing various permutations, the best performance is achieved using XGB as the meta-learner with DT and RF as base learners. After applying 10-fold CV, the hyperparameter-tuned two-stage meta-ensemble stacking model demonstrated stable and consistent performance on the validation dataset. The corresponding results are presented in Table3.8. The corresponding confusion matrix and ROC-AUC curve for the stacked model concerning DF-1 and DF-2 are represented in Figs. 3.10 and 3.11. In conclusion, the proposed layered architecture aims to deliver

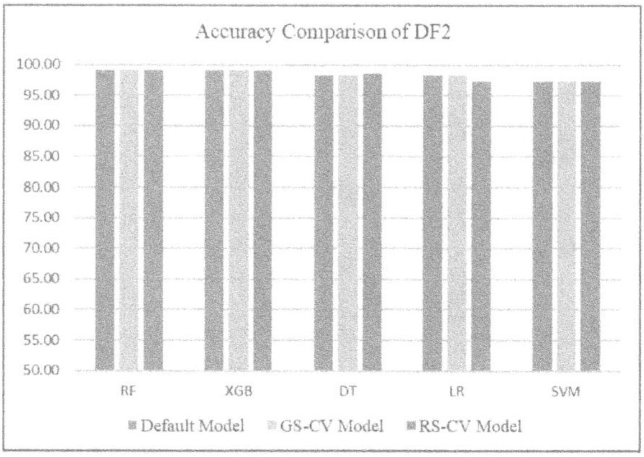

Figure 3.9: Comparative accuracy of the deployed models for DF-2

more reliable heart disease risk predictions. It mitigates overfitting, enhances generalization through optimization, and improves robustness by integrating the complementary strengths of diverse models.

Stacked Model (RF, DT, XGB) - CV-10							
# Dataset	Ac (Ma)	Pr	Re	Fs	Cks	Sd	Ra
DF-1	97.78	0.98	0.98	0.97	0.96	2.37	0.97
DF-2	99.13	0.98	1.00	0.99	0.98	0.89	0.99

Table 3.8: The two-stage meta-ensemble stacking models' experimental results

To combat the overfitting issue, the proposed model took into account the standard deviation (Sd), optimization methods, and ten-fold cross-validation. The outcomes demonstrate that no such circumstance occurs, and the proposed model is more accurate based on both actual and validation data. Additionally, hyperparameter tuning with GridSearchCV and RandomizedSearchCV posed significant challenges due to the time required to identify optimal estimator values for each parameter. Furthermore, the tuning process employs a cloud engine to run each model, which consumes a lot of power. Thus, one of the main challenges in this research study is fitting the five models with the appropriate parameters. To create a quick-response disease prediction recommender decision-making system, this work specifically concentrated on using the traditional machine learning based classification model with an ensemble generalization model to predict HD from the standpoint of resource-constrained devices.

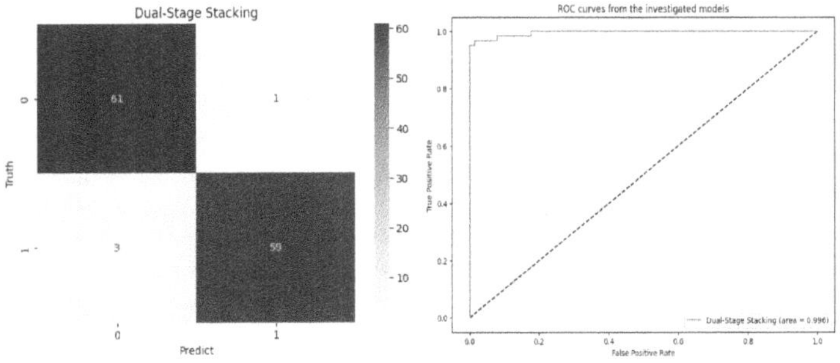

(a) The confusion matrix of the stacking model for DF-1

(b) The ROC-AUC curve of the stacking model for DF-1

Figure 3.10: The CM and ROC-AUC curve of the proposed tuned stacking model for DF-1

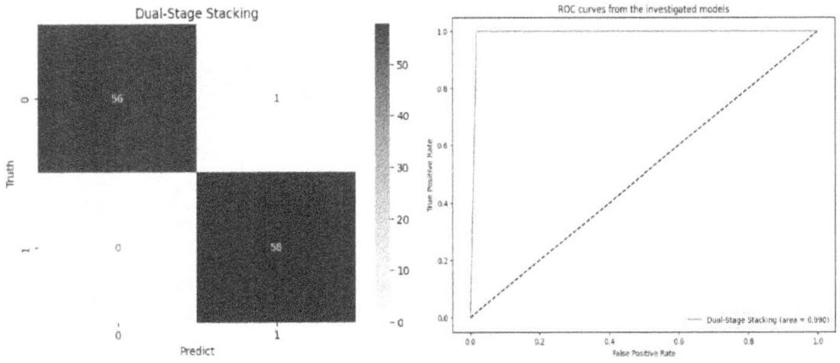

(a) The confusion matrix of the stacking model for DF-2

(b) The ROC-AUC curve of the stacking model for DF-2

Figure 3.11: The CM and ROC-AUC curve of the proposed tuned stacking model for DF-2

3.5 Result Analysis and Discussion

This section provides a thorough comparison and performance assessment of the proposed framework for predicting heart disease. The experimental results of this study are thoroughly examined in this chapter, along with the observable results from related literature under their explained test conditions. The IEEE comprehensive HD dataset [60] and CVD Mendeley dataset [75] are used, and the well-known performance metrics that are previously mentioned are taken into consideration. It has been observed that only a few

researchers reported ROC–AUC values in their results, while most studies primarily considered accuracy, precision, recall, and F1 score. Moreover, none of them evaluated prediction model performance using k-fold cross-validation mean accuracy (Ma) and standard deviation (Sd) to effectively address overfitting concerns. All these factors are taken into account in this study's analysis of the presented framework's model performance.
The stacked model has superior recall and ROC-AUC values compared to any other literature, and it is more accurate when compared to the literature [72] and [52]. Table 3.9 displays the findings of the proposed stacking model analysis along with the investigations conducted by all other scholars. The empty cell signifies that the writers have not offered any outcomes that align with the metrics. After applying the same data preprocessing methods and deploying the models, the same experiment is repeated over the Mendeley dataset, considering all the parameters and the test circumstances. The experimental results, which have a 99.13% accuracy rate and ROC-AUC values of 0.99, are much superior to the SOTA literature. The two open-source datasets mentioned above are the most suitable and up-to-date for predicting heart disease-related risks that are utilized in research.

# Ref	Methods	Ac (Ma)	Pr	Re	Fs	Cks	Sd	Ra	Dataset # Instances	
									DF-1	DF-2
									1190	1000
[[72]]	Majority	93.39	0.99	0.88	0.90	-	-	-	✓	
[[72]]	Voting	96.75	0.98	0.96	0.97	-	-	-		✓
[[52]]	CART	87.25	0.88	0.89	-	-	-	-	✓	
[[69]]	Stacking	92.34	0.92	0.93	0.93	-	-	0.92	✓	
[[73]]	Soft voting	95.00	-	-	-	-	-		✓	
Proposed Study	**Stacking**	**99.13**	**0.98**	1.00	**0.99**	**0.98**	**0.89**	**0.99**		✓
		97.78	**0.98**	0.98	**0.97**	**0.96**	**2.37**	**0.97**	✓	

Table 3.9: The comparison analysis of the study with the literature results.

This section provides a thorough comparison and performance assessment of the proposed framework for predicting heart disease. Three important viewpoints are used in the analysis: (i) the impact of optimization concerning default versus hyperparameter-tuned models; (ii) the performance generalizability of stacking ensemble versus individual base models; and (iii) the effect of target class balancing with and without the hybrid sampling method SMOTETomek. The IEEE and Mendeley datasets are used for these comparisons to evaluate the models' efficiency, generalizability, and resilience. The outcomes are quantified using a variety of metrics, including accuracy, precision, recall, F1-score, and AUC-ROC. The objective is to confirm how well ensemble learning techniques and model optimization may enhance the prediction of heart disease risk. The IEEE comprehensive HD and Mendeley CVD datasets are used for these comparisons to evaluate the models' efficiency, generalizability, and resilience. The outcomes are quantified using a variety of metrics,

including accuracy, precision, recall, F1-score, Cohen's kappa, standard deviation, and AUC-ROC. The objective is to confirm how well ensemble learning techniques and model optimization may enhance the prediction of heart disease risk.
The hyperparameter-tuned models consistently perform better in both datasets than their default counterparts. The model's capacity to learn optimal decision boundaries is greatly improved by tuning, which improves performance and generalization. Recall and ROC-AUC show notable improvements, which are important for identifying cases of high-risk heart disease. This confirms the significance of optimizing model-specific parameters with tools like GridSearchCV and RandomizedSearchCV.
The stacking ensemble model outperforms any single classifier by combining tuned RF and DT as base learners with XGB as the meta learner. The ensemble can compensate for the shortcomings of individual models and capture a variety of data patterns thanks to the layered learning approach. The benefit of meta-learning in clinical risk prediction tasks is thus confirmed by the stacking model, which obtains the maximum accuracy, recall, and F1-score across both datasets.
The impact of applying hybrid sampling SMOTETomek is that the class balance greatly enhances prediction performance, especially for the minority class (HD: 1). Models with no sampling exhibit biased predictions that favour the majority class, which lowers the recall for true positive detection. By balancing class distributions and improving the learning of decision boundaries, SMOTETomek improves the sensitivity and fairness of the model. This demonstrates how important preparation is for unbalanced medical datasets.

3.5.1 Effect of Dual-Stage Hyperparameter Tuning on Hybrid Ensemble

Dual-stage hyperparameter tuning significantly enhances the effectiveness of hybrid ensemble architectures by optimizing both individual model learning and ensemble-level decision fusion. In stacking-based ensembles, tuning base learners in the first stage improves their predictive quality, reduces bias and variance, and produces well-calibrated outputs that serve as high-quality meta-features. In the second stage, tuning the meta-learner enables optimal aggregation of base predictions through effective weighting and nonlinear error correction. This two-level optimization significantly improves stacking-based ensembles, where the quality of meta-features directly depends on base learner outputs. It prevents error propagation, improves generalization, and yields substantial gains in accuracy, recall, and ROC-AUC. In this study, the dual-stage tuned stacking framework achieved accuracies of 97.78% and 99.13%, outperforming default and single-stage tuned models and demonstrating superior stability across cross-validation folds.

Similarly, in bagging and voting-based hybrid architectures, dual-stage tuning strengthens ensemble performance by ensuring that each base learner is both diverse and individually optimized. Hyperparameter tuning reduces weak or biased learners within the ensemble, while optimized soft voting improves confidence calibration and balanced decision-making. As a result, bagging and voting ensemble methods exhibit reduced variance, improved sensitivity to the minority class, and lower standard deviation across cross-validation folds. Overall, dual-stage hyperparameter tuning enhances robustness, mitigates overfitting, and ensures consistent performance on imbalanced clinical datasets, making hybrid ensemble architectures particularly suitable for reliable heart disease risk prediction.

In conclusion, dual-stage hyperparameter tuning enhances hybrid ensemble models by optimizing both individual learners and ensemble fusion. This results in improved accuracy, robustness, and generalization on imbalanced medical datasets, confirming the effectiveness of the proposed approach.

3.6 Key Findings and Summary

This chapter addressed the first study goal by providing a thorough analysis of the presented framework for predicting heart disease (HD). Two benchmark datasets are used in a sequential model development and evaluation technique as part of the methodology. Five popular machine learning models, LR, XGB, DT, RF, and SVM, are first chosen and put into use with default settings, both with and without SMOTETomek class balancing. Following that, GridSearchCV and RandomizedSearchCV are used to optimize the hyperparameters, which greatly improved model performance and decreased the likelihood of overfitting. XGB is employed as the meta-learner, and RF and DT are employed as base learners in a two-stage meta-ensemble stacking structure that included the optimized models. Comparing this ensemble approach to individual classifiers, it showed better prediction accuracy and greater generalization.

An in-depth evaluation of performance showed key findings that:

- Significant gains in performance accuracy over default models are achieved by hyperparameter tuning.
- In every evaluation metric, the hyperparameter-tuned stacking-based ensemble method proved to be superior to individual models with a mean accuracy of 97.78% and 99.13% for DF-1 and DF-2, respectively. Also, in disease prediction, the recall value is observed to be great with a near-zero false negative (FN) rate for DF-2 and 2.41% for DF-1.
- The application of sampling SMOTETomek for class imbalance handling contributed to balanced learning and increased sensitivity, especially for the minority class.
- Utilization of two datasets with the employed optimization methods improves the prediction model generalization, preventing overfitting issues using the k-fold cross-validation technique.
- The thorough assessment metrics provide an insightful, comprehensive evaluation and superior framework for HD prediction compared to the literature.

The chapter demonstrated the robustness, interpretability, and clinical utility of the dual-stage, hyperparameter-tuned ensemble framework for heart disease prediction, validating its efficacy and generalization in real-world decision-support systems. While the ensemble framework achieved high accuracy and generalization, limitations remain, including the inability to address long-term CHD mortality, limited adaptability of deep learning models, and challenges in handling complex class imbalance. The next chapter 4 overcomes these challenges through a dual-phase CHD framework: Phase I applies boosting ensembles, while Phase II introduces an optimized ANN with advanced sampling. Together, these approaches enhance predictive reliability and clinical relevance, laying the groundwork for robust, scalable CHD risk assessment.

4

Risk Prediction Framework for Coronary Heart Disease

This study extends the previous ensemble-based framework to address long-term CHD mortality. To overcome the limitations of generalization and complex risk factor interactions, the next phase introduces a dual-phase predictive approach. Primarily, CHD remains one of the world's primary causes of death and a major contributor to the burden of cardiovascular-related mortality worldwide. The intricate relationships between clinical, behavioural, and genetic risk factors make it difficult to detect CHD early and accurately, even with advances in healthcare technology. Consequently, early CHD risk prediction is essential for prompt intervention, lowering the death rate, and preventing long-term health issues. This chapter proposes a thorough two-phase risk prediction system that uses cutting-edge ML and DL techniques to improve diagnostic precision and interpretability to resolve this important healthcare issue.

The study makes use of the Framingham Heart Study (FHS) dataset, which comprises 4,240 person records with 15 attributes that indicate risk factors related to behaviour, health, and demographics. The dataset is significant for long-term risk prediction because its outcome variable shows whether a person is at risk of CHD within the next ten years. Following the second research goal of this thesis, the proposed approach is implemented in two stages:
In Phase I, sophisticated ensemble learning methods are investigated to increase generalization and prediction accuracy. Initially, thirteen machine learning classifiers are implemented and assessed using the SMOTE technique, both with and without class imbalance enhancement. After that, hyperparameter optimization techniques like RandomizedSearchCV are used to fine-tune the top-performing models. Finally, the five leading boosting classifiers, like XGB, LGBM, HGB, GB, and CB, are included in a novel ensemble architecture that is created utilizing both soft and hard voting techniques. This ensemble strategy aims to improve diagnostic accuracy through model diversity and voting mechanisms.
Phase II aims to develop a deep learning approach using a tailored ANN architecture. The ANN model is trained using a variety of optimization techniques, such as Adam, AdaDelta, RMSProp, and SGD, as well as activation functions (ReLU, LeakyReLU), and

optimized through different hyperparameter configurations. Before model training, a variety of sophisticated resampling strategies like SMOTE, SMOTETomek, SMOTEENN, and a proposed hybrid two-stage sampling method are used to address class imbalance. The model is fine-tuned by analyzing the effectiveness of various activation functions and tuning parameters, including the number of hidden layers, neurones, learning rate, batch size, and momentum. The purpose of this model is to improve generalizability and prediction accuracy even more.

This chapter proposes an extensive predictive framework for CHD that combines deep neural networks' and ensemble learning's advantages. The remainder of the chapter is structured as follows: The motivation and objective of the research are addressed in the next section, 4.1, which is followed by the chapter contributions aligned with the second research objective in Section 4.2. Next, the information about the dataset and preprocessing strategies in Section 4.3, and a thorough description of both phases. The ensemble learning-based framework of phase I in Section 4.4, and the deep learning approach of phase II in Section 4.5. The methods, experimental configurations, result analysis, and the comparison with the SOTA learning methods are discussed in the above two sections in detail. The advantages of ensemble learning and the DL-based ANN framework used for CHD prediction are illustrated in Section 4.6. The chapter concludes with the main key findings, summary, and insights in Section 4.7. Extensive experimentation and performance evaluation show that the presented models are successful in lowering false positives and increasing the precision of early coronary heart disease detection.

4.1 Motivations, Research Gaps, and Objectives

Coronary Heart Disease (CHD) remains a leading global health concern and major cause of cardiovascular deaths. Despite advances in care and diagnostics, early prediction is challenging due to varied risk factors like age, blood pressure, cholesterol, lifestyle, and genetics. While traditional machine learning shows promise in predicting cardiac disease, challenges remain in generalization, handling imbalanced data, overfitting, and accuracy. Many studies rely on single models or classical methods, which often lack robustness for real-world CHD datasets. Scientific and technical limitations still hinder reliable early-stage CHD prediction.

A thorough review of current research on CHD prediction identifies several important areas that require more investigation:

- **Target Class Data Imbalance:** The Framingham Heart Study and most real-world CHD datasets are naturally unbalanced, with fewer cases of favourable CHD outcomes. By favouring the majority class and ineffectively capturing minority class patterns, this mismatch frequently distorts model performance.
- **Model Generalization:** The inability of many conventional machine learning algorithms to generalize effectively over a range of patient demographics and risk factor distributions results in inconsistent prediction results.

- **Overfitting and Limited Robustness:** Overfitting is still a serious issue if models are not carefully adjusted and validated, particularly when sophisticated models are trained on noisy or high-dimensional data.

- **Lack of Comprehensive Integration:** Despite the potential of individual models, there is a dearth of research on a cohesive framework that integrates deep learning and ensemble learning techniques for CHD risk prediction.

This study proposes a two-phase prediction framework for CHD to address existing limitations. The primary objective is to develop a sophisticated and reliable risk prediction model for early detection, aiming to reduce CHD-related mortality. This study overcomes the shortcomings of previous efforts by combining deep learning and ensemble learning techniques, and it suggests a two-stage approach to improve prediction performance. The following specific objectives are established to approach the research goal methodically:

1. To establish an effective framework for predicting CHD utilizing sophisticated ensemble learning techniques, with a focus on soft and hard voting classifiers built from boosting algorithms (XGB, LGBM, CB, HGB, and GB).

2. To optimize prediction performance by utilizing RandomizedSearchCV to hyperparameter tune the best-performing machine learning models.

3. To design a customized ANN model capable of effectively capturing complex feature interactions within the dataset and achieving high predictive accuracy.

4. To evaluate how different activation functions (ReLU, LeakyReLU) and optimization strategies (Adam, RMSProp, AdaDelta, SGD) influence the performance of the ANN-based CHD prediction model.

5. Additionally, the proposed ANN models can undergo tuning of the learning rate, weights, and other parameters to optimize the loss function and boost overall performance.

6. To address class imbalance challenges by incorporating advanced sampling techniques such as SMOTE, SMOTETomek, SMOTEENN, and a hybrid two-stage sampling approach, ensuring fair prediction across all classes.

4.2 Research Contributions

This chapter concentrates on the two main phases of methodological contributions to close these research gaps and tackle the real-world difficulties in CHD prediction:

4.2.1 Phase I: Emphasis on Ensemble Learning Methods

This phase aims to enhance the performance and reliability of the CHD prediction system by leveraging the predictive power of ensemble machine learning models.

1. **Deployment of Multiple Classifiers:** Initially, thirteen baseline machine learning classifiers are deployed on the FHS dataset, incorporating 10-fold cross-validation and data balancing techniques like SMOTE to address class imbalance.

2. **Model Optimization:** To increase model precision and recall, RandomizedSearchCV is used to optimize hyperparameters and avoid overfitting in the top ten classifiers.

3. **Voting Classifier Ensemble:** Also, this phase proposes a novel ensemble voting approach for CHD prediction, combining five boosting classifiers (XGB, LGBM, CB, GB, and HGB), a first in the existing literature. The method incorporates both hard and soft voting to significantly enhance model robustness and predictive accuracy. This integrated boosting strategy demonstrates strong potential for early CHD risk prediction.

4.2.2 Phase II: Development of ANN Framework

The second phase involved creating a customized ANN to further enhance forecast performance by taking advantage of the non-linear correlations among CHD risk factors.

1. **Customized ANN Design:** To overcome the drawbacks of traditional models that concentrate on optimizing learning depth without overfitting, a customized ANN architecture is proposed to better capture non-linear correlations among risk factors.

2. **Optimization Techniques:** To find the best configuration and predictive performance, several optimizers (Adam, RMSProp, AdaDelta, SGD) and activation functions (ReLU, LeakyReLU) are examined for their impact on model convergence.

3. **Hyperparameter Tuning of ANN Architecture:** To reduce the loss function and improve prediction accuracy, crucial parameters, including learning rate, batch size, momentum, epochs, number of hidden layers, and neurones per layer, are adjusted.

4. **Advanced Resampling:** To address data imbalance, advanced techniques such as SMOTE, SMOTETomek, SMOTEENN, and a novel hybrid two-stage sampling strategy (SMOTEENN + SMOTETomek) are integrated during ANN training. This approach ensures fair representation of data and prevents biased learning towards a particular class.

To successfully handle the challenges of CHD risk prediction, these contributions together propose a thorough methodology that integrates the preparation of data, model optimization, ensemble learning, and deep learning. In addition to contributing substantially to the existing literature and practical clinical decision support, this work adopts a two-phase research approach that combines ensemble learning and deep learning techniques. This integrated approach enables more comprehensive, accurate, and generalizable early prediction of CHD risk.

Two peer-reviewed research publications are the outcome of the intensive experiments that confirmed the contributions made in this chapter. The first phase is published in a conference article in the IEEE Explore Digital Library [114] and focuses on ensemble machine learning techniques for early CHD prediction. In the second phase, which focuses on the optimization and deployment of an ANN model based on deep learning, a journal article is published in Scientific Reports, Nature Portfolio [115]. These publications support the promise of sophisticated AI-driven models in assisting early and precise CHD risk assessment, as well as the originality and efficacy of the proposed dual-phase methodology.

4.3 Dataset Description and Preprocessing

This study utilizes the FHS dataset to develop an effective CHD risk prediction model. To guarantee data quality and enhance learning performance, several preprocessing procedures are carried out before the model is developed. These include resolving class imbalance using sophisticated sampling strategies, standardizing numerical features, handling missing values, and dividing the data for reliable analysis.
The dataset, sourced from the WHO's HME workshop, is used to analyze and predict the presence of CHD in individuals [90]. It is publicly accessible for analyzing patterns and aiding in the prediction of an individual's likelihood of developing CHD. The data is collected from research conducted on the residents of Framingham, Massachusetts, USA, by recording the responses of almost four thousand patients to fifteen distinct questions posed to everyone. Every inquiry is a crucial element that can impact the designated class, with all features being statistical, developmental, and therapeutic. Finally, the dataset consists of information from 4,240 patients, covering 15 potential risk factors categorized as demographic, behavioural, and medical. The target attribute is a binary variable indicating whether the patient developed CHD within the next 10 years (1: CHD, 0: Normal). The risk factors are depicted in Table 4.1, which displays the descriptions of the different aspects as well as occurrences of null values during EDA. The features in the dataset are categorized as follows:

- Demographic attributes: age, gender, education
- Behavioural factors: smoking habits, alcohol intake
- Clinical metrics: systolic and diastolic blood pressure, BMI, total cholesterol, glucose level, heart rate
- Medical history: prevalent stroke, hypertension, diabetes

4.3.1 Null Values Replacement

Null values significantly impact the accuracy and reliability of machine learning and neural network models. If not handled properly, they can introduce bias, cause overfitting, and hinder generalization. Consequently, early detection and appropriate handling are essential. Once identified, null values are addressed using the 'fillna' function, followed by imputation techniques. For numerical columns, missing entries are replaced with the column *mean*, ensuring consistent data representation. In the data analysis phase, missing values are found in seven attributes, accounting for 15.21% of the data. While numerical

#	Risk Factors	# Null Values	Feature description
0	gender	0	Patients gender M (1) or F (0)
1	age	0	Patients' age, numeric values
2	education	105	Education stages, numeric valuers
3	currentsmoker	0	Smoking status, binary either o or 1
4	cigsperday	29	Count of cigarettes, numeric values
5	bpmeds	53	Either consume blood pressure medicine or not
6	prevalentstroke	0	History of stroke, either 0 or 1
7	prevalenthyp	0	Patients are hypertensive or not, numeric values.
8	diabetes	0	Diabetic patients or not, binary values
9	totchol	50	Count of cholesterol
10	sysbp	0	Lower BP level, numeric values
11	diabp	0	Upper BP level, numeric values
12	bmi	19	Body mass, values
13	heartrate	1	Heart bit-level values
14	glucose	388	Blood glucose measurements in numeric values
15	**tenyearchd**	0	Binary target values of ten-year risk of future CHD

Table 4.1: Feature descriptions of the FHS dataset (CHD) with null value counts

attributes are imputed using the mean, categorical features such as "bpmeds" and "education" are handled using the mode. It is crucial to verify that all null and missing values have been properly resolved. Fig. 4.1 illustrates the missing data values.

4.3.2 Data Correlation Analysis

The correlation heat map is created among attributes, assessing linear correlation and multicollinearity, and assessing the model's integrity by verifying the correlated values of each cell, as illustrated in Fig. 4.1. The Pearson correlation coefficient (r) between the two variables is computed using formula 4.1, yielding a value between -1 and 1.

$$r = \frac{\sum(x_i - \bar{x})(y_i - \bar{y})}{\sqrt{\sum(x_i - \bar{x})^2 \sum(y_i - \bar{y})^2}} \tag{4.1}$$

Where: r : Correlation coefficient, x_i : Values of the attributes X, $\bar{x}$: Mean of the attribute's values X. y_i : Values of the target class Y, and $\bar{y}$: Mean of the Y values.

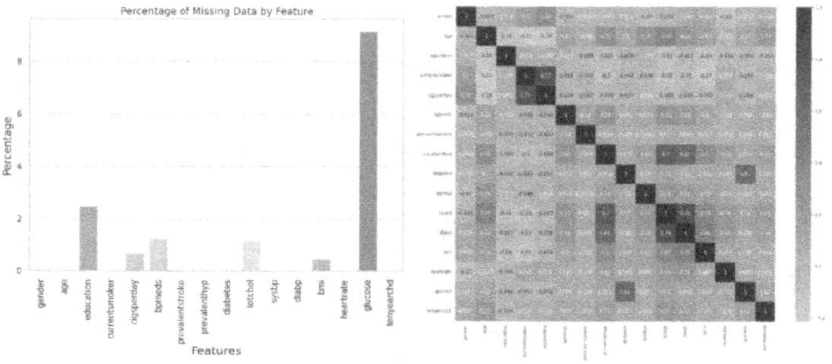

(a) Missing values count percentage (b) Correlation heat map

Figure 4.1: Missing Value Attributes and Their Correlation Heat map

4.3.3 Label Encoding Technique

To achieve higher accuracy during training, outputs can be represented numerically. Since the dataset is already in numerical form and contains no categorical features, there's no need to apply label encoding to convert categorical values into numeric format.

4.3.4 Feature Scaling or Normalization Technique

Optimizing model performance requires running the model on a dataset with minimal variance. Normalizing and scaling input features ensures consistent contribution from each feature, improves convergence speed, and enhances numerical stability. This process addresses feature range disparities and outliers, helping reduce execution time. For this purpose, the *"StandardScaler"* is used, a mean-centric scaling method that transforms the data to have a mean of 0 and a standard deviation of 1. The mathematical formula for scaling each variable is given below: where x_i represents the instance value of an attribute, x_{mean} (μ) denotes the mean value of the training samples, and σ signifies the standard deviation of X attributes as stated accordingly. The following Eqs. 4.2, 4.3, and 4.4 are used to calculate the mean and standard deviation for this purpose.

$$x_{\text{scaled}} = \frac{x_i - x_{\text{mean}}(\mu)}{\text{Standard Deviation}(\sigma)} \tag{4.2}$$

$$\mu = \frac{1}{N}\sum_{i=1}^{N} x_i \tag{4.3}$$

$$\sigma = \sqrt{\frac{1}{N}\sum_{i=1}^{N}(x_i - \mu)^2} \tag{4.4}$$

4.3.5 Balancing Target Classes

A balanced dataset is crucial for ML to effectively build accurate models such as networks, trees, and graphs. Achieving balance among target classes in a neural network model reduces bias towards majority classes, enhances minority class predictions, and mitigates biased outcomes. An oversampling strategy developed in 2002, the SMOTE, is used to achieve this. The SMOTETomek oversampling method, developed in 2003, combines SMOTE with Tomek's Link to address the imbalance between minority and majority classes. This method eliminates duplicate data points, balances the dataset without compromising original data integrity, and mitigates overfitting or underfitting difficulties in ensemble and neural network models. The synthetic data sample is generated using the following formula.

Let it x_i be a minority sample, and the nearest chosen neighbour is x_{ik}. If they $x_{ik1}, x_{ik2}, \ldots, x_{ikn}$ are the neighbours of m, the syntactic values x_{smote} are generated by the formula in Eq. 4.5.

$$x_{\text{smote}} = x_i + \delta \cdot (x_{ik} - x_i) \tag{4.5}$$

Where δ is a random number within the range of $[0, 1]$, determining the position of the synthetic sample along the line segment connecting x_i and x_{ik}. The process is repeated until the desired class balance is obtained.

$$d(x_i, x_j) < d(x_i, x_k) \tag{4.6}$$

Furthermore, employing the Tomek connection between the two instance pairs (x_i, x_j), where x_i and x_j are nearest neighbours from disparate classes, facilitates the elimination of overlapping instances after SMOTE. The Tomek connection of the pair (x_i, x_j) is established using another formula of 4.6 for all other instances x_k, where $d(x_i, x_j)$ denotes the distance between the two points and x_k represents the other occurrence.

In 2004, the SMOTEENN technique is introduced to address class imbalance in datasets. While SMOTE alone can produce noisy or irrelevant samples that hinder model generalization, combining it with ENN helps generate cleaner, more representative samples of the minority class, enhancing generalization. Additionally, SMOTEENN and SMOTETomek work together to improve data quality by removing noise and refining class boundaries using Tomek links.

After applying SMOTEENN, the dataset is further enhanced using SMOTETomek. This two-stage process, first oversampling and then undersampling, leverages the strengths of both methods. SMOTEENN removes noise, while SMOTETomek sharpens class boundaries, resulting in a well-balanced, high-quality, and clearly separated dataset.

The data distribution of the target class before and after the implementation of the sampling strategies SMOTE, SMOTETomek, SMOTEENN, and SMOTEENN + SMOTETomek is illustrated in Figs. 4.2 and 4.3. Furthermore, the instances of the target class in class 1 and class 0, after the application of sampling procedures, are illustrated for enhanced comprehension in Table 4.2.

Target Class Level tenyearchd (Yes/No)	# Before Sampling	# After Sampling			
		SMOTE	SMOTETomek	SMOTEENN	SMOTEENN + SMOTETomek
0	3596	3596	3568	1971	3326
1	644	3596	3568	3326	3326
# Total Instances	4240	7192	7136	5297	6652

Table 4.2: The effect of sampling techniques on the target class data instances.

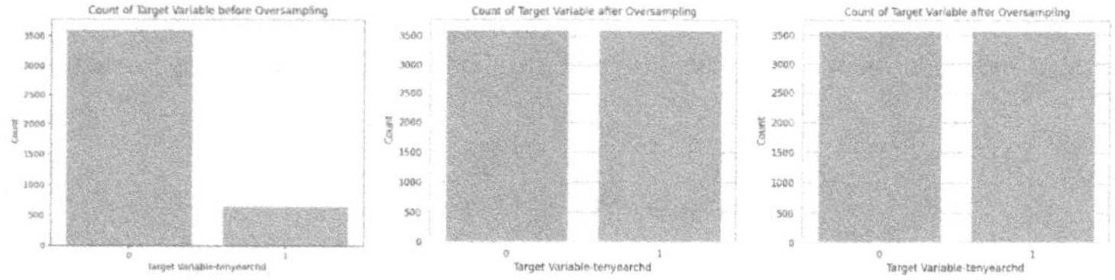

(a) Before applying oversampling (b) After oversampling SMOTE (c) After oversampling SMOTETomek

Figure 4.2: The target class data distribution.

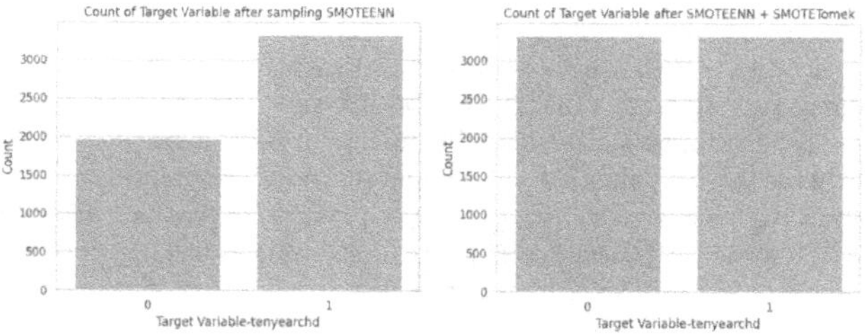

(a) After applying SMOTEENN separately (b) After SMOTEENN + SMOTETomek

Figure 4.3: The proposed sampling target class data distribution

After applying the required data cleaning procedures to the acquired raw dataset, it is prepared for subsequent two-phase model deployment. To train and evaluate the ensemble voting approach and the proposed artificial neural network model by employing various optimization techniques to enhance predictive performance and generalization. It is essential to partition the complete dataset into training and testing subsets. The hold-out and the k-fold CV methods are considered for this purpose in each instance's model deployment. In each instance, before and after the application of SMOTE, SMOTETomek, SMOTEENN, and the proposed two-stage sampling approach, the complete dataset is partitioned in a 0.90:0.10 ratio for training and testing purposes. Also, for validation methods, the ten-fold CV method is employed in each phase model implementation.

4.4 Proposed CHD Risk Prediction Framework – Phase I: Ensemble Learning

The first phase of this study proposes a robust ensemble-based framework for predicting CHD risk utilizing advanced machine learning algorithms. This phase seeks to improve early prediction accuracy by utilizing various classifiers and ensemble techniques. A collection of base classifiers is first trained on the preprocessed dataset by applying a 10-fold cross-validation method. Next, the hyperparameter tuning is conducted using RandomizedSearchCV to enhance prediction accuracy and generalization. Finally, a unique ensemble voting method that integrates both soft and hard voting is developed by combining the highest-performing boosting classifiers. This ensemble approach capitalizes on the unique capabilities of each classifier while mitigating the shortcomings of individual models in managing intricate, unbalanced health data. The entire process flow diagram of the proposed boosting-based voting ensemble approach is depicted in Fig. 4.4.

4.4.1 Baseline Classifier Deployment

This research employs thirteen established ML classifiers to provide a robust foundational baseline for predicting CHD. These classifiers include several learning paradigms, such as probabilistic, tree-based, instance-based, and boosting models. The main objective of this phase is to assess the predictive performance of each classifier on the preprocessed and balanced dataset, applying default parameter configurations. The ML models that are employed initially in this stage include CB, AB, GB, XGB, LGBM, HGB, KNN, Gaussian NB (GNB), Bernoulli NB (BNB), DT, RF, SVM, and LR classifiers. Additionally, to address class imbalance in the CHD dataset, SMOTE is applied prior to model training. A 10-fold cross-validation ensures reliable performance evaluation. Metrics like accuracy, precision, recall, F1-score, Cohen's kappa, and ROC-AUC are used for model comparison on the test set. The experimental results are tabulated in Table 4.3 with the default hyperparameter setting.

This baseline deployment presents a thorough assessment of each classifier's performance under comparable settings, creating a benchmark for further optimization using hyperparameter tuning and ensemble techniques in later stages.

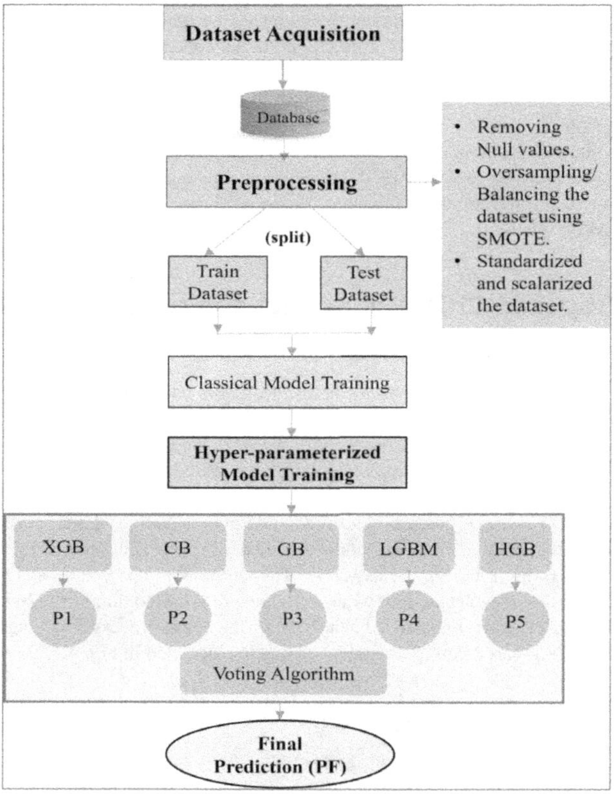

Figure 4.4: Proposed workflow of the boosting-based voting ensemble CHD model

4.4.2 Hyperparameter Tuning Deployment

Next, upon assessing the baseline performance of thirteen machine learning classifiers, the 10 models demonstrating the highest performance metrics are selected for further enhancement via hyperparameter tuning. Hyperparameter tuning is crucial for optimizing model performance and enhancing generalization by determining the optimal parameter combinations. The RandomizedSearchCV method is adopted for hyperparameter optimization to improve model performance. In contrast to GridSearchCV, which conducts a comprehensive search, RandomizedSearchCV randomly selects a predetermined number of parameter configurations from designated distributions. This approach is more computationally efficient and better suited for extensive search spaces. Table 4.4 shows the

Model Name	Ac (%)	Ma (%)	Pr	Re	Fs	Cks	Ra
RF	90.69	91.29	0.94	0.87	0.90	0.81	0.907
CB	88.33	90.30	0.95	0.81	0.87	0.77	0.883
LGBM	89.17	90.03	0.97	0.81	0.88	0.78	0.892
HGB	88.33	89.85	0.94	0.82	0.88	0.77	0.883
GB	87.08	88.26	0.94	0.79	0.86	0.74	0.871
XGB	86.67	87.59	0.94	0.79	0.85	0.73	0.867
AB	82.22	84.15	0.80	0.86	0.83	0.64	0.822
DT	83.75	84.01	0.86	0.80	0.83	0.68	0.838
KNN	81.81	81.78	0.75	0.95	0.84	0.64	0.818
SVM	77.50	78.12	0.78	0.77	0.77	0.55	0.775
LR	66.81	67.65	0.66	0.71	0.68	0.34	0.668
BNB	65.69	64.23	0.67	0.63	0.65	0.31	0.657
GNB	62.64	60.94	0.76	0.37	0.50	0.25	0.626

Table 4.3: The initial deployed models' outcomes without hyperparameter tuning

experimental results analysis for the top ten tuned model performances. The ROC-AUC curve with the default and the tuned models' probabilistic AUC values is depicted in Fig. 4.5.

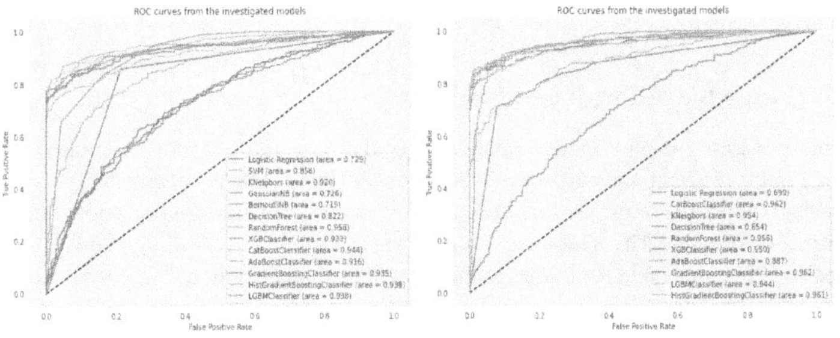

(a) The default model's ROC-AUC curve (b) The tuned models ROC-AUC curve

Figure 4.5: The Default and tuned model ROC-AUC curve with probabilistic values

Furthermore, post-tuning, substantial performance enhancements are noted across nearly all models. Boosting algorithms outperformed non-boosting classifiers after examining

Model Name	Ac (%)	Ma (%)	Pr	Re	Fs	Cks	Ra
GB	90.97	92.12	0.94	0.87	0.91	0.82	0.910
CB	90.69	92.10	0.95	0.86	0.90	0.81	0.907
HGB	90.97	91.80	0.94	0.88	0.91	0.82	0.910
XGB	90.97	91.42	0.98	0.84	0.90	0.82	0.910
LGBM	88.19	91.39	0.94	0.82	0.87	0.76	0.882
RF	89.44	91.07	0.93	0.85	0.89	0.79	0.894
KNN	85.14	87.25	0.79	0.95	0.86	0.70	0.851
DT	80.14	83.05	0.81	0.79	0.80	0.60	0.801
AB	79.72	80.04	0.81	0.77	0.79	0.59	0.797
LR	63.89	67.34	0.63	0.66	0.65	0.28	0.639

Table 4.4: The initial deployed models' outcomes with hyperparameter tuning by RandomizedSearchCV

the tuned model outcomes. The accuracy and ROC-AUC scores improved by an average of 2% to 4%, based on the model. The optimization resulted in an improved precision-recall equilibrium, particularly for the minority class. Furthermore, overfitting in boosting and tree-based models is mitigated by adjusting the depth and learning rate parameters. This stage of model optimization is essential, as it yields fine-tuned models for subsequent usage in the ensemble learning phases. The five most optimized models (GB, CB, XGB, HGB, and LGBM) are chosen for the building of a voting-based ensemble in the subsequent section.

4.4.3 Ensemble Voting-based Model

Ensemble learning is an effective methodology that integrates several base classifiers to create a more resilient and precise model. After analyzing the experimental outcomes in the initial two phases of prediction, the ensemble is an alternative approach to enhance the performance of models by averaging the prediction accuracy. Accordingly, this study employed a voting ensemble technique to improve the early prediction of coronary heart disease (CHD), concentrating on soft and hard voting processes leveraging high-performing boosting classifiers. In voting, there are two kinds of classifiers: hard voting (HV) and soft voting (SV). In hard voting, each base classifier votes for the predicted class, and the final output is decided by majority rule. It handles all classifiers uniformly and is straightforward, although it lacks informativeness when classifiers yield probabilistic outputs. On the other side, SV computes the mean of the expected probabilities from the base classifiers and chooses the class label corresponding to the highest averaged probability. It generally outperforms hard voting when the basis classifiers are well-calibrated and probabilistic.

Soft voting depends on base model performance; thus, the top five tuned boosting models are used for hard and soft voting with ten-fold cross-validation. The ensemble models are trained on the SMOTE-resampled dataset and assessed using measures such as accuracy, precision, recall, F1-score, and ROC-AUC.
The soft voting classifier produced better results, with a mean accuracy of 92.26% and ROC-AUC and F1 scores of 0.917 and 0.91, respectively. The outcomes of the voting procedure on the model with hyperparameter adjustments are shown in Table 4.5. The derived soft and hard voting are represented by the voting classifiers model's confusion matrix in Fig. 4.6.

Model Name	Ac (%)	Ma (%)	Pr	Re	Fs	Cks	Ra	Sd
SV	91.67	92.26	0.96	0.87	0.91	0.83	0.92	0.99
HV	91.11	92.09	0.96	0.86	0.91	0.82	0.91	1.16

Table 4.5: Final results of the deployed voting ensemble model

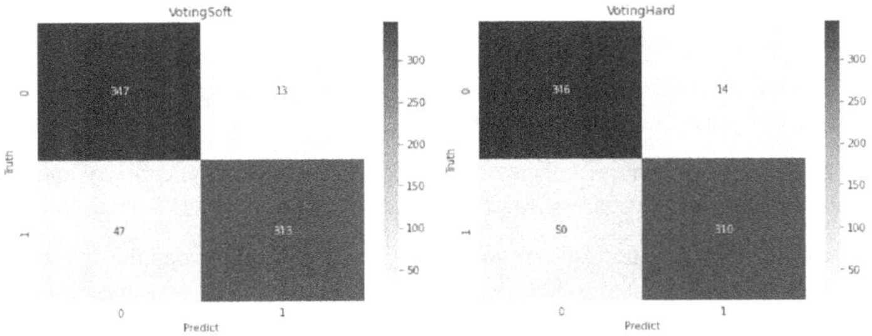

(a) The CM of Soft Voting Ensemble (b) The CM of Hard Voting Ensemble

Figure 4.6: The CM of Voting Ensemble Classifier

4.4.4 Comparative Analysis and Key Findings

The efficacy of the proposed CHD risk prediction framework adopting ensemble learning is assessed through several experimental circumstances to confirm its validity.
Initially, thirteen machine learning classifiers are implemented, applying default hyperparameters. While some models exhibited satisfactory accuracy, additional optimization is required to get consistent performance across evaluation metrics.

- RandomizedSearchCV is employed on the ten highest-performing models as determined by cross-validation outcomes.
- Post-tuning, notable enhancements are detected in mean accuracy, ROC-AUC, and F1-score across the majority of classifiers.

- Particularly, all boosting models like XGB enhanced their accuracy from 87.59% to 91.42%, LGBM improved from 90.03% to 91.39%, and GB increased from 88.26% to 92.12%.
- ROC-AUC values for optimized models improved by 2–5% relative to their default configurations.

This highlighted that hyperparameter adjustment is essential for enhancing model generalization and prediction accuracy for CHD risk.
Moreover, the dataset (FHS) is fundamentally imbalanced, featuring fewer CHD-positive cases than normal cases. In the absence of sampling, models demonstrated good accuracy but low recall, reflecting inadequate sensitivity to CHD-positive cases. SMOTE sampling methods are employed to overcome this issue. Consequently, class rebalancing techniques are essential in enhancing model equality and diminishing biased predictions favouring the majority class.

Finally, the outcomes of the voting models are contrasted with individually optimized classifiers to evaluate the efficiency of the ensemble.

- Soft voting achieved superior performance, attaining an accuracy of 92.26% and a ROC-AUC score of 0.92, surpassing all individual models.
- Hard voting, while marginally less effective than soft voting, nonetheless outperformed the majority of individual classifiers.
- The ensemble technique enhanced the model's generalization capacity and robustness, particularly in addressing intricate patterns within the CHD dataset.

The ensemble method, especially the soft voting technique, illustrated the advantages of integrating various boosting classifiers. As a result, the proposed boosting-based voting ensemble configuration enhanced predicted accuracy and dependability in CHD risk assessment. In conclusion, boosting models consistently outperform alternative approaches for CHD prediction. They are frequently ranked among the top-performing methods and exhibit strong generalization capabilities, even when applied to imbalanced clinical datasets.

4.5 Proposed CHD Risk Prediction Framework – Phase II: Deep Learning Approach

In continuation of the ensemble learning-based predictive modelling established in Phase I, this second phase of the study leverages DL techniques further to enhance the accuracy and reliability of CHD risk prediction. Medical data, particularly in heart disease diagnosis, are complex and highly non-linear. ANNs can provide a powerful alternative by capturing hidden patterns and complex feature interactions that traditional ML models may overlook.
The proposed framework in this phase incorporates a tailor-made ANN architecture, carefully developed and optimized for CHD prediction employing the FHS dataset. The ANN

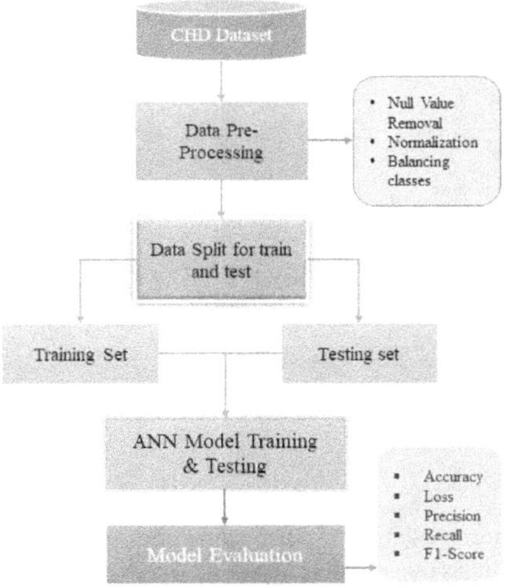

Figure 4.7: The workflow diagram of the proposed methodology for CHD prediction.

model analyzed these inputs to forecast the 10-year risk of acquiring CHD as an outcome variable. To handle challenges like class imbalance, model generalization, and nonlinear data patterns, the proposed ANN incorporates various activation functions (ReLU, LeakyReLU), multiple optimizers (Adam, RMSProp, SGD, and AdaDelta), hyperparameter tuning (learning rate, epochs, batch size, etc.), and advanced sampling techniques (SMOTE, SMOTE-Tomek, SMOTEENN, and the proposed two-stage hybrid). This phase is to develop a high-performance, clinically effective decision-support system that can accurately identify at-risk patients, facilitate early intervention, and perhaps decrease worldwide mortality linked to CHD.
This section outlines the methodology for developing ANN-based CHD prediction models using various optimizers. It includes dataset preprocessing, model deployment strategy, optimization techniques, evaluation methods, and key components. A high-level workflow of the entire process is shown in Fig. 4.7.

4.5.1 ANN Architecture Design

This is a crucial phase in the whole workflow and is of paramount significance in this research study. This section introduces a tailored ANN architecture to enhance the prediction accuracy for CHD. The approach focuses on capturing complicated nonlinear patterns in the data while maintaining model generalization and decreasing overfitting. The framework is built in many stages of dense layers, with the parameters for these levels detailed below. Fig. 4.8 illustrates the specifics of the tailored deployed model framework following the preprocessing of the collected dataset input into the neural network model.

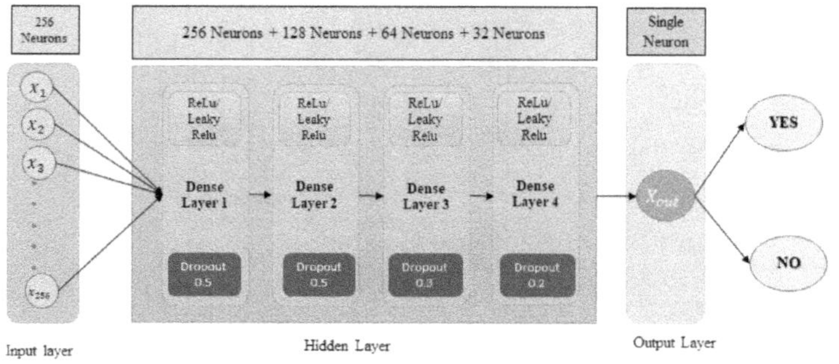

Figure 4.8: The implemented framework of the proposed ANN methodology

This is the main approach used to train the neural network model, utilizing an advanced method that involves importing multiple libraries. The "Keras" and "TensorFlow" libraries are used for establishing the model, followed by the "Sequential ()" API for constructing the stacking layers of the network. It is essential to establish many nodes within the dense levels of the network, with each layer incorporating an activation function. The data traverse the input dense layers, and through the many hidden dense layers, the neurones receive input from the preceding layer's neurones. The dense layer constitutes a completely connected network and culminates in an output layer. Additionally, dropout layers may be be implemented with a specified dropout rate to effectively filter values, consequently enhancing the training of a node. During each training phase, the dropout rate can be incrementally increased by 1 to mitigate model overfitting.

The proposed architecture utilizes dense layers that ensure full connectivity between neurons in consecutive layers. Thus, it enhances the model's ability to capture complex and hierarchical patterns for effective feature extraction. Incorporating four dense layers enables the network to learn intricate relationships within the input data progressively. This design maintains a balance between complexity and computational efficiency, promoting generalization while minimizing overfitting and unnecessary computational overhead. Dropout layers are included to randomly deactivate neurones during training, reducing over-reliance on specific neurones and further mitigating overfitting.

Activation functions like ReLU are employed to efficiently handle non-linearities by passing only positive values, helping avoid vanishing gradients and enabling faster training. LeakyReLU complements ReLU by allowing a small gradient for negative inputs, thus addressing the "dying neurone" problem and improving learning where negative correlations exist. Using both ReLU and LeakyReLU across input and hidden layers improves the model's robustness and performance. Given the binary nature of the target variable, the output layer includes a single neurone with a sigmoid activation function, paired with binary cross-entropy as the loss function for accurate performance evaluation.

To ensure efficient training and faster convergence of the ANN model, multiple optimization strategies are explored – Adam: Used for its adjustable learning rate and momentum features. SGD (Stochastic Gradient Descent): Incorporated to evaluate the performance of conventional optimizers. RMSProp: Efficient for managing non-stationary objectives. AdaDelta: An improvement over AdaGrad, notably useful in regulating learning rate decay. Each optimizer is assessed regarding training stability, convergence rate, and ultimate prediction accuracy.

4.5.2 ANN Tuning and Optimization

To enhance the accuracy and robustness of the proposed ANN model for CHD prediction, this subsection emphasizes the systematic tuning and optimization of the model architecture. Once the structure is finalized, the model is compiled using the *"compile"* function. During this step, an appropriate optimizer is selected to update the weights based on the loss function and gradients. Given the binary classification nature of the task, binary cross-entropy is used as the loss function to measure the difference between actual and predicted values, with accuracy chosen as the evaluation metric. The optimization procedure sought to reduce this loss over epochs utilizing chosen optimizers, including Adam, RMSProp, AdaDelta, and SGD. The learning rate scheduling is utilized to prevent overfitting and mitigate vanishing gradients.

This process is repeated multiple times, each with adjustments to either the activation function or the optimization strategy. The ANN model employs activation functions such as ReLU and LeakyReLU to improve predictive accuracy. To minimize the loss during training, optimizers like Adam, RMSProp, SGD, and AdaDelta are used. Various learning rates, ranging from 0.001 to 0.1, are tested to determine the optimal rate that allows for quick convergence without overshooting the minimum loss. Learning rate plays a key role in controlling the extent of weight updates during backpropagation.

Higher dropout rates, starting at 0.5 in the initial layers, remove more connections, promoting diverse feature learning. In contrast, lower dropout rates of 0.2 in the deeper layers help retain learnt patterns while still providing regularization. This strategic variation in dropout rates across layers helps reduce overfitting while preserving essential features.

The training process is carried out using the *"fit"* method on the dataset. During this phase, the optimizer updates model weights across several epochs based on the loss function. Epochs determine how many full passes the model makes over the dataset, while batch size dictates how many samples are processed before updating the weights. Training is conducted over 35, 50, and 100 epochs to accommodate different dataset sizes, increasing variability and improving accuracy. A batch size of 32 is used, meaning the model processes 32 samples at a time, calculates the loss, and updates the weights before moving on. This smaller batch size supports stable weight updates and a steady learning process. The complete workflow of the ANN model training and execution is detailed in the accompanying algorithms in 1.

The model undergoes training across multiple epochs to determine a training score and accuracy. The model's training with diverse data segments enhances accuracy by supplying varied information during each iteration. The division of the dataset into training and testing subsets is advantageous, as it enables the model to learn and make predictions from

Algorithm 1: Define, compile, train, evaluate, and predict with the artificial neural network model.

Step 1: Define the model architecture
Initialize the sequential model
Add Dense layer with 256 neurons, ReLU / LeakyReLU activation, and input shape ($input\_dim$)
Add Dense layer with 256 neurons and ReLU / LeakyReLU activation
Add Dropout layer with a rate of 0.5
Add Dense layer with 128 neurons and ReLU / LeakyReLU activation
Add Dropout layer with a rate of 0.5
Add Dense layer with 64 neurons and ReLU / LeakyReLU activation
Add Dropout layer with a rate of 0.3
Add Dense layer with 32 neurons and ReLU / LeakyReLU activation
Add Dropout layer with a rate of 0.2
Add Dense layer with 1 neuron and "Sigmoid" activation **# for binary classification**
Step 2: Compile the model: "compile()"
Compile model with:
  Optimizer = Adam(learning_rate=0.001) **or** SGD **or** RMSProp **or** AdaDelta
  Loss = Binary Cross-entropy **# For binary classification**
  Metrics = Accuracy
Display model summary: "sequential": model.summary()
Step 3: Train the model: "fit()"
Fit model on training data (X_{train}, y_{train}) **# With and without oversampling (SMOTE/SMOTETomek)**
Parameters:
  Epochs = 100
  Batch size = 32
  Validation data = (X_{test}, y_{test})
Step 4: Evaluate the model: "evaluate()"
Evaluate model on training data (X_{train}, y_{train})
Evaluate model on test data (X_{test}, y_{test})
Step 5: Make predictions
Predict using the trained model on new input data (new_data)

distinct portions of the same data.

4.5.3 Experimental Setup

The experiment is executed within the Anaconda environment, utilizing the Python programming language for the tests. Optimal performance is attained by utilizing the proposed model with a *i5 processor, an Nvidia GeForce RTX GPU, and the Windows 11* operating system. Developing a model that incorporates the NumPy library for image array computations, together with Anaconda Navigator and Shell for configuring the backend environment and installing essential supporting libraries. The transfer function and activation function are utilized to create hidden layers in the ANN model, which is developed using Keras, an open-source neural network toolkit built on TensorFlow. TensorFlow provides both high-level and low-level APIs to enhance the user-friendliness of Keras.

4.5.4 Experimental Result

This section illustrates the results of the implemented artificial neural network following the application of data preparation procedures. The experiment aimed to mitigate overfitting and underfitting by utilizing several parameters, including a batch size of 32, a maximum of 100 epochs, and dropout rates varying from 0.2 to 0.5 across different layers. The preliminary prediction model is implemented before the balancing of the target class after suitable data cleansing techniques. The Adam optimizer, with a learning rate of 0.01 and utilizing the ReLU and LeakyReLU activation functions (AF), is employed to attain the output illustrated in Table 4.6. The implemented ANN model utilizing the Adam optimizer with LeakyReLU achieves a validation accuracy of 86.79%. Fig. 4.9 illustrates the appropriate confusion matrix (CM), the training accuracy (TA) compared to validation accuracy, the training loss (TL) against validation loss (VL) throughout epochs (E), and the validation accuracy (VA) concerning loss. The FN value is recorded at 54, constituting 12.74% of the total text data in the CM.

AF	E	TA (%)	TL	VA (%)	VL
	35	85.22	0.3692	85.38	0.3864
ReLU	60	86.27	0.3491	85.85	0.3953
	100	86.84	0.3211	85.61	0.4069
	35	85.32	0.3692	86.08	0.3797
Leaky-ReLU	60	85.88	0.3595	86.08	0.3857
	100	87.00	0.3287	86.79	0.3875

Table 4.6: The outcomes before oversampling using Adam optimizer (lr=0.01)

In the second step of model deployment on the preprocessed dataset, following the use of the initial oversampling strategy with *SMOTE*, the target class exhibited equal instances across each category. An analogous experimental configuration is employed to implement the ANN model utilizing several optimization strategies, including Adam, SGD, RMSProp, and AdaDelta, to attain improved accuracy in findings. Optimization strategies are employed to refine the parameters and architecture of neural networks for enhanced outcome efficiency. The results of the initial Adam optimization method applied to the proposed ANN model for CHD prediction are presented in Table 4.7. The optimization

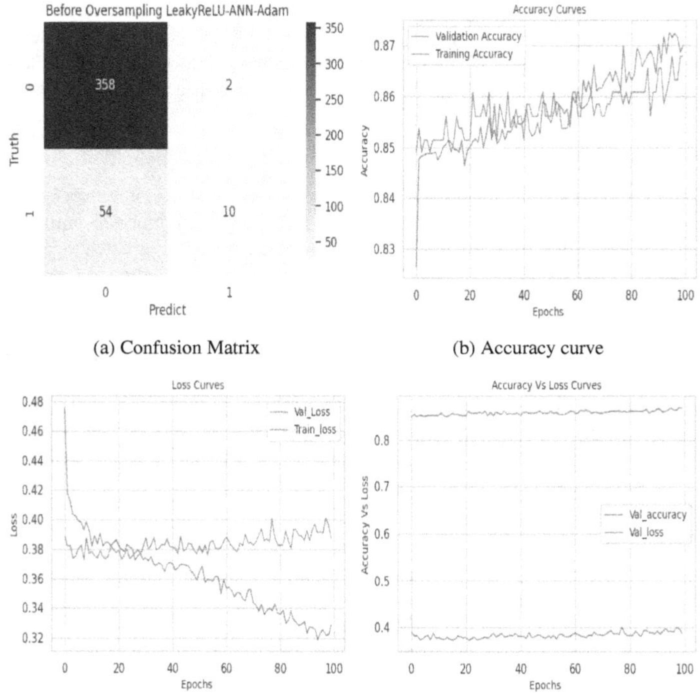

(a) Confusion Matrix

(b) Accuracy curve

(c) Loss curve

(d) Accuracy Vs Loss curve

Figure 4.9: The performance curves of the ANN model before Oversampling using LeakyReLU-Adam optimizer

findings for the subsequence for SDG, RMSProp, and AdaDelta under identical experimental conditions are provided in Tables 4.8, 4.9, and 4.10, respectively.

Furthermore, after analyzing the experimental results from the second phase of model deployment with the SMOTE oversampling technique, the Adam optimizer exhibited superior performance compared to other optimizers. The SMOTETomek oversampling technique is applied to address dataset imbalance by removing redundant majority instances and balancing classes. This technique is employed to ascertain the importance of its application in addressing the severely unbalanced target class. Additionally, the recently created sampling approach *SMOTEENN*, a variant of SMOTE combined with Edited Nearest Neighbour, is selected to eliminate noise from the majority class and appropriately man-

AF	E	TA (%)	TL	VA(%)	VL	Pr	Re	Fs
ReLU	35	98.28	0.0495	89.86	0.3578	0.88	0.96	0.93
	60	99.40	0.0190	91.25	0.3966	0.89	0.96	0.93
	100	99.98	0.0177	**93.75**	0.4905	0.91	0.97	0.94
LeakyReLU	35	98.01	0.0583	88.75	0.3177	0.86	0.96	0.91
	60	99.69	0.0148	90.97	0.3867	0.87	0.97	0.91
	100	100	0.0002	**92.36**	0.4165	0.92	0.96	0.92

Table 4.7: The Adam optimizer results after SMOTE (lr=0.001)

AF	E	TA (%)	TL	VA (%)	VL	Pr	Re	Fs
ReLU	35	96.40	0.1001	88.75	0.3519	0.87	0.92	0.91
	60	100	0.0236	92.50	0.4319	0.88	0.96	0.92
	100	100	0.0132	92.50	0.5211	0.89	0.97	0.93
LeakyReLU	35	98.11	0.0538	86.94	0.3524	0.88	0.92	0.91
	60	99.51	0.0143	91.67	0.3682	0.88	0.95	0.91
	100	100	0.0003	92.50	0.4500	0.89	0.97	0.93

Table 4.8: The SDG optimizer results after SMOTE (lr=0.001, momentum=0.9)

AF	E	TA (%)	TL	VA (%)	VL	Pr	Re	Fs
ReLU	35	98.39	0.0509	89.86	0.4025	0.86	0.91	0.88
	60	99.18	0.0274	90.83	0.5347	0.87	0.93	0.88
	100	99.64	0.0142	91.53	0.6969	0.88	0.96	0.91
LeakyReLU	35	97.87	0.0691	88.19	0.4754	0.85	0.90	0.89
	60	99.37	0.0284	90.97	0.5609	0.88	0.91	0.91
	100	99.57	0.0218	92.08	0.6241	0.90	0.94	0.92

Table 4.9: The RMSProp Optimizer outcomes after SMOTE (lr=0.01, rho=0.9)

AF	E	TA (%)	TL	VA (%)	VL	Pr	Re	Fs
ReLU	35	65.54	0.6560	66.11	0.6528	0.67	0.69	0.68
	60	66.30	0.6262	66.25	0.6235	0.67	0.69	0.68
	100	67.86	0.6032	66.81	0.6047	0.67	0.69	0.68
LeakyReLU	35	66.67	0.6462	64.31	0.6521	0.64	0.66	0.66
	60	67.26	0.6297	65.28	0.6382	0.64	0.67	0.66
	100	68.68	0.6013	66.25	0.6182	0.66	0.68	0.67

Table 4.10: The AdaDelta Optimizer results after SMOTE (lr=0.001, rho=0.95)

age the minority class. These strategies are employed to ascertain the significance of usage in managing highly unbalanced target class data instances and to evaluate the superiority of these techniques. Comparable experimental settings are evaluated to implement the ANN model utilizing the optimal Adam optimizer with the same parameters previously employed in conjunction with SMOTE and Adam. The testing findings indicated a high accuracy of 93.98% and 94.53% for ReLU with Adam, after the sampling effects of SMOTETomek and SMOTEENN. The relevant results are reported in Tables 4.11 and 4.12, respectively, for enhanced comprehension of their insights.

After evaluating SMOTEENN and SMOTETomek, a two-stage sampling strategy is adopted to address class imbalance and improve decision boundary separation. The synergistic effect exhibited the best accuracy of 96.25% in conjunction with the Adam-ReLU combination. The observable results are depicted in Table 4.13.

AF	E	TA (%)	TL	VA (%)	VL	Pr	Re	Fs
ReLU	35	98.65	0.0395	91.74	0.3914	0.91	0.97	0.93
	50	99.49	0.0181	92.86	0.3569	0.93	0.97	0.94
	100	100	0.0000	**93.98**	0.5001	0.94	0.97	0.94
LeakyReLU	35	98.56	0.0426	91.46	0.3245	0.91	0.96	0.94
	50	98.58	0.0366	92.02	0.3932	0.92	0.96	0.94
	100	100	0.0000	93.70	0.5084	0.93	0.97	0.94

Table 4.11: The Adam Optimizer results after SMOTETomek (lr = 0.001)

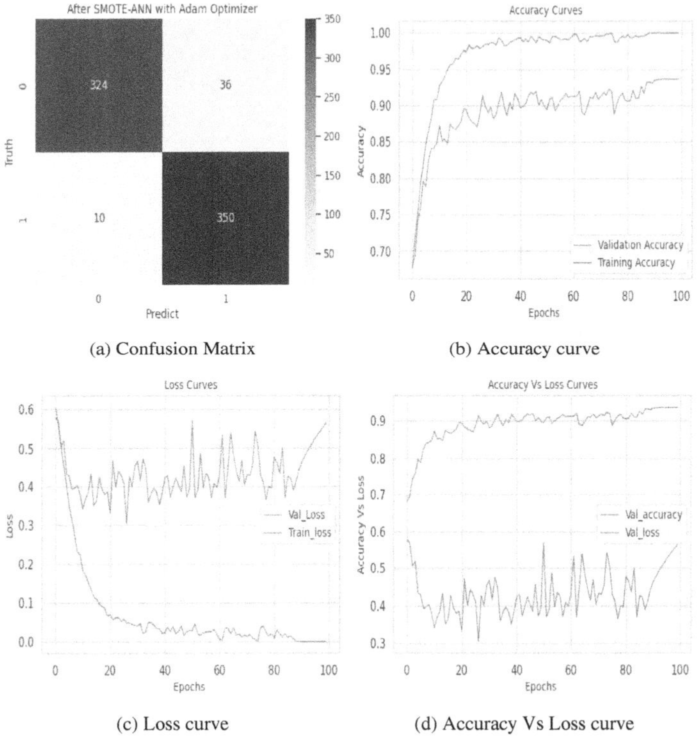

(a) Confusion Matrix

(b) Accuracy curve

(c) Loss curve

(d) Accuracy Vs Loss curve

Figure 4.10: The performance curves of the proposed ANN model after oversampling (SMOTE) with Adam optimizer & ReLU activation function

4.5.5 Results Analysis and Discussion

The most effective optimization method, employing the Adam optimizer, following the target class oversampling via SMOTE and utilizing the ReLU activation function, attained an accuracy of 93.75%. The validation loss is approximately 0.4905, while other measures, such as recall, are elevated, signifying prediction stability at 0.97. The anticipated accuracy and loss during training and validation throughout epochs, along with the confusion matrix (CM) for binary classification, are illustrated in the following images. Fig. 4.10 illustrates the corresponding confusion matrix, the training and validation accuracy, the training and validation loss throughout epochs, and the validation accuracy with loss. The associated false negative (FN) value is markedly reduced in this instance, as noted

AF	E	TA (%)	TL	VA (%)	VL	Pr	Re	Fs
ReLU	35	99.92	0.0075	93.96	0.3197	0.90	0.98	0.95
	50	100	0.0000	94.34	0.5481	0.91	0.98	0.96
	100	100	0.0000	**94.53**	0.7601	0.92	0.99	0.96
LeakyReLU	35	98.76	0.0484	92.82	0.3335	0.90	0.97	0.93
	50	99.63	0.0108	93.77	0.3176	0.92	0.99	0.95
	100	100	0.0000	94.34	0.7002	0.92	0.99	0.95

Table 4.12: The Adam Optimizer results after SMOTEENN (lr = 0.001)

AF	E	TA (%)	TL	VA (%)	VL	Pr	Re	Fs
ReLU	35	99.32	0.0189	94.59	0.3017	0.92	0.97	0.95
	50	100	0.0000	96.10	0.4212	0.94	0.98	0.96
	100	100	0.0000	**96.25**	0.4364	0.94	0.98	0.96
LeakyReLU	35	99.06	0.0282	94.44	0.2751	0.91	0.97	0.93
	50	100	0.0000	95.20	0.3371	0.93	0.98	0.95
	100	100	0.0000	95.35	0.5005	0.93	0.98	0.95

Table 4.13: The Adam Optimizer results after Two-Stage sampling (SMOTEENN + SMOTETomek), (lr = 0.001)

with 10, representing 1.39% of the test data.
The impact of alternative sampling strategies, such as SMOTETomek and SMOTEENN, is favourable when utilized with the Adam optimizer in conjunction with the ReLU activation function. The observed validation accuracy is 93.98% and 94.53%, with recall values of 0.97 and 0.99, respectively. The performance curves for SMOTETomek and SMOTEENN models are illustrated in Figs. 4.11 and 4.12, respectively. The FN rates are adequately recorded for SMOTETomek and SMOTEENN at 1.26% and 0.56%, respectively.

Furthermore, the combined application of SMOTEENN and SMOTETomek utilizing the ReLU activation function with the Adam optimizer yielded superior performance compared to all previously deployed models, in contrast to the effects of SMOTETomek and SMOTEENN used independently. The integrated model attained a performance accuracy of 96.25% with a loss function value of 0.5364. Furthermore, the LeakyReLU achieved marginally lower accuracy than ReLU; yet, both models are extremely efficient predictors,

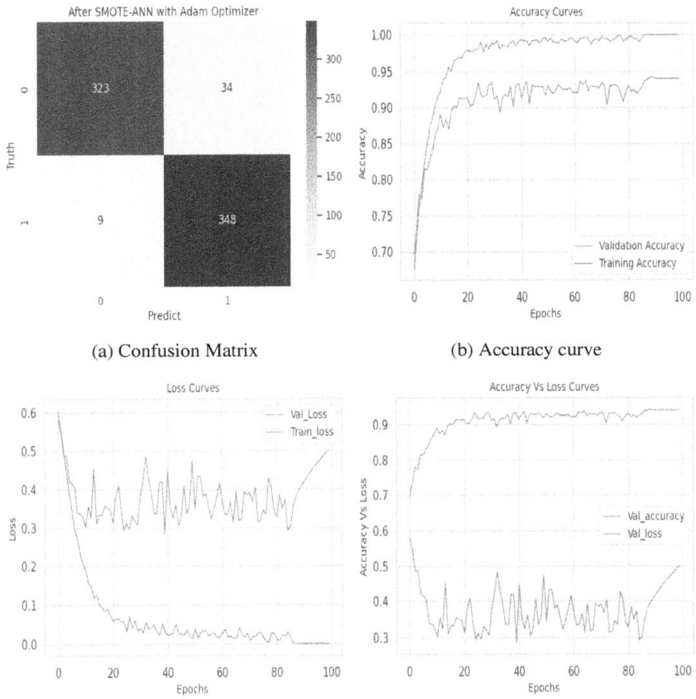

(a) Confusion Matrix (b) Accuracy curve

(c) Loss curve (d) Accuracy Vs Loss curve

Figure 4.11: The performance curves of the proposed ANN model after oversampling (SMOTETomek) with Adam optimizer & ReLU activation function

each exhibiting a recall value of 0.98. This demonstrates the reliability and efficacy of the proposed approaches for predicting CHD in highly imbalanced medical datasets. Owing to the elevated recall values, the effective FN rate is 0.75%, signifying that 99.25% of positive observations are accurately forecasted as positive. Fig. 4.13 illustrates the accuracy versus loss curves for training and validation over 100 epochs, incorporating CM and the validation accuracy versus loss curves, while accounting for the impact of SMOTEENN combined with SMOTETomek.

The employment of those optimizers indicates that the model relies on freshly discovered techniques. Utilizing several gradient descent methods, it demonstrates remarkable accuracy when implemented with LeakyReLU. This outcome indicates that the new optimizer

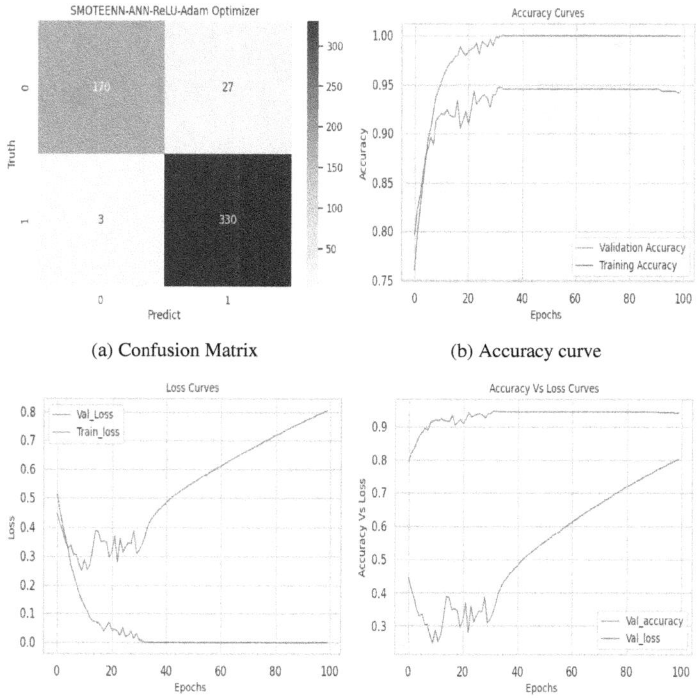

(a) Confusion Matrix (b) Accuracy curve

(c) Loss curve (d) Accuracy Vs Loss curve

Figure 4.12: The performance curves of the proposed ANN model after oversampling (SMOTEENN) with Adam optimizer & ReLU activation function

libraries significantly aid in the development of the CHD prediction model. The Adam Optimizer enhances the precision and fitting of the ANN model, resulting in more stable outcomes. The results obtained via the optimizers SGD and RMSProp are only proximate to the final proposed solutions due to their analogous mechanisms. Conversely, the AdaDelta exhibits a significantly larger disparity.

The outcomes obtained with two activation functions provide superior performance throughout several tests conducted with various parameters. Each tuning parameter influences the output; nonetheless, the function remains intact despite all technicalities. LeakyReLU is an alternative activation function for training, and it is evident that its results are comparable to those obtained by ReLU, including instances when it outperforms ReLU. This demonstrates that a comparable working style employing a similar implementation may

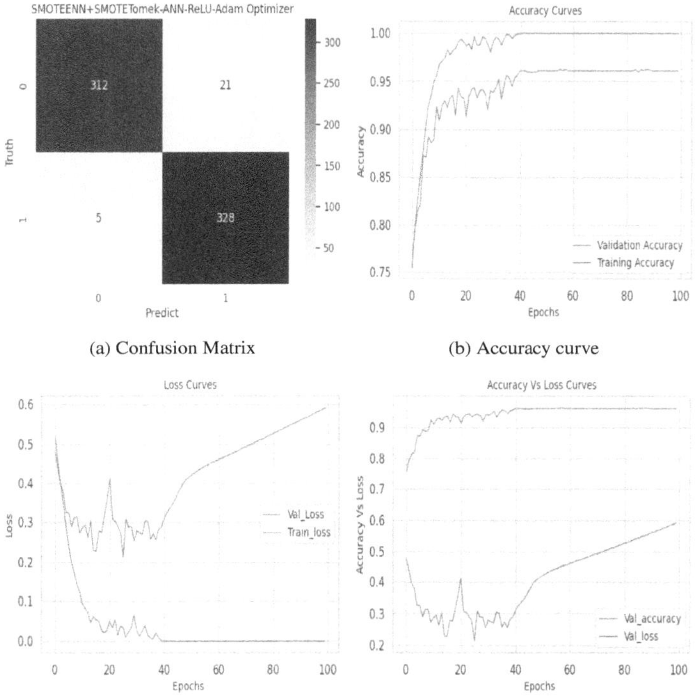

(a) Confusion Matrix (b) Accuracy curve

(c) Loss curve (d) Accuracy Vs Loss curve

Figure 4.13: The proposed ANN model's performance curves after sampling SMOTEENN+SMOTETomek with Adam optimizer & ReLU activation function

only enhance accuracy.

Fig. 4.14 illustrates the comparative performance of the evaluated optimizers regarding activation functions, focusing on validation accuracy and loss function following the use of the SMOTE approach. The insights provided by the optimizers are crucial for predicting coronary heart disease in neural networks, highlighting key aspects. The efficacy of the sampling approaches SMOTE, SMOTETomek, SMOTEENN, and SMOTEENN + SMOTETomek is significantly affected by the application of the optimal Adam optimizer in conjunction with ReLU and LeakyReLU activation functions. Also, Fig. 4.14 illustrates the comparative performance of several sampling methodologies for clarity and comprehension of their effects.

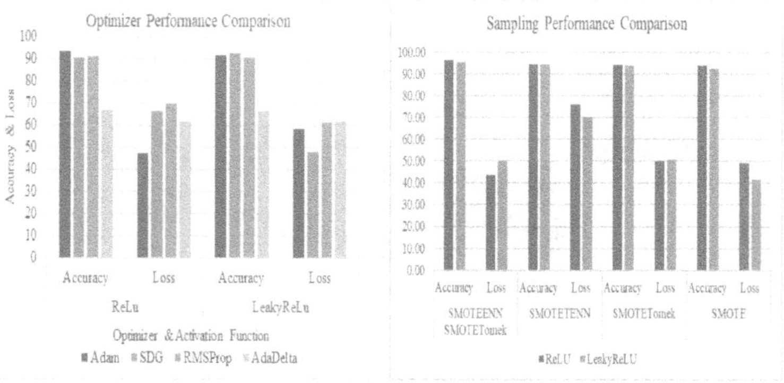

(a) Optimizer Techniques Comparison (b) Sampling Techniques Comparison

Figure 4.14: The effect of Optimizers and Sampling techniques performance comparison (Adam) concerning validation accuracy and loss function

4.5.6 Comparison with the SOTA Learning Techniques

This study compares experimental findings with an alternative solution using the FHS dataset. The research focuses on mitigating overfitting by parameter adjustment rather than feature selection or removal techniques. The proposed methodology produces more precise outcomes compared to the latest research. The study emphasizes the impact of oversampling and optimization strategies on ANNs for generalized illness prediction models. The model's tailored architecture, dropout rates, activation functions, and optimal optimizer choice yield superior outcomes. The study also addresses data preparation methods and the use of sophisticated sampling techniques. The proposed innovative two-stage sampling method, incorporating SMOTEENN and SMOTETomek together with their sequential combined effects, achieved significant experimental findings. Due to their capacity to handle complex non-linear correlations among input features and their automated feature extraction from raw datasets, ANN-based CHD prediction models can improve effectiveness in modern healthcare decision-making systems. Table 4.14 shows that the proposed methodology yields more accurate results compared to recent research using the FHS Dataset.

4.6 Advantages and Reliability of ML and DL Models for CHD Risk Prediction

Traditional statistical models used for CHD risk prediction, such as linear regression and Cox proportional hazards models, are limited by strong assumptions, including linearity, feature independence, and predefined interactions. These constraints restrict their ability to

# Ref	Dataset	Techniques used	Ac (%)
[116]	FHS	Boosted Decision Tree Classifier combined with R-Studio	85.00
[117]	FHS	RF without feature selection	91.60
		RF with GA as a feature selection	90.70
[64]	FSH	ANN based on a sparse autoencoder (SAE)	90.00
[118]	Hospital	RF Classifier (ML Model)	92.04
[119]	Hospital	KELM with salp swarm algorithm (SSA)	84.40
[80]	FSH	MLP based on a Neural Network model without a feature selection approach	92.87
[120]	FHS	RF with Recursive Feature Elimination (RFE) feature selection method	89.00
Proposed Model		**Customized ANN model with the combination of SMOTEENN+SMOTETomek-ReLU-Adam Optimizer**	**96.25**

Table 4.14: Comparison of the proposed technique with the previous studies conducted on FHS

capture the complex, nonlinear relationships that exist among demographic, behavioural, and clinical risk factors. In contrast, ML- and DL-based ANN techniques offer a data-driven modelling paradigm capable of learning intricate patterns and high-order feature interactions directly from clinical data, thereby improving predictive accuracy and robustness.

Ensemble learning approaches, particularly boosting and voting-based classifiers, enhance prediction reliability by aggregating the decisions of multiple optimized learners. This aggregation reduces individual model bias and variance, leading to more stable and generalized predictions. In this study, ensemble-based CHD prediction models consistently outperformed individual classifiers and conventional statistical baselines, achieving superior accuracy of 92.26% and ROC-AUC scores of 0.92. Furthermore, hyperparameter optimization using RandomizedSearchCV significantly improved model generalization by identifying optimal learning configurations and reducing overfitting.

Furthermore, deep learning models, while powerful, are often susceptible to overfitting, especially when applied to small or imbalanced medical datasets. To address this challenge, several overfitting control strategies are systematically integrated into the proposed framework. Advanced sampling techniques, including SMOTE, SMOTETomek, SMOTEENN, and a proposed two-stage novel sampling, are employed to balance class distributions and improve minority class learning. Additionally, the ANN architecture is carefully optimized through controlled network depth, neurone configuration, learning rate adjustment, batch size tuning, activation function, and optimizer selection. Among the evaluated optimizers, Adam demonstrated superior convergence stability and generalization capability. Cross-validation and validation-based performance monitoring further ensured that the model maintained robust performance across unseen data.

As a result of these combined strategies, the optimized ANN model achieved a validation accuracy of 96.25%, a recall of 0.98, and low validation loss. It indicates effective overfitting mitigation and reliable learning. These findings demonstrate that properly optimized and regularized ML and DL models surpass traditional statistical approaches in predictive accuracy. Moreover, they offer enhanced reliability and clinical applicability for CHD risk prediction.

4.7 Key Findings and Summary

This chapter introduced a dual-phase prediction framework for evaluating the risk of CHD employing sophisticated ML and DL strategies. Phase I concentrated on ensemble-based classifiers, whereas Phase II utilized a tailored ANN for improved prediction. The key findings and overall contributions from both phases are summarized here.

- **Ensemble Learning Enhances Predictive Accuracy (Phase I):** A soft voting ensemble of five optimized boosting classifiers (XGB, LGBM, HGB, CB, GB) attained a mean accuracy of 92.26% and a ROC-AUC of 0.92, surpassing the performance of most individual classifiers. As a result, it affirms the ensemble strategy as an effective method for early CHD prediction.
- **Hyperparameter Tuning is Crucial:** RandomizedSearchCV significantly enhanced the performance of the top ten classifiers. This result validates that thorough optimization of learning models improves generalization and reduces classification error.
- **Effective Handling of Class Imbalance:** The utilization of sophisticated sampling methods such as SMOTE, SMOTETomek, SMOTEENN, and a dual-stage hybrid approach significantly enhanced the classification of minority CHD cases. These techniques mitigated bias and enhanced overall model reliability.
- **Deep Learning Surpasses Traditional Models (Phase II):** An optimized ANN enhanced with optimizers such as Adam, SGD, RMSProp, and AdaDelta demonstrates strong capability in learning complex patterns. It achieves a validation accuracy of 96.25%, a recall of 0.98, and minimal validation loss through the use of a two-stage sampling strategy, the Adam optimizer with ReLU activation, and optimized hyperparameter tuning.
- **Activation and Optimizer Impact:** The implementation of ReLU and LeakyReLU mitigated vanishing gradient issues in further layers. Among optimizers, Adam with optimal parameters demonstrated superior convergence and learning stability.

- **Advanced Optimization Minimizes Overfitting/Underfitting:** The appropriate selection of learning rate, batch size, epochs, and momentum is essential for optimizing training and validation performance.
- **New Performance Benchmark Achieved:** The ANN model, combined with a synergistic oversampling strategy using SMOTEENN and SMOTETomek, demonstrates a superior benchmark performance in CHD prediction. When supported by suitable optimization methods, it outperforms traditional ML-based approaches in terms of efficiency.

In both phases contributed to developing a comprehensive decision-support system for early CHD risk assessment. By combining ensemble learning and neural networks, the framework achieved high accuracy, generalizability, and clinical relevance in addressing real-world healthcare prediction challenges. In summary, Chapter 4 fulfilled the second research objective via a thorough two-phase methodology. The initial phase revealed that ensemble learning, leveraging optimized boosting classifiers and voting methodologies, substantially improves the accuracy of CHD predictions. The next phase enhanced the model with a customized ANN architecture, wherein the selection of optimizers, activation functions, and hyperparameter tuning is crucial in improving predictive performance. The proposed models demonstrated exceptional performance on the FHS dataset, establishing a robust foundation for real-world CHD risk prediction systems.

Despite these promising outcomes, certain limitations remain. First, the framework primarily focused on long-term CHD risk, without addressing short-term survival outcomes in acute clinical settings. Second, while ANN and ensemble models enhanced predictive accuracy, their computational complexity may hinder real-time clinical deployment. Third, dynamic and rapidly changing patient parameters, critical in ICU scenarios, are not considered in this phase. Finally, the generalizability of the models to high-risk environments such as intensive care units requires further validation.

Leveraging this achievement, the next chapter expands the scope of cardiovascular risk assessment by focusing on short-term mortality prediction in HF patients admitted to intensive care units (ICUs). Given the clinical urgency and complexity of ICU settings, Chapter 5 explores a predictive framework that incorporates automatic feature selection through regularization techniques to identify critical risk factors influencing survival outcomes, thereby enhancing the reliability and practical applicability of predictive healthcare systems.

5

Assessment of Risk Factors for Mortality Prediction in Heart Failure Patients

The previous chapter presented a dual-phase framework for CHD risk prediction, integrating ensemble learning and deep neural networks to improve accuracy, generalization, and clinical relevance. While this approach effectively addressed long-term CHD mortality, it did not capture the urgent dynamics of short-term outcomes in acute care settings. In real-world clinical practice, particularly in intensive care units, rapid and accurate mortality prediction becomes equally critical. Cardiovascular disorders, especially CHD and HF, continue to be primary contributors to global mortality. This chapter extends the predictive modelling techniques discussed earlier and focuses on short-term mortality prediction in critically ill HF patients hospitalized in ICUs. Long-term CHD risk prediction supports early intervention and preventive care strategies. In contrast, in-hospital mortality prediction is crucial for timely clinical decision-making, optimized treatment planning, efficient allocation of healthcare resources, and effective patient prioritization. The precise and prompt identification of high-risk ICU patients can significantly decrease unnecessary deaths and enhance treatment strategies. In this context, risk factor analysis is crucial, as it identifies the major factors affecting mortality outcomes. Nonetheless, challenges such as high-dimensional clinical data, significant class imbalance, and limited interpretability often hinder the performance of predictive models in real-world healthcare applications.

The study presents a data-driven predictive modelling methodology to identify ICU patients with HF at high risk of mortality. The research employs the MIMIC-III (v1.4) dataset, comprising 1,177 patients and 48 clinical, laboratory, and demographic factors. The technique consists of three primary stages: Implementing 11 conventional machine learning classifiers, both boosting and non-boosting, to achieve baseline predictive performance. Next, employing Lasso (L1 penalty) and Ridge (L2 penalty) regularization methods for automated feature selection to mitigate overfitting and decrease model complexity. Also, the use of the SMOTE technique to rectify class imbalance, consequently enhancing the representation of mortality instances during the training process. Finally, followed by alpha tuning to enhance performance further. The research assesses the execution time and memory consumption of each classifier to investigate its suitability for resource-constrained clinical environments.

The main aim is to develop a resource-efficient, clinically relevant decision-support system for predicting mortality in ICU-admitted HF patients by integrating risk factor reduction with predictive modelling. It advances the broader goal of building robust, interpretable, high-performing models for short- and long-term cardiovascular risk management.

The chapter is arranged as follows: Section 5.1 discusses the chapter motivation and objectives, and in Section 5.2 defines the major contributions that have aligned with the 3rd objective of this thesis. The proposed methodology is discussed in Sections 5.3 and 5.4 concerning data preprocessing and the implementation approaches. Also, Section 5.5 highlights the advantages of ML-based performance metrics over traditional scoring methods. Finally, Section 5.6 concludes with a chapter summary and the key findings.

5.1 Motivations and Objectives

Despite ML advances in clinical care, predicting in-hospital mortality remains challenging due to complex interactions among physiological, laboratory, and demographic factors. Present prediction models frequently exhibit inadequate generalizability, overfitting, and insufficient interpretability when implemented on high-dimensional ICU datasets. The prognosis for mortality in heart failure patients admitted to the ICU remains challenging owing to:

- High-dimensional and heterogeneous medical data. The 48-feature clinical dataset poses challenges in training effective models, which often leads to increased computational burden and overfitting.
- Severe class imbalance, where mortality cases are under-represented. Additionally, imbalanced data and the need for real-time prediction demand lightweight and highly efficient models.
- Risks of model overfitting and poor generalization, especially when many irrelevant features are present.
- Limited studies focusing on resource-efficient models in terms of computation time and memory usage for clinical environments.

The third objective of the thesis is addressed through the development of a robust and scalable framework that ensures high accuracy using feature selection and resource-aware deployment. This framework enables interpretable risk assessment and efficient mortality prediction for ICU-admitted HF patients.

1. To evaluate the performance of multiple classical ML classifiers for predicting mortality among heart failure ICU patients using real-world data.
2. To apply feature selection using regularization techniques (Lasso and Ridge) to identify key predictors and reduce model complexity.
3. To tune the regularization hyperparameter alpha (α) in L1 and L2 models to enhance generalization and reduce overfitting.

4. To mitigate data imbalance using SMOTE, ensuring improved predictive performance and fairness across classes.
5. To assess execution time and memory consumption of each model to propose efficient models suitable for deployment in resource-constrained environments.

5.2 Research Contributions

This chapter proposes a systematic and thorough strategy for forecasting in-hospital mortality in HF patients admitted to the ICU, employing classical ML algorithms and feature selection methods. The key contributions of this study are highlighted below:

1. **Comprehensive Evaluation of Classical ML Models:** Eleven ML models, comprising boosting techniques (XGB, LGBM, CB, GB, HGB, AB) and classical classifiers (SVM, RF, DT, KNN, LR), are implemented as baseline models. The performance metrics include k-fold mean accuracy, standard deviation, precision, recall, and F1-score.
2. **Integration of Regularization-Based Feature Selection:** Two notable regression-based regularization techniques, LASSO (L1) and Ridge (L2), are employed to systematically remove extraneous features and improve model generalization.
3. **Hyperparameter Optimization:** The α regularization parameter value is tuned to determine appropriate feature subsets, enhancing prediction stability and interpretability. This improved classification performance while significantly reducing computational complexity.
4. **Addressing Class Imbalance through SMOTE:** The SMOTE technique is employed to address target class imbalance, enhancing recall and minimizing false negatives in forecasts for the minority class.
5. **Resource-Aware Model Analysis:** The study analyses and contrasts the computational efficiency (execution time and memory utilization) of each model, confirming their appropriateness for low-resource clinical environments.

The contributions establish a solid and comprehensible prediction framework that guarantees high classification accuracy while also handling practical issues such as feature redundancy, data imbalance, and computational efficiency. The subsequent section elaborates on the proposed technique, outlining the sequential process employed to execute the ML pipeline, encompassing data preparation, feature selection, model training, and evaluation. This chapter's contributions have been published in an article of the IEEE conference, and it is available at [121] for reference.

5.3 Proposed Methodology: Dataset and Preprocessing

In predictive modelling, particularly within the field of health care, the quality and preparation of the dataset are essential in establishing model efficiency. This section offers a

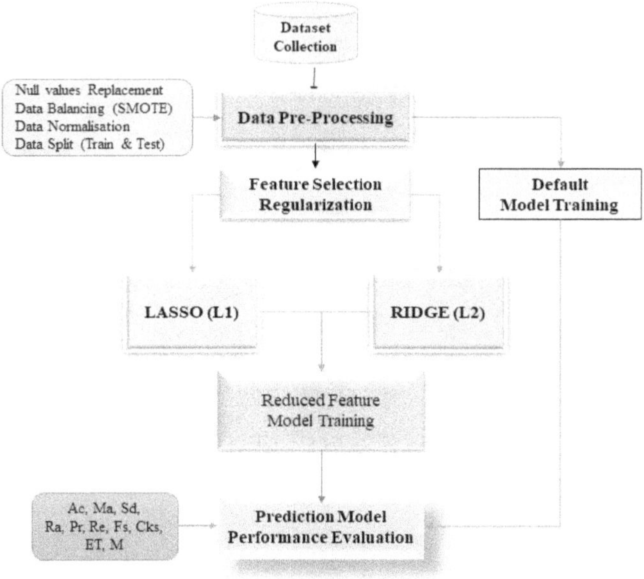

Figure 5.1: The proposed High-level workflow diagram of In-hospital Mortality

thorough review of the dataset utilized for mortality prediction in ICU-admitted heart failure patients, along with an in-depth discussion of the critical preprocessing techniques implemented to guarantee model robustness and generalizability. The presented models based on initial and feature selection outline the methodology and assessment technique described in the methods and implementations section. The proposed high-level workflow diagram of the risk assessment for HF patients' mortality prediction is illustrated in Fig. 5.1.

5.3.1 Dataset Description

The research employs the publicly accessible MIMIC-III, v1.4 (Medical Information Mart for Intensive Care) dataset, concentrating on a subset assembled for predicting in-hospital mortality, available on Kaggle [122]. The dataset consists of 1177 patient records, each corresponding to an ICU-admitted heart failure (HF) patient. The dataset has 51 columns; among them, two columns are irrelevant, like "ID" and "group", which need to be removed. The other features encompass vital signs, demographic information, co-morbidities, and laboratory findings. The objective is binary; mortality is classified as either 'living' or 'dead', denoted by 0 and 1. All specified properties are documented as numerical values, with no category values included. Certain attributes, including gender, hypertension, atrial fibrillation, coronary heart disease, and diabetes, are binary, but others, such as BMI, blood sodium, and blood calcium, are expressed in decimal format. The description of mortality factors concerning the dataset is tabulated in Table 5.1.

#	Features Name	#Non-Null	Dtype	#	Features Name	#Non-Null	Dtype
0	outcome	1177		25	RDW	1177	
1	age	1177	int64	26	Leucocyte	1177	
2	gendera	1177		27	Platelets	1177	
3	BMI	962	float64	28	Neutrophils	1033	
4	hypertensive	1177		29	Basophils	918	
5	atrialfibrillation	1177		30	Lymphocyte	1032	
6	CHD with no MI	1177		31	PT	1157	
7	diabetes	1177		32	INR	1157	
8	deficiencyanemias	1177	int64	33	NT-proBNP	1177	
9	depression	1177		34	Creatine kinase	1012	
10	Hyperlipemia	1177		35	Creatinine	1177	
11	Renal failure	1177		36	Urea nitrogen	1177	float64
12	COPD	1177		37	glucose	1159	
13	heart rate	1164		38	Blood potassium	1177	
14	Systolic blood pressure	1161		39	Blood sodium	1177	
15	Diastolic blood pressure	1161		40	Blood calcium	1176	
16	Respiratory rate	1164		41	Chloride	1177	
17	temperature	1158		42	Anion gap	1177	
18	SP O2	1164	float64	43	Magnesium ion	1177	
19	Urine output	1141		44	PH	885	
20	hematocrit	1177		45	Bicarbonate	1177	
21	RBC	1177		46	Lactic acid	948	
22	MCH	1177		47	PCO2	883	
23	MCHC	1177		48	EF	1177	int64
24	MCV	1177					

Table 5.1: Feature Description of the MIMIC-III Dataset

5.3.2 Data Preprocessing

The dataset contains numerous points that can be adjusted to enhance the findings; consequently, various preprocessing procedures are necessary. The initial step is eliminating specific columns from the dataset, including the 'ID' and 'Group No.' of each patient, with the "outcome" designated as a target variable. This decreases 51 columns to merely

48, consequently simplifying the work, as these columns may have impacted the model's integrity. Upon concluding the comprehensive preprocessing phase, the data is dispatched for subsequent steps. It is observed that all the feature values are numerical, so no encoding methods are applied to the features.

Handling Null/Missing Values

During the exploratory data analysis phases, the dataset is analyzed to ascertain the presence of any missing or null values that require replacement. It is imperative to remove all null values from the dataset, since they may lead to model overfitting or underfitting and biased prediction. To enhance this circumstance, a widely utilized statistical method, imputation approaches, namely the *Mean*, are employed for numerical data to augment data quality without compromising its integrity.

Target Class Imbalance

The dataset exhibits imbalanced outcome classes, with one class containing five times the number of values compared to the other label. This results in the model exhibiting bias towards a specific class, potentially compromising prediction accuracy. The labels can be well balanced; otherwise, the data may be biased, and oversampling or augmenting the samples could result in repetitive data, compromising the integrity of the dataset. To avert such a scenario, the oversampling approach known as SMOTE is employed, which enhances the instances of the minority class without compromising the dataset's integrity. The effect of SMOTE is represented in Table 5.2, which illustrates the instances of the outcome class, whereas Fig. 5.2 depicts the distribution of target "outcomes" before and after the sampling method.

Target Outcome	# Before Balancing	# After SMOTE
0 = Death	1018	1018
1 = Alive	159	1018

Table 5.2: Target outcome distribution before and after SMOTE

Normalization or Feature Scaling

After the sampling method, it has been noticed that the feature values are in different ranges of distribution. The feature density distribution is depicted in Fig.5.3. To handle this situation, the *MinMax* scaling method is utilized for data standardization and result enhancement. It is recognized for its capacity to normalize feature values from 0 to 1. This normalization is performed to enhance data efficiency by reducing the volume of each data point the model can evaluate. This facilitates expedited model training, and the reduction in value magnitude, when appropriately scaled, also leads to diminished resource consumption. After that, the normalized feature correlation heat map has been generated

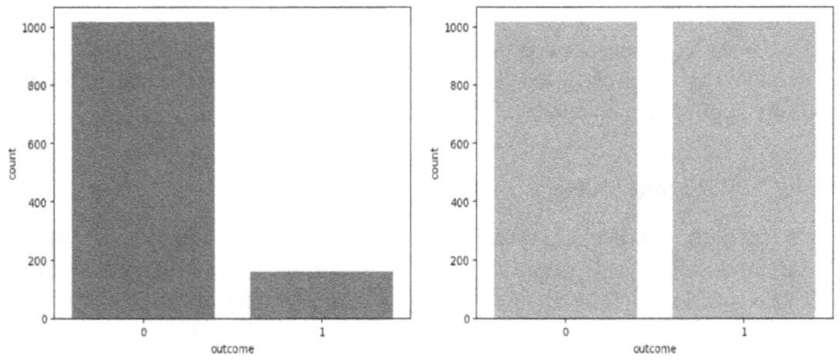

(a) Before Sampling (b) After Sampling (SMOTE)

Figure 5.2: The target class level data distribution

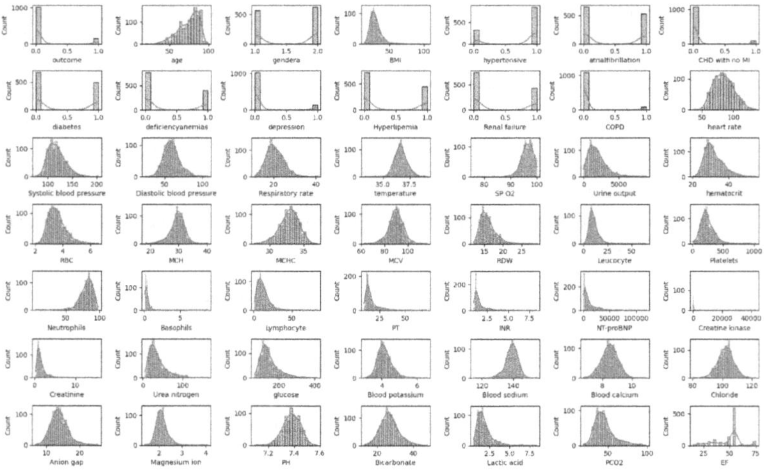

Figure 5.3: Feature density distribution

to check the intricate relationship between the feature and the target class and is depicted in Fig. 5.4.

After performing requisite data preprocessing methods, the complete oversampled dataset is divided into two segments as training and testing sets. The training procedure constitutes 80%, while testing accounts for 20% of the total cases in the balanced dataset as a hold-out method. Also, the k-fold cross-validation method is used to split the dataset into ten folds

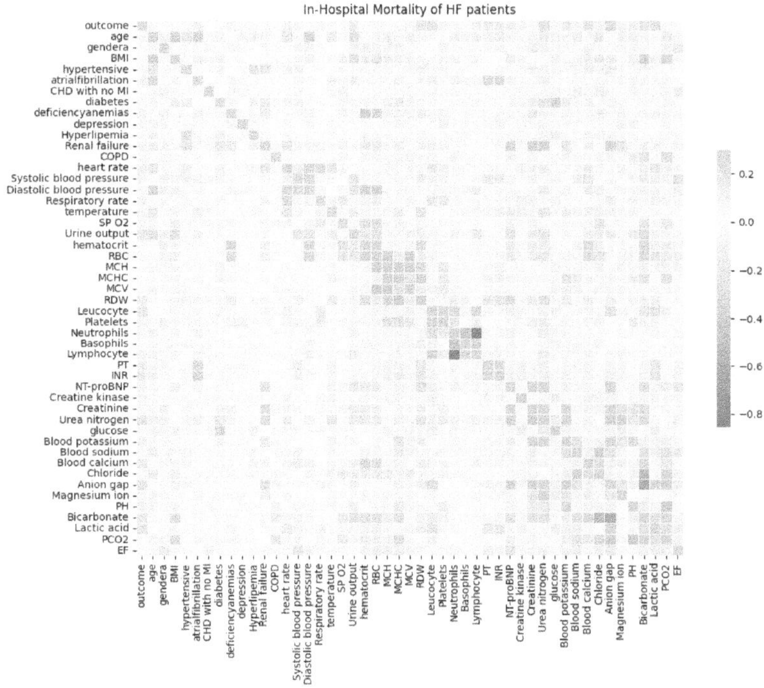

Figure 5.4: Feature Correlation Heat Map

as a validation method to ensure unbiased performance evaluation across different folds. These two validation methods are considered to overcome the model overfitting issues and improve generalization. This strategy also helped in overcoming the limitations of a small dataset size. Now, the preprocessing pipeline guarantees that the input data is cleaned up, balanced, and appropriate for machine learning model training, as a result enhancing prediction performance in subsequent analyses.

5.4 Proposed Methodology and Implementations

Widely used classifiers, including tree-based and linear models, SVM, RF, DT, LR, KNN, and boosting methods (XGB, AB, GB, HGB, LGBM, and CB), are employed to train and evaluate model performance. The technique is accurate and yields adequate predictions, facilitating improved training and evaluation of the model. The boosting model is a widely utilized approach for model training, as it integrates ensemble learning to mitigate biases and variance in supervised learning. It is utilized for the conversion of a weak learner into a strong learner. The training data is utilized by the model to comprehend the information and apply it during the prediction phase. This is conducted to evaluate and choose the superior system yielding optimal results. Model performance is assessed through the classification report, which includes Ac, Pr, Re, and Fs. Additionally, ten-fold cross-validation mean accuracy (Ma), standard deviation (Sd), Cks, ROC-AUC values (Ra), as well as the model's execution time (ET) and memory usage (M) are analyzed to elucidate the performance trade-offs among the models.

5.4.1 Experimental Setup

To maximize flexibility and repeatability, this study used cloud-based and local systems. Python packages like Scikit-learn, Imbalanced-learn, and Matplotlib assisted model creation, training, and evaluation. Google Collaboratory's high-RAM environment with GPU support sped up model training and evaluation for most tests. Tests on a local system with an *Intel Core i5 CPU, 8GB RAM, and Windows 10 OS* assessed resource efficiency and execution time in limited-compute scenarios. All model runs are consistent and balanced with 10-fold stratified cross-validation and a fixed random seed. This hybrid setup shows the proposed approaches' adaptability in high-performance and resource-constrained contexts.

5.4.2 Baseline Model Deployment (N)

This part employs an entire range of eleven conventional machine learning classifiers for predicting the mortality risk of heart failure patients. The primary objective of employing multiple classifiers is to create a flexible and comparable baseline model that can effectively handle complex medical datasets and achieve high sensitivity in mortality prediction. These models differ in their foundational learning mechanisms; some deploy decision-tree ensembles, while others employ distance metrics or probabilistic models, resulting in a diversity of predictive behaviour. During model training, classifiers are evaluated using default hyperparameters.

The experimental outcomes of the default model, utilizing the optimal configurable simulation environment based on the performance parameters, are provided in Table 5.3. The efficacy of each classifier is assessed according to its predictive accuracy, generalization capacity, and computing resources. To enhance reliability, 10-fold cross-validation is included in the experiments, and models are initially trained on the entire feature set without feature selection to determine their baseline effectiveness. The SMOTE technique is employed during preprocessing to address the unequal distribution of target classes, consequently preventing classifiers from exhibiting bias towards the majority class.
The HGB model achieved 96.57% accuracy with 22.71s ET, low standard deviation, and the highest recall, demonstrating stability and efficacy. The duration required for execution to assess model performance is a trade-off between accuracy and consumption time. The depicted Fig. 5.5 illustrates the confusion matrix (CM) of the HGB model and the ROC-AUC curve together with the probabilistic values of all the evaluated deployment

models.

Model	Ac	Ma	Pr	Re	Fs	Cks	Sd	Ra	ET	M (MiB)
HGB	96.57	93.43	0.96	0.97	0.97	0.93	1.74	0.97	22.71	598.95
CB	95.59	93.67	0.94	0.97	0.96	0.91	2.04	0.96	175.48	598.79
RF	95.10	93.92	0.97	0.93	0.95	0.90	1.77	0.95	24.56	598.56
LGBM	94.36	93.37	0.93	0.96	0.95	0.89	2.18	0.94	22.82	598.96
XGB	94.36	92.32	0.93	0.96	0.95	0.89	2.13	0.94	20.67	595.68
SVM	93.63	92.38	0.93	0.95	0.94	0.87	2.64	0.94	18.11	600.52
GB	92.16	91.15	0.93	0.92	0.92	0.84	2.64	0.92	43.16	599.45
LR	88.48	86.42	0.87	0.91	0.89	0.77	2.67	0.88	15.59	598.37
KNN	87.75	86.55	0.81	1.00	0.89	0.75	1.79	0.87	16.66	598.92
AB	87.25	85.32	0.87	0.89	0.88	0.74	2.79	0.87	23.56	598.75
DT	84.07	82.74	0.85	0.84	0.84	0.68	2.86	0.84	15.95	599.59

Table 5.3: Performance comparison of ML models without feature selection

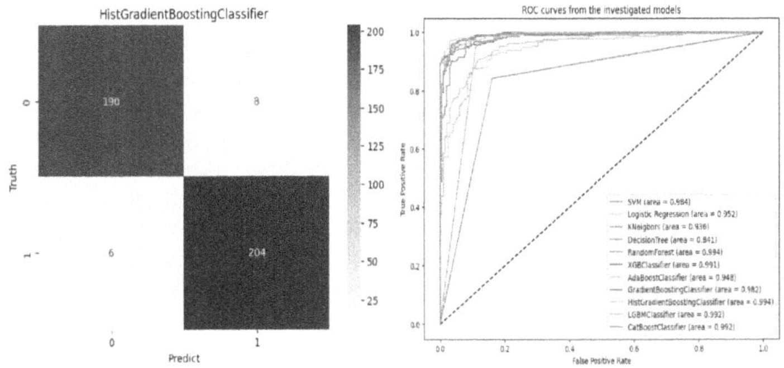

(a) The CM of HGB Model (b) The ROC-AUC curve of all models

Figure 5.5: The CM of HGB and the ROC-AUC curve of default deployed models

5.4.3 Feature Importance Model

To address the high dimensionality of the obtained datasets and mitigate overfitting, two regularization techniques based on regression are employed: Lasso and Ridge. This simplifies the study, as the impact of each feature in the model is assessed using these methods, facilitating the automatic selection of the most effective ones. This minimizes the likelihood of eliminating any essential feature that could compromise the integrity of the data and the trained model. The primary purpose is to streamline the model for application to new datasets, as a result improving its generalizability and performance. Regularization is a statistical approach employed to construct models for analyzing and comprehending the interdependence among numerous characteristics. The feature selection process follows a cost function for a basic regression model presented in Eq. 5.1.

$$\sum_{i=1}^{M}(y_i - \hat{y}_i)^2 = \sum_{i=1}^{M}\left(y_i - \sum_{j=1}^{p}(w_j \times x_{ij})\right)^2 \tag{5.1}$$

The formula contains critical variables that can be considered while assessing the cost function, including the weights of the investigated attributes. The variable y_i in the provided formula represents the actual value, whereas it $\hat{y}_i$ is the anticipated output. The coefficient w_j corresponds to the weight of each feature, which x_{ij} signifies the feature itself. The bias is essential to the model, as it aids in optimizing the fit. The complexity of linear regression, in contrast to multicollinearity, is minimal. The simplification of the model can be achieved by the utilization of alpha (α). This may enhance the model's performance with increased efficiency. Alpha (α) is a hyperparameter utilized to modify algorithmic performance through tuning to enhance outcomes. If this parameter is defined with the appropriate value, the L1 and L2 regression algorithms can yield optimal results. A linear form is essential for model training, as it reduces complexity.

Lasso regression is a widely utilized and streamlined method for constructing a robust model with chosen characteristics while preserving data integrity. It is a generalization method that eliminates superfluous features by assigning them a coefficient of 0. It is employed for feature selection to influence outcomes, as it multiplies alpha (α) by the mean weight with the least absolute value, resulting in a reduction of the slope to zero. The hyperparameter facilitates the characterization of complicated multicollinearity in linear regression, as shown by L1 in Eq. 5.2 below. This can aid in diminishing complexity and optimizing the model's performance while mitigating the issue of overfitting.

$$\sum_{i=1}^{M}(y_i - \hat{y}_i)^2 = \sum_{i=1}^{M}\left(y_i - \sum_{j=1}^{p}(w_j \times x_{ij})\right)^2 + \alpha \sum_{j=1}^{n} |w_j| \tag{5.2}$$

Ridge regression is employed for estimating multicollinearity in data characterized by interdependence. Alpha (α) is a hyperparameter that calibrates the severity of a user-defined penalty term to eliminate features with the least number of affected dependent variables. The alpha (α) value is multiplied by the mean squared weight of each feature. The L2 regression method aims to minimize the penalty term by squaring each value as indicated in the following formula 5.3. Given that the value is absolute due to squaring, the regression can converge towards zero.

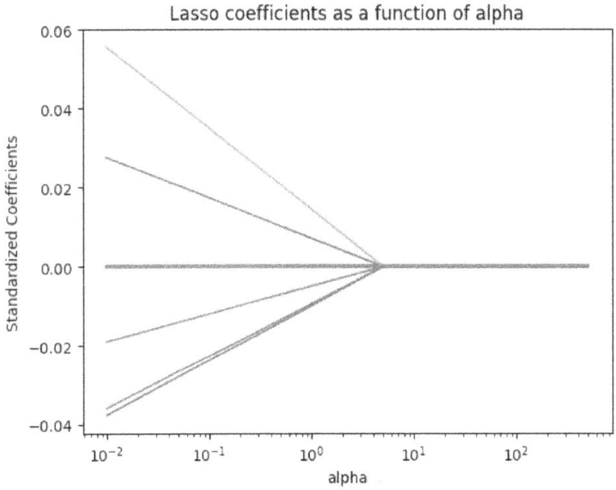

Figure 5.6: Lasso coefficients optimized alpha value

$$\sum_{i=1}^{M}(y_i - \hat{y}_i)^2 = \sum_{i=1}^{M}\left(y_i - \sum_{j=1}^{p}(w_j \times x_{ij})\right)^2 + \alpha \sum_{j=1}^{n} w_j^2 \tag{5.3}$$

5.4.4 Lasso Regression Model Deployment (L)

In Lasso regression, 15-fold cross-validation is used to determine the optimal alpha values for the L1 term in the equation. This facilitates accurate feature importance assessment and automatically selects the minimal features through the Lasso regression feature selection method. Fig. 5.6 illustrates the plot of the optimized alpha values. In Lasso regression, the non-zero coefficient values of each feature are identified as significant factors. The corresponding automatic feature selection plot, illustrated in Fig. 5.7, is then utilized for additional model training and validation to enhance outcomes. The model is trained and validated using the 32 features selected by Lasso with optimum alpha values, employing an L1 penalty, and the performance of the experimental findings is given in a manner analogous to that in Table 5.4.

The ROC-AUC curve for all deployed models and the confusion matrix of the best-performing XGB model are illustrated in Fig. 5.8 concerning the lasso regression feature selection model.

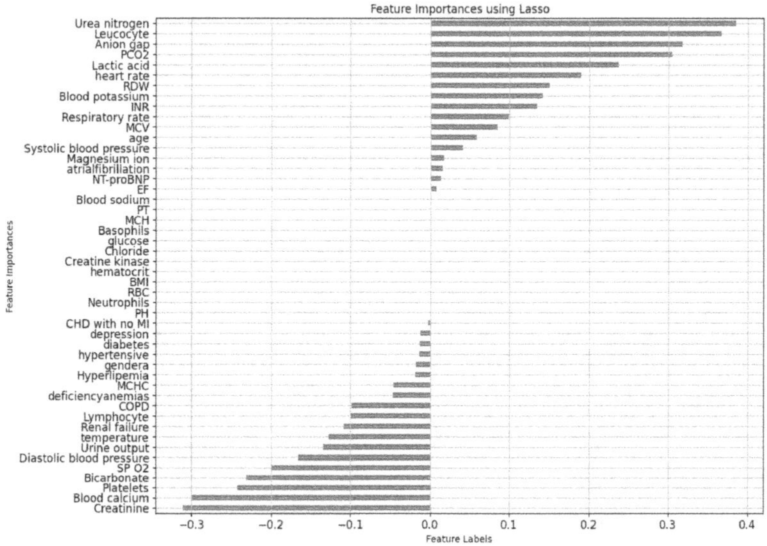

Figure 5.7: Feature importance in Lasso with coefficient values for each feature

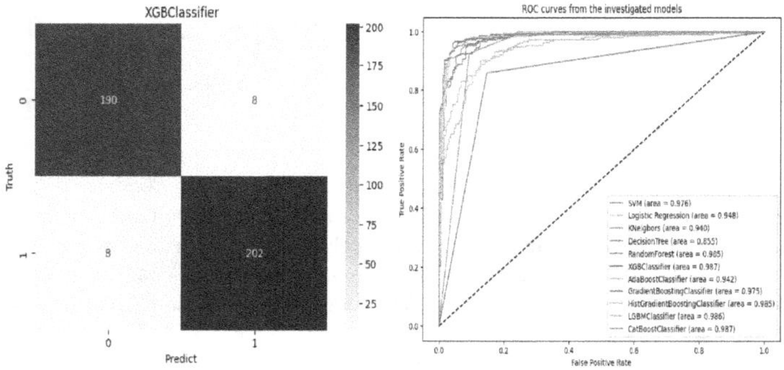

(a) The CM of Lasso XGB Model (b) The ROC-AUC curve of Lasso models

Figure 5.8: The CM of the LGBM model and the ROC-AUC curve of all the deployed models concerning Lasso

Model	Ac	Ma	Pr	Re	Fs	Cks	Sd	Ra	ET	M (MiB)
XGB	96.08	92.88	0.96	0.96	0.96	0.92	1.89	0.96	5.60	618.72
CB	95.10	92.75	0.94	0.97	0.95	0.90	1.84	0.95	106.43	623.82
LGBM	94.36	92.45	0.94	0.95	0.95	0.89	2.09	0.94	5.54	623.82
HGB	94.36	92.45	0.94	0.95	0.95	0.89	2.50	0.94	9.05	623.82
SVM	93.38	91.22	0.92	0.95	0.94	0.87	2.40	0.93	4.96	618.72
RF	92.89	93.37	0.95	0.91	0.93	0.86	2.60	0.93	10.23	618.72
GB	91.42	90.30	0.91	0.93	0.92	0.83	2.35	0.91	21.56	623.82
AB	88.24	84.21	0.88	0.89	0.89	0.76	3.36	0.88	6.92	623.82
KNN	87.99	86.73	0.82	0.99	0.89	0.76	2.21	0.88	3.15	618.72
LR	87.50	85.93	0.86	0.90	0.88	0.75	2.91	0.87	3.00	618.72
DT	85.54	81.39	0.86	0.86	0.86	0.71	3.82	0.86	2.40	618.72

Table 5.4: Performance comparison of models after hyperparameter tuning by Lasso Regression feature selection

5.4.5 Ridge Regression Model Deployment (R)

In contrast to Lasso, Ridge regression does not completely remove features; rather, it reduces the magnitude of their coefficients. It is advantageous in scenarios when multicollinearity exists and all input variables possess predictive capability. Ridge imposes a penalty proportionate to the square of the coefficients, yielding a model that equilibrates bias and variance. Similar to Lasso, the Ridge regression feature selection method utilizes identical optimized alpha values across all dataset features, from which the coefficients of each feature are calculated. Ultimately, the non-negative coefficient values for 23 features are chosen for subsequent model implementation. This section demonstrates ridge-based feature contributions using coefficient plots, facilitating a comparative analysis of each feature's impact on the outcome. The feature significance plot generated by the Ridge model is illustrated in Fig. 5.9.

The experimental results utilizing L2 penalty through ridge regression applied to the identical environmental simulation, along with the outcomes of each model, are presented in Table 5.5. Similar to Lasso, Fig. 5.10 illustrates the CM and ROC-AUC curve of the optimal XGB model alongside all deployed models concerning the ridge feature selection approach.

5.4.6 Execution Time and Memory Usage

In addition to prediction performance, evaluating the computational efficiency of machine learning models is essential, especially in real-world healthcare applications where time and resource constraints are critical. This section analyzes the execution time (ET) and

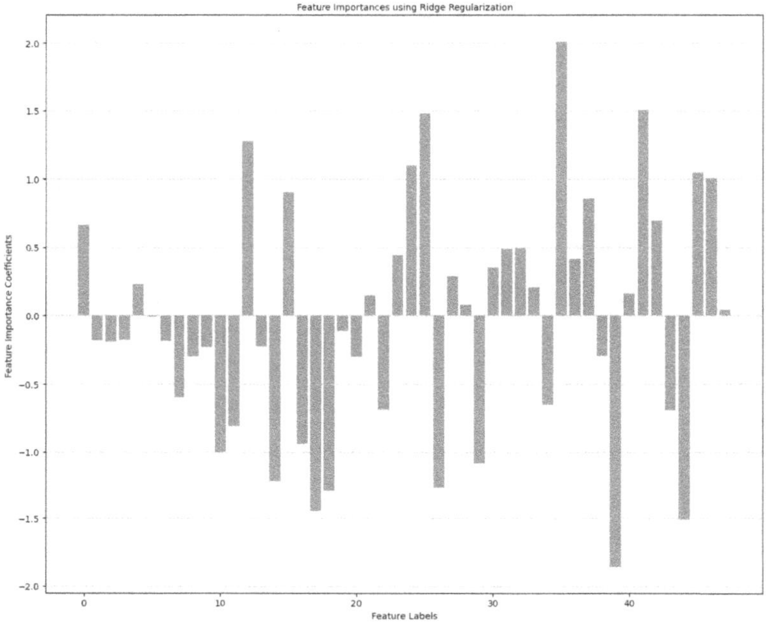

Figure 5.9: Ridge regression feature importance with their coefficient values

memory (M) usage of each deployed classifier under three scenarios: default model with all 51 features, after Lasso-based feature selection (L1 penalty), and after Ridge-based feature selection (L2 penalty) for the deciding factors of the in-hospital mortality prediction for the heart failure patients. Table 5.6, illustrates the execution time and memory consumption for each model type from a resource-constrained perspective.

5.4.7 Performance Analysis and Discussion

The model trained on all selected features is presented in the dataset, attaining the best accuracy in each instance. The HGB classifier attained an accuracy of 96.57%, whereas the XGB achieved 94.36%. The values derived from each evaluation technique demonstrate model stability, achievable only with well-refined data. The findings indicate that the model's integrity remains intact despite oversampling or the elimination of null values. Numerous evaluations demonstrate that employing feature selection through regression techniques yields enhanced and efficient outcomes. The XGB model achieved the highest accuracy of 96.08% with lasso and 94.12% with ridge after feature selection. Also, the ET is reduced drastically after feature selection: 5.60 seconds for the lasso and 6.41 seconds

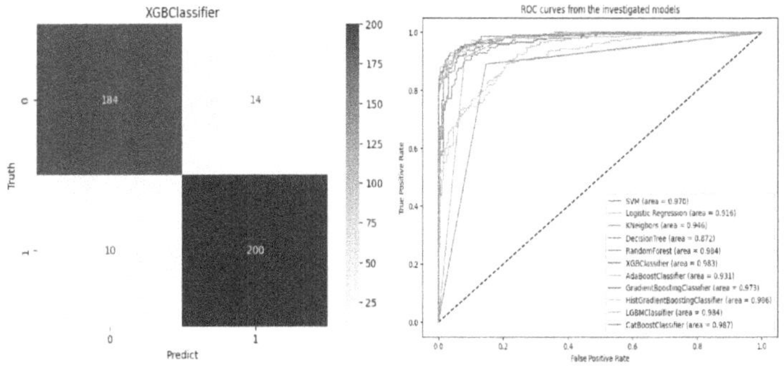

(a) The CM of Ridge LGBM Model (b) The ROC-AUC curve of Ridge models

Figure 5.10: The CM of XGB and the ROC-AUC curve of all the deployed models concerning Ridge

Model	Ac	Ma	Pr	Re	Fs	Cks	Sd	Ra	ET	M (MiB)
XGB	94.12	91.52	0.93	0.95	0.94	0.88	2.27	0.94	6.41	619.74
CB	93.87	91.28	0.93	0.95	0.94	0.88	2.69	0.94	92.77	624.07
LGBM	93.38	91.52	0.93	0.95	0.94	0.87	2.48	0.93	6.49	624.07
HGB	93.38	91.34	0.91	0.97	0.94	0.87	2.39	0.93	6.63	624.07
RF	92.89	92.14	0.95	0.91	0.93	0.86	1.92	0.93	9.61	619.74
SVM	92.40	89.74	0.93	0.92	0.93	0.85	3.23	0.92	5.64	619.73
GB	90.93	87.53	0.91	0.92	0.91	0.82	2.89	0.91	21.83	624.07
KNN	88.97	86.61	0.83	0.98	0.90	0.78	2.14	0.89	3.70	619.74
DT	87.25	82.92	0.87	0.89	0.88	0.74	2.79	0.87	2.63	619.74
LR	83.33	81.26	0.84	0.83	0.84	0.67	3.09	0.83	1.91	619.74
AB	82.35	82.31	0.83	0.82	0.83	0.65	5.00	0.82	5.91	624.07

Table 5.5: Performance comparison of models using Ridge-based feature selection

for the ridge-based XGB model deployment. The performance evaluators give a representation of both the L1 and L2 regression models and their impact on the characteristics chosen by each model. Fig. 5.11 illustrates the accuracy and ET comparison between the standard and feature selection models.

A comparative table or bar chart is employed to illustrate the variances in execution time and memory consumption among the three configurations (Default, Lasso, and Ridge).

Model	ET (Second)			Peak Memory (MiB)		
	N	L	R	N	L	R
XGB	20.67	5.60	6.41	595.68	618.72	619.74
CB	175.48	106.43	92.77	598.79	623.82	624.07
LGBM	22.82	5.54	6.49	598.96	623.82	624.07
HGB	22.71	9.05	6.63	598.95	623.82	624.07
SVM	18.11	4.96	5.64	600.52	618.72	619.73
RF	24.56	10.23	9.61	598.56	618.72	619.74
GB	43.16	21.56	21.83	599.45	623.82	624.07
AB	23.56	6.92	5.91	598.75	623.82	624.07
KNN	16.66	3.15	3.70	598.92	618.72	619.74
LR	15.59	3.00	1.91	598.37	618.72	619.74
DT	15.95	2.40	2.63	599.59	618.72	619.74

Table 5.6: Execution Time (Seconds) and Peak Memory (MiB) for each model across Normal (N), Lasso (L), and Ridge (R) scenarios

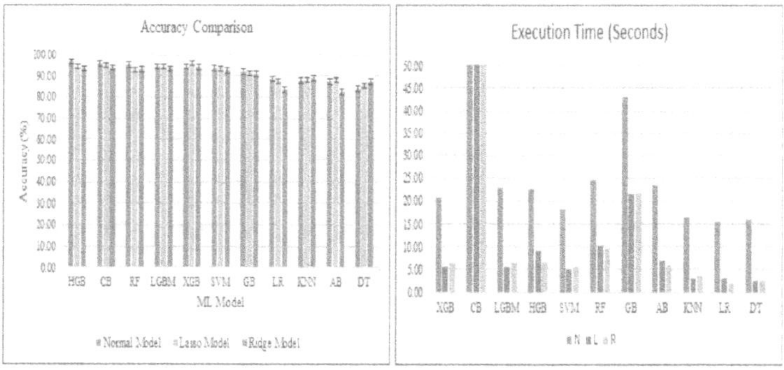

(a) The accuracy comparison of models (b) The ET comparison of models

Figure 5.11: Performance comparison among the different types of deployed models concerning accuracy and ET

The Lasso-selected models typically provided the optimal combination of performance and resource efficiency, making them appropriate for low-latency, high-throughput applications. This study guarantees that the resulting models are accurate, interpretable, lightweight, and scalable, meeting the requirements for practical and deployable solutions in clinical environments.

5.5 Advantages over Clinical Scoring Systems and Evaluation Metrics

Traditional clinical scoring systems, such as the New York Heart Association (NYHA) Functional Classification and the Seattle Heart Failure Model (SHFM), rely on predefined clinical rules and a limited set of physiological variables. Although widely used to assess heart failure severity, their predictive capability is limited by linear assumptions and an inability to capture complex interactions in high-dimensional ICU data. In contrast, ML models such as RF, SVM, XGB, GB, and HGB effectively capture nonlinear relationships among demographic, laboratory, and vital parameters, enabling more accurate mortality risk prediction. By learning complex, patient-specific patterns from high-dimensional ICU data, these models consistently outperform traditional heart failure scoring systems.

In this study, eleven machine learning classifiers are deployed on the MIMIC-III dataset to predict in-hospital mortality in HF patients. Among them, boosting-based models such as HGB and XGB demonstrated superior predictive performance, achieving accuracies of 96.57% and 94.36%, respectively, significantly outperforming traditional rule-based clinical scoring approaches. The integration of feature selection using Lasso and Ridge further enhanced model efficiency by identifying the most influential risk factors, reducing model complexity while maintaining high predictive accuracy.

To ensure clinical relevance and reliability, multiple performance metrics are employed, including accuracy, precision, recall (sensitivity), specificity, ROC-AUC, Cohen's Kappa score, standard deviation, and k-fold mean accuracy. Sensitivity is emphasized as a critical metric due to its importance in identifying high-risk patients who may require immediate clinical intervention. ROC-AUC is used to assess discrimination capability across varying decision thresholds, supporting risk stratification in ICU settings. Furthermore, cross-validation and standard deviation analysis are applied to minimize overfitting and ensure consistent generalization across patient subsets. Finally, sensitivity and ROC-AUC are prioritized for clinical decision-making, while accuracy, k-fold mean accuracy, and standard deviation ensure robustness and generalization.

The optimization of these metrics through class imbalance handling using SMOTE, regularization based feature selection, and hyperparameter tuning resulted in robust, interpretable, and computationally efficient models. The observed reduction in execution time, from over 20 seconds to under 6 seconds after feature selection, demonstrates the suitability of the proposed framework for real-time or resource-constrained clinical environments. Collectively, these findings confirm that ML-based mortality prediction models provide a more accurate, reliable, and clinically actionable alternative to traditional HF risk scoring systems.

5.6 Key Findings and Summary

This chapter provided an extensive analysis focusing on the assessment of risk factors for the mortality forecasting in HF patients admitted to the ICU, using the MIMIC-III dataset. The primary objective is to assess the performance and efficiency of classical ML models enhanced with feature selection methods and data balancing techniques.

1. A total of eleven classical ML classifiers are deployed to predict in-hospital mortality using 51 clinical features, achieving strong baseline performances.

2. Histogram-based Gradient Boosting (HGB) emerged as the best-performing default model, achieving 96.57% accuracy, while XGB followed closely at 94.36%.

3. To reduce model complexity and resource overhead, Lasso (L1) and Ridge (L2) regularization techniques are applied for automatic feature selection, effectively identifying the most influential predictors.

4. After applying Lasso, the XGB classifier achieved an improved accuracy of 96.08%, while Ridge-based XGB recorded 94.12%, indicating strong generalization capability even with reduced feature sets.

5. Execution time (ET) improved significantly after feature selection; in the case of XGB, training time dropped from 20.67s (default) to 5.60s (Lasso) and 6.41 s (Ridge). Similarly, HGB dropped from 22.71 s to under 6.63 seconds, showcasing the computational benefits of dimensionality reduction.

6. SMOTE oversampling proved effective in addressing the severe class imbalance, balancing the minority class to match the majority without sacrificing predictive accuracy.

This chapter illustrated that the incorporation of feature selection using Lasso and Ridge with resilient ML classifiers can produce high-performance, resource-efficient models for mortality prediction. The experimental findings demonstrated that lowering feature dimensionality improves model interpretability. It also significantly reduces execution time and memory consumption, making these models suitable for real-time or resource-constrained healthcare environments. These insights provide a basis for feasible decision-support systems in ICUs and facilitate the incorporation of lightweight predictive models into comprehensive clinical processes.

Despite these promising outcomes, several limitations persist. First, the study primarily relied on regularization-based feature selection (L1 and L2), without evaluating a broader range of methods for identifying key predictors. Second, the approach focused on a single dataset (MIMIC-III), raising questions about generalizability across diverse clinical populations. Third, while the models are computationally efficient, their interpretability in terms of individual feature contributions requires further enhancement for clinical adoption. Finally, the influence of feature selection strategies beyond regularization, such as filter, wrapper, and embedded-based methods, remains underexplored.

Expanding on the insights obtained from mortality prediction in ICU-admitted HF patients, the subsequent chapter 6 explores the impact of multiple factors on heart disease risk prediction. It presents a framework combining filter, wrapper, and embedded feature selection methods to identify key risk factors, improving accuracy, interpretability, and clinical relevance in heart disease prediction.

6

Interpretable HDP Framework with Feature Selection and XAI

The previous chapter showed that Lasso and Ridge effectively reduced feature dimensionality for ICU mortality prediction, yielding efficient and accurate models. However, it is limited to regularization-based methods and did not explore broader feature selection techniques needed for greater interpretability and clinical relevance. These limitations highlight the need to move beyond single-method feature reduction toward an integrated framework that systematically analyze feature influence. Heart disease continues to be one of the most widespread and life-threatening health concerns worldwide, highlighting the importance of early detection and precise prediction in medical research. ML models have shown strong potential for HD prediction. However, their effectiveness largely relies on the quality and relevance of the most influential features. So, feature selection is crucial in enhancing model accuracy, reducing computational complexity, minimizing dimensionality, and improving interpretability. Accurately forecasting HD and recognizing its risk factors are essential for early diagnosis and prompt medical intervention. This chapter expands the focus beyond predictive model development and mortality risk estimation, as discussed in Chapters 3 and 5. It introduces a feature influence predictive framework that examines the factors most significantly affecting HD prediction.

This study employs a multifaceted approach to feature selection, utilizing various strategies from the filter, wrapper, and embedding categories to assess and improve the efficacy of predictive models. This employs a real-world dataset from the Mendeley Data Portal to ensure robustness and generalizability, encompassing a variety of patient variables related to HD. The assessment procedure is based on a multi-stage experimental framework that incorporates fifteen ML classifiers to establish a baseline performance. Subsequently, six feature selection techniques: Chi-Square, Mutual Information Gain, Fisher Score, Recursive Feature Elimination, BorutaShap, and Lasso Regression, are applied to identify the most significant features. Finally, the eight superior predictive classifiers' performance is analyzed using comprehensive performance indicators. A comparative analysis of complete and reduced feature sets is conducted, providing the basis for a robust and interpretable HDP system. To improve transparency and trust in the model, XAI tools – SHAP and LIME – are utilized to explain the influence of individual features on model predictions. This chapter aims to develop a feature-optimized and explainable predictive system that can support clinicians in making data-informed decisions regarding HD risk.

This chapter is arranged as follows: In Sections 6.1 and 6.2, the research objectives and the corresponding contributions of this chapter are stated. Also, Sections 6.3 and 6.4 discuss the dataset, preprocessing, and the proposed methodology. Next, Sections 6.5 and 6.6 demonstrate the experimental outcomes and explain the interpretability of the model predictions. Finally, Section 6.7 addresses the feature selection and XAI significance, and Section 6.8 summarizes the key findings and summary of this chapter.

6.1 Motivations and Objectives

Despite the existence of robust machine learning methodologies, numerous heart disease prediction models suffer from high-dimensional feature spaces. This can introduce noise, elevate the chance of overfitting, and reduce interpretability. Feature selection mitigates these issues by identifying the most relevant risk factors, improving model accuracy, and facilitating interpretation. In healthcare, especially for life-threatening diseases like HD, understanding the main risk factors is as important as making accurate predictions. Conventional ML models frequently depend on all available features, potentially leading to higher complexity, extended training durations, and a higher risk of overfitting. Moreover, black-box models frequently exhibit an issue in interpretability, restricting their use in real healthcare environments. Nevertheless, limited research offers a comparative and systematic assessment of feature selection methodologies and their overall impact on predictive accuracy, particularly within the medical field.

This research is motivated by the need to identify the most critical predictive factors influencing heart disease diagnosis. It aims to reduce feature redundancy and improve model generalization through optimal feature selection strategies. The study also seeks to enhance clinical interpretability by employing XAI techniques, which provide transparent and understandable insights into model predictions. In addition, the findings are validated across diverse classifiers and datasets to ensure robustness and generalizability. Improved transparency and interpretability are emphasized, as they play a vital role in strengthening physicians' trust and confidence in AI-assisted clinical decision-making systems. Thus, there is an interesting motivation to identify key risk factors using advanced selection methods and validate their relevance using explainable AI approaches.

This chapter aligns with the third research objective of the thesis, which focuses on identifying the most influential risk factors for HD using comprehensive feature selection techniques. The primary objectives of this chapter are as follows:

1. To evaluate the effectiveness of different feature selection techniques, specifically Chi-square, Mutual Information Gain, Fisher Score (Filter Method); Recursive Feature Elimination, BorutaShap (Wrapper Method); and Lasso Regression (Embedded Method) in identifying key HD risk predictors.

2. To compare the performance of fifteen ML classifiers (boosting and non-boosting)

using both full and reduced feature sets.

3. To construct a robust HD prediction system using the top eight best-performing classifiers trained on optimal feature subsets derived from the considered methods.
4. To interpret and justify model decisions using XAI tools like SHAP and LIME.
5. To assess models with a comprehensive set of evaluation metrics, including accuracy (Ac), precision (Pr), recall (Re), F1-score (Fs), ROC-AUC (Ra), Cohen's Kappa (Cks), standard deviation (Sd), and mean accuracy (Ma) using k-fold cross-validation.

6.2 Research Contributions

This chapter advances heart disease prediction by integrating diverse feature selection strategies. The study helps identify the most important risk factors by assessing filter, wrapper, and embedding techniques across several classifiers and a real dataset. These contributions help to build a reliable, interpretable, and accurate cardiac disease prediction framework. To fulfil the stated goals, this research study's main contributions are as follows:

1. **Deployment of Diversified Machine Learning Classifiers:** Initially, fifteen diverse ML classifiers, including ensemble, neural, and traditional models, are implemented on a real-world heart disease dataset. Advanced data preprocessing, including SMOTETomek oversampling, is applied to address severe target class imbalance and enhance training data quality.
2. **Comprehensive Feature Selection Analysis:** A comparative analysis of six feature selection methodologies Chi-square (Chi-2), Mutual Information Gain (MIG), Fisher Score (Fisher), Recursive Feature Elimination (RFE), BorutaShap, and Lasso Regression (Lasso) are employed to extract and rank the most significant HD risk factors. These methods utilize filter, wrapper, and embedding feature selection methodologies.
3. **Performance Evaluation and Comparison:** Based on performance assessment, eight superior classifiers are shortlisted and redeployed using the optimal feature subsets to form a refined decision support system. Through validation employing k-fold cross-validation to evaluate model robustness and generalization, while mitigating for overfitting and underfitting.
4. **XAI Interpretation:** Additionally, SHAP and LIME are employed to interpret the prediction model results. This approach reveals the importance of essential risk factors and enhances the model's transparency for clinical application.

In summary, this chapter comprehensively examines how feature selection strategies affect heart disease prediction accuracy. The study identifies the most important clinical features and improves model interpretability and efficiency by aligning with the third research ob-

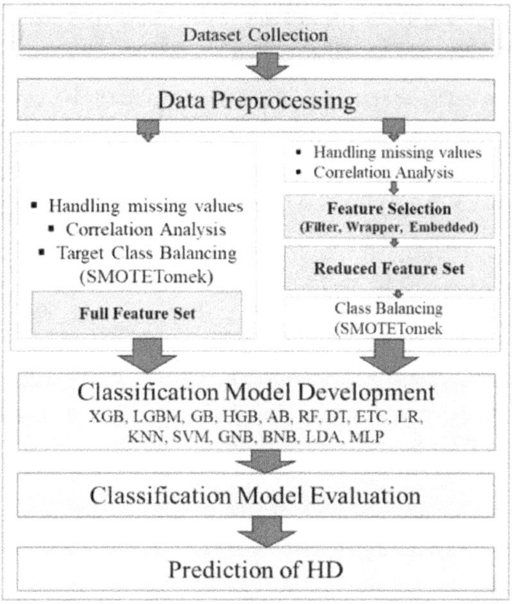

Figure 6.1: The workflow diagram of the Feature Influence predictive framework

jective. These efforts help create a reliable and explainable predictive system for heart disease diagnosis and risk assessment.

6.3 Methodology: Dataset and Preprocessing

This research study examines the significance of features in the HD classification model. Various feature selection strategies are employed to identify the most significant risk indicators from the collected dataset. This section details the description of the acquired raw medical dataset utilized for precise heart disease prediction. The constraints and shortcomings of the dataset are examined by EDA employing necessary data cleaning procedures. The feature influence predictive framework of the proposed methodology is illustrated in Fig. 6.1 for the entire model deployment process.

6.3.1 Dataset Description

The medical dataset is obtained from the Mendeley data port [75] to examine the impact of various features or risk factors on the incidence of HD, sourced from a hospital in India. To develop an ML-based decision support system for HD detection, namely the

CVD dataset comprising 1000 instances and 12 risk variables, is utilized. The risk factors for cardiovascular disorders are classified into demographics (age, gender), medical factors (cholesterol, blood pressure, fasting blood sugar), and lifestyle factors (chest pain, smoking, exercise-induced angina, etc.). The dependent variable is a binary classification, signifying the existence or non-existence of HD. This dataset has been widely used in research for developing predictive models for CVD and assessing feature relevance. The detailed description of the features with data types as either numerical (N) or categorical (C) in nature, along with the null values observed during EDA, is presented in Table 6.1.

6.3.2 Data Preprocessing

The data preprocessing is an essential phase in the ML lifecycle, as it facilitates data analysis and enhances the precision and efficiency of ML algorithms to ensure data uniformity and quality. Before performing further analysis, preprocessing steps are executed to address missing values and data outliers. During the EDA, an initial verification and numerical transformation of the categorical variables are conducted. In the target class, "1" and "0" signify the "presence" and "absence" of HD, respectively. Moreover, since absent values can significantly impact overall performance, it is crucial to identify and either eliminate or substitute them. The collected dataset revealed absent values and class imbalance issues; therefore, various preprocessing strategies are implemented to address these challenges.

Handling Null/Missing Values

Handling missing data is essential to maintaining the integrity of the dataset. It had observed some abnormal or null values in the dataset, as depicted in Table 6.1. To handle this situation, during EDA, the numerical feature "chol" had some values of "0". These values were initially replaced with "NaN". After that, the *mean* imputation method was applied to the missing values. For categorical features, no imputation techniques, such as *mode* imputation, were applied, as no missing or anomalous values were observed.

Feature Density Distribution

Feature density distribution plays a crucial role in understanding the underlying structure and distribution of each feature's data, especially for numerical features. Feature density distribution plots are generated to analyze the statistical behaviour of numerical features. This visualization aided in detecting outliers, understanding skewness, and identifying the need for scaling or transformation techniques. The kernel density overlay provided a smoothed approximation of the underlying data distribution, facilitating better preprocessing decisions, as depicted in Fig. 6.2. Based on these distributions, no significant outliers were identified, and the degree of skewness was found to be within acceptable limits.

#	Feature Name/Attributes	Descriptions	DTypes	# Null
1	age	Years (20 to 80)	N	0
2	Sex (Gender)	1: Male, 0: Female	C	0
3	cp (chest-pain type)	1: typical angina, 2: atypical, 3: non-anginal, 4: asymptotic	C	0
4	trestbps (resting blood pressure)	mmHg during hospital admission (94 to 200)	N	0
5	chol (serum cholestrol)	mg/dl (0 to 602)	N	53
6	fbs (fasting blood sugar >120 mg/dl)	1: true 0: false	C	0
7	restecg (resting ECG)	0: normal, 1: having ST-T wave abnormality, 2: left ventricular hypertrophy	C	0
8	thalach (max heart rate achieved)	71 to 202	N	0
9	exang (exercise induced angina)	1: yes 0: no	C	0
10	oldpeak (ST depression induced by exercise relative to rest)	0 to 6.2	N	0
11	slope (peak exercise ST segment)	0: normal, 1: upsloping 2: horizontals, 3: downsloping	C	0
12	noofmajorvessels (Number of major vessels)	0, 1, 2, 3	C	0
13	target (diagnosis of heart disease)	0: Absence (HD) 1: Presence (HD)	C	0

Table 6.1: The feature description of the dataset with missing values

Feature Encoding

In ML, models require numerical inputs, but datasets often contain categorical features like "gender", "chest pain type", "fbs", "ECG results", and "slope". To convert these into a suitable format, encoding techniques are required. But, from the feature distribution plot, it has been noticed that the categorical features are already in numerical values. Conse-

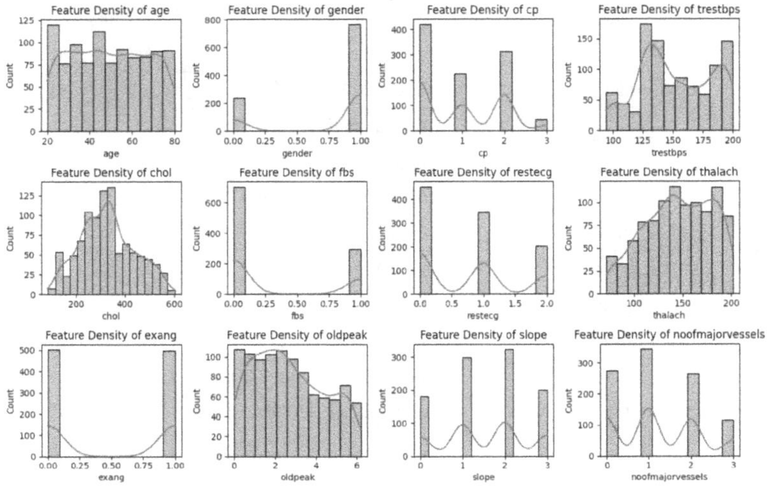

Figure 6.2: The feature density distribution of the CVD dataset

quently, there is no need to apply any label encoding techniques. This step ensured that ML algorithms could effectively process categorical information without introducing unintended bias or ordinal assumptions.

Correlation Heat Map Analysis

A correlation heat map is created to evaluate multicollinearity among features and the target class. The values indicate the positive and negative correlation between the attributes, from -1 to 1. It visually depicts the relationships among all variables within the dataset. In a heat map, value -1 signifies the absence of correlation, 1 denotes perfect correlation, and 0 indicates no connection. The heat map also identifies outliers and reveals linear or nonlinear relationships. It helps to detect multicollinearity, i.e., highly correlated features that may provide redundant information, and select relevant features that contribute uniquely to the prediction model. High correlations exceeding a threshold, such as 0.9, are eliminated to diminish redundancy, reduce model complexity, and enhance generalizability. This phase is essential to prevent overfitting and guarantee the retention of only independent, significant features. During analysis, the Pearson correlation coefficient is used to find the multicollinearity for the HD risk factors and is represented computationally in the following formula: 6.1. The heat map is depicted in Fig. 6.3.

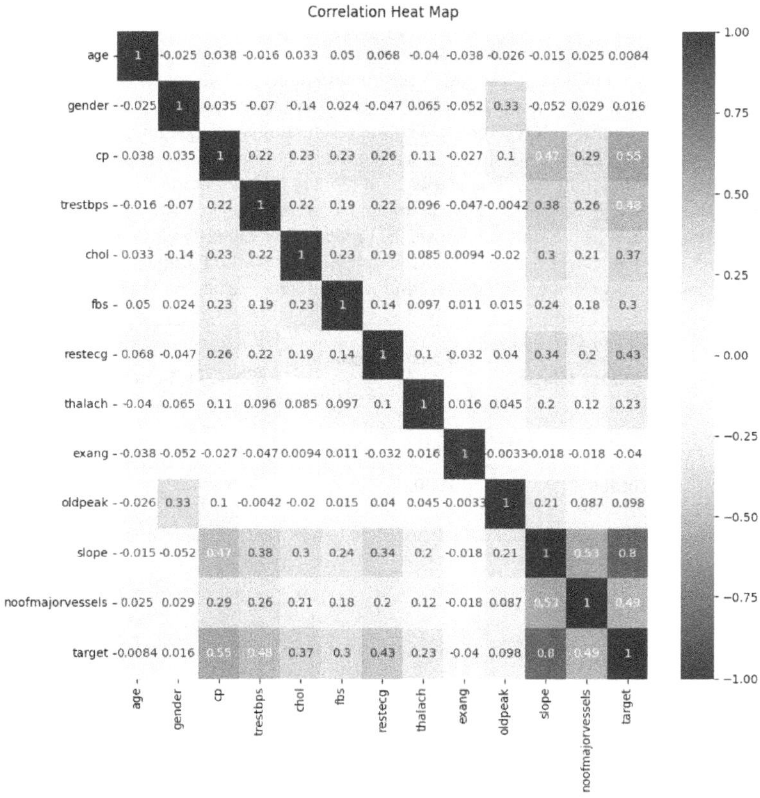

Figure 6.3: The feature correlation heat map.

$$\rho_{ij} = \frac{\sum_{k=1}^{n}(x_{ki} - \bar{x}_i)(x_{kj} - \bar{x}_j)}{\sqrt{\sum_{k=1}^{n}(x_{ki} - \bar{x}_i)^2} \cdot \sqrt{\sum_{k=1}^{n}(x_{kj} - \bar{x}_j)^2}} \tag{6.1}$$

Where, x_{ki} and x_{kj} are the kth observations of features X_i and X_j, $\bar{x}_i$ and $\bar{x}_j$ are the mean values of features X_i and X_j, and $\rho_{ij} \in [-1, 1]$ indicates the linear correlation between features X_i and X_j.

Handling Class Imbalance

In predictive modelling, particularly within medical datasets utilized for HDP, class imbalance is a prevalent difficulty. The target class distribution exhibited an imbalance, characterised by a significantly lower number of negative instances (patients without heart disease). To resolve this, SMOTETomek, a hybrid resampling technique integrating SMOTE with Tomek connections, is utilized. This facilitated an effective balancing of class distribution and refining of class boundaries by removing noisy or borderline samples. This hybrid methodology enhances model learning and generalization, mitigates bias towards the majority class, and eventually boosts the prediction of minority class outcomes, such as identifying patients at risk for HD. After applying the SMOTETomek, the class distribution instance is presented in Table 6.2 and a pictorial representation in Fig. 6.4.

Target Class Level (Binary Class)	# Before Sampling	# After Sampling (SMOTETomek)
0	420	538
1	580	538
Total #	**1000**	**1076**

Table 6.2: The target class data distribution before and after sampling technique

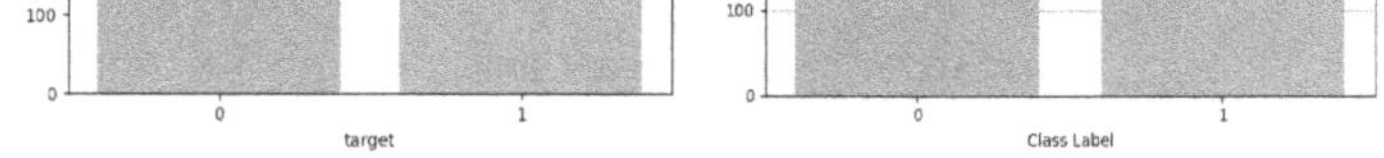

(a) The target class before sampling (b) The target class after sampling

Figure 6.4: The target class distribution before and after sampling

Normalization of Numerical Features

Normalization is an essential preprocessing step in ML that ensures numerical features contribute proportionately to the model. In HDP, features like "age", "cholesterol", "blood pressure", "old peak", and "heart rate" frequently possess varying units and scales. In the absence of normalization, features with greater numeric ranges may overshadow model training and influence the learning process. This study employs *MinMax* scaling to normalize all numerical features. This method normalizes each feature to a predetermined range, usually [0,1], while maintaining the relationships between the data points. The transformation is defined as follows in Eq. 6.2:

$$x' = \frac{x - x_{\text{min}}}{x_{\text{max}} - x_{\text{min}}} \tag{6.2}$$

Where: x is the original feature value, x_{min} and x_{max} are the minimum and maximum values of the feature, and x' is the normalized value.

By applying "MinMax" scaling, all features are rescaled to a uniform range. This improves the performance of distance-based algorithms and gradient boosting-based models by ensuring faster convergence and avoiding numerical instability during training. The scaling also helps in maintaining fairness in how each feature influences the model.

In summary, the data preprocessing phase improved the overall quality and suitability of the dataset for model development. This is achieved by handling class imbalance using the SMOTETomek technique, and null or invalid values are appropriately managed. Also, numerical features are normalized using "Min-Max" scaling, and categorical variables are encoded to ensure compatibility with machine learning algorithms. These measures are designed to enhance model learning, mitigate bias, and boost generalization. To ensure dependable performance evaluation and reduce the likelihood of overfitting or underfitting, k-fold cross-validation is employed as the validation method. Also, the hold-out validation method is considered to split the dataset into a 0.80:0.20 ratio as a training and testing dataset for model deployment and performance evaluation.

6.4 Proposed Methodology and Implementation

This research study examines two types of methodologies by analyzing every feature of HD risk factors inside the datasets, primarily for the training of a default ML model. Subsequently, feature selection techniques are employed to identify the most significant aspects related to the methodologies, resulting in the selection of the highest-performing ML classifiers to implement an accurate predictive model for HD. This section discusses the model training approach, justifying its application in an organized manner.

6.4.1 Experimental Setup

The experiment is simulated in the *Python 3.7, Jupyter Notebook 6.5.2 environment on a 13th Gen Intel(R) Core(TM) i5-1334U CPU @ 1.30 GHz PC.* Also, the high resource requirement is fulfilled by setting the GPU T4 into the Google Collaboratory Compute Engine backend using a Python 3 simulation environment.

6.4.2 Baseline Prediction Models Deployment

Initially, all features related to HD risk factors for the binary classification are assessed for the deployment of baseline prediction models. Upon implementing the aforementioned data preprocessing procedures on the dataset, it is now prepared to train the ML classifiers using the training data instances. The fifteen ML classifiers are selected for the preliminary construction of the prediction model, taking into account the test dataset. A total of 15 different ML classifiers are evaluated, encompassing both boosting and non-boosting algorithms, with ensemble methods and linear/non-linear models. These classifiers are chosen to facilitate a thorough assessment of various learning paradigms for HDP. The implemented classifiers are as follows: boosting models (LGBM, HGB, GB, XGB, and AB); bagging and other ensemble models (RF, DT, ETC); linear and kernel-based models (LR, SVM, and LDA); instance-based and probabilistic models (KNN, GNB, and BNB); and also a neural network-based model (MLP) are implemented using the default parameters, specifying *random_state* = 0. Each model is initially deployed using the full feature set without sampling the target class to assess their performance and establish a baseline before applying feature selection. Performance metrics, including accuracy (Ac), precision (Pr), recall (Re), F1-score (Fs), Cohen's Kappa score (Cks), standard deviation (Sd), and the ROC-AUC (Ra) probabilistic values, are also considered to measure the classification model's performance to support a detailed comparison.
Furthermore, the low-instance datasets are managed using the k-fold cross-validation method, which mitigates overfitting issues and assesses the efficacy of the classification model. K-fold cross-validation derives its name from the parameter k, which denotes the number of folds or groups into which the sample data is divided. This study evaluates the efficacy of the proposed method on balanced data by 10-fold cross-validation, resulting in a mean accuracy (Ma).

6.4.3 Feature Selection Models Deployment

The fundamental objective of this research is to determine the medical risk factors associated with HD that can enhance the predicted accuracy of HDP models. Feature selection is the process of identifying the most influential features from a larger range of original features. The objective of employing feature selection is to improve model interpretability, reduce dimensionality, enhance data quality, decrease computational time, minimize overfitting, and enhance overall prediction performance by retaining only the most relevant features.
The subsequent phases involve analyzing the features through various feature selection techniques, including filter-based, wrapper-based, and embedding methods. Various techniques from distinct methods are employed to figure out feature importance for heart disease risk factors. It includes filter methods such as Chi-square, Mutual Information Gain, and Fisher Score; wrapper methods like Recursive Feature Elimination and BorutaShap; and an embedded method, Lasso regression.

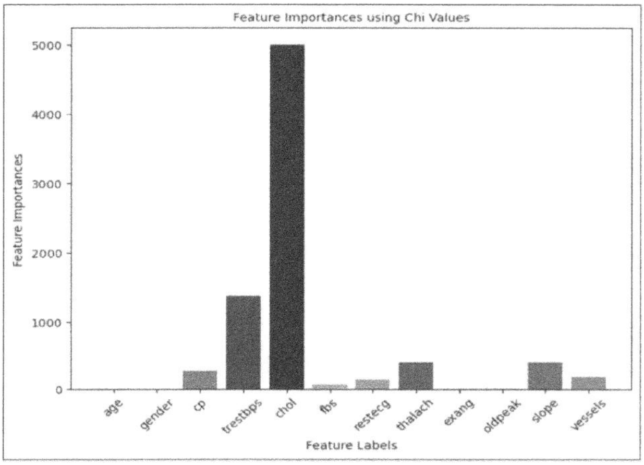

Figure 6.5: The Chi-square values of each feature

Chi-Square (χ^2)

The chi-squared feature assessment alone reflects the significance of each original feature concerning the target class. It is feasible to determine which features to retain and eliminate based on the labelled data and category attributes. The *Chi2()* function in the scikit-learn library computes chi-square scores, reflecting the degree of independence between two characteristics. Features with higher chi-square scores have stronger associations with heart disease presence. In chi-square testing, the p-value indicates the likelihood of witnessing a test statistic as extreme or more extreme than the computed chi value, assuming the null hypothesis is true. A p-value of < 0.05 indicates a significant relationship between variables, rejecting the null hypothesis of independence. The chi- and p-values of each feature are plotted in Figs. 6.5 and 6.6. According to the scores, the features with higher values are selected first, and lower-score-achieving features are eliminated.

Mutual Information (MI)

Mutual information (MI) is a statistical metric that assesses the degree of interdependence or reduction of uncertainty between two random variables within a dataset. The correlation of a feature with the target variable is assessed using it. A non-negative gain value between two random variables signifies the degree of dependence between them. Elevated values signify more dependence, and it equals zero if and only if the two random variables are independent. Consequently, it has employed the *mutual_info_classif()* method to compute the MI scores, thereby assessing the link between the features and the target. The traits are prioritized in descending order based on MI values, selecting those with higher scores as more significant, as depicted in Fig. 6.7.

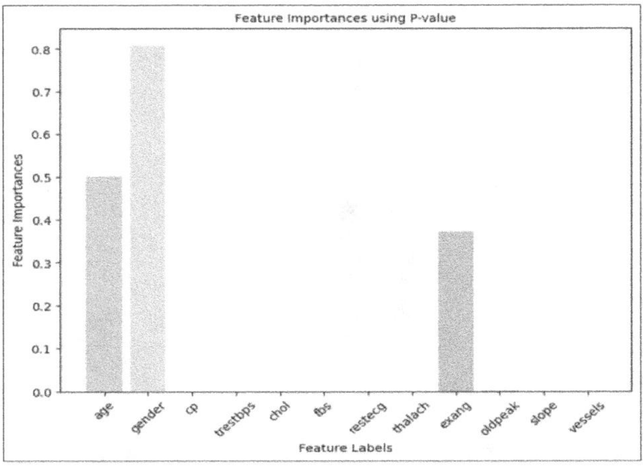

Figure 6.6: The p-values of each feature

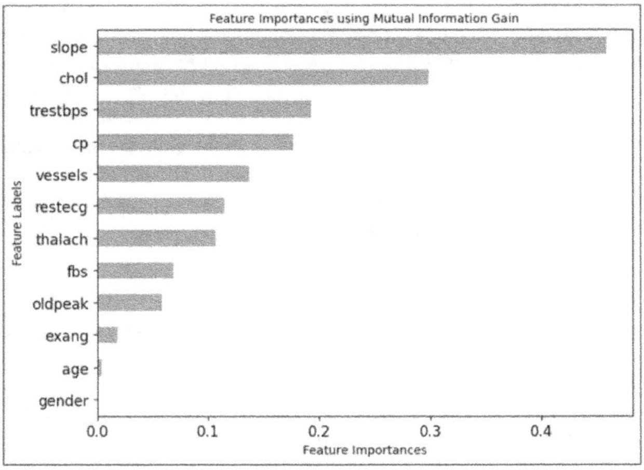

Figure 6.7: The feature importance by the MI according to scores

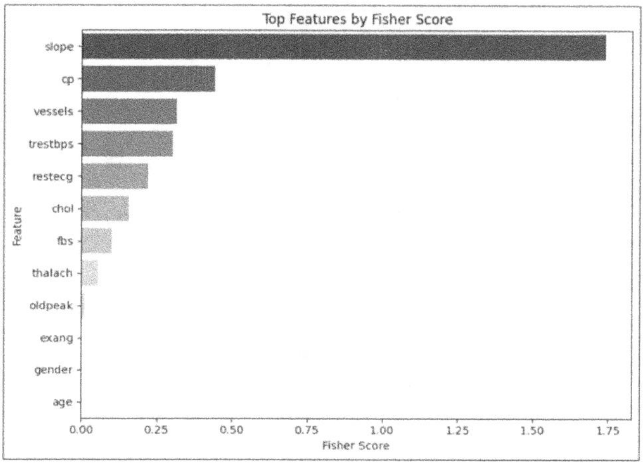

Figure 6.8: The feature important fisher score in descending order

Fisher Score (FS)

Fisher's Discriminant Ratio, or Fisher's Score, is a feature selection technique that ranks features based on their efficacy in differentiating between distinct classes within a dataset. In a classification problem, it may apply to continuous variables. The ratio of between-class variation to within-class variance is utilized to calculate Fisher's Score. An elevated Fisher's Score signifies that a characteristic is more beneficial and distinctive for classification purposes. It works well for classification problems, especially when dealing with multiple features. For each feature, the Fisher score is calculated according to formula 6.3.

$$\text{Fisher Score}(f) = \frac{\sum_{i=1}^{c} n_i(\mu_i - \mu)^2}{\sum_{i=1}^{c} n_i\sigma_i^2} \tag{6.3}$$

Where: c : Number of classes, n_i : Number of samples in class i, μ_i : Mean of feature f in class i, μ : Overall mean of feature f, σ_i^2 : Variance of feature f in class i.
Additionally, Fisher's Score was applied for feature selection by calculating a score for each feature and ranking them accordingly using the $fisher_score()$ library function. Features exhibiting a greater Fisher's Score are considered more meaningful by the model. The ranks of the variables, based on Fisher's score, are presented in descending order in Fig. 6.8.

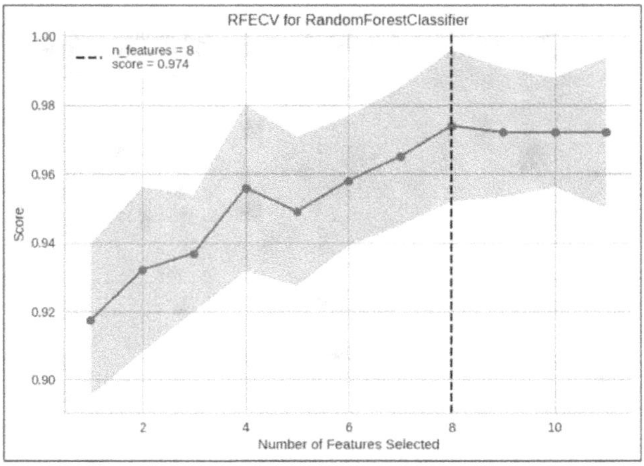

Figure 6.9: The features selected by the REFCV concerning the RF classifier

Recursive Feature Elimination (RFE)

Recursive feature elimination iteratively trains the model by utilizing the algorithm's weights as a criterion for each iteration, consequently eliminating the least significant feature. The objective of RFE is to select features by systematically evaluating increasingly smaller subsets of features. Systematically eliminating elements with minimal impact on the model produces the most essential attributes for forecasting accuracy. The RFE function evaluates feature significance, discards the least significant features, and reconstructs the model until a preferred subset of features is achieved. The *coef_* attribute is utilized to rank features while reducing dependency and collinearity effects, with the RF classifier serving as the estimator in the model. Subsequently, the features are ranked using the *ranking_* function. In addition, feature importance is further evaluated by applying the *RFECV()* function with the RF classifier, employing "Stratified K-Fold" cross-validation to ensure robust and balanced feature selection. Initially, a predetermined quantity of characteristics can be preserved; however, the quantity of valid features is sometimes indeterminate in advance. Cross-validation is employed alongside RFE to evaluate different feature subsets and identify the collection of features that yields the highest score, consequently determining the optimal number of features. The RFECV visualizer illustrates the quantity of features in the model, their variability, and their cross-validated test score, as well as the number of selected features depicted in Fig. 6.9.

BorutaShap

BorutaShap integrates the Boruta feature selection method with the SHAPley (SHapley Additive exPlanations) metric to increase feature importance evaluation. Instead of find-

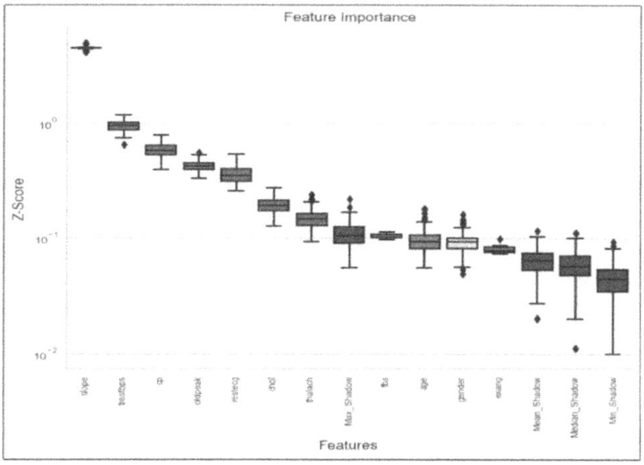

Figure 6.10: The selected relevance features by the BorutaShap method

ing every relevant feature, the Boruta algorithm seeks a minimal optimal feature set. It is an elegant wrapper strategy based on the Random Forest model as a foundation learner, which eliminates features with Gini impurity relevance scores too low to be useful. Also, it is a reliable feature selection method; however, it relies on model-based feature importance, which may be biased or unsuitable for the data.
To address the above challenges, BorutaShap computes scrambled versions of all input features algorithmically and then uses a machine learning model to establish a tentative set of significant features. After that, the above-selected model (typically a tree-based Random Forest or Gradient Boosting Machine) determines Shapley values for these tentative features. Shapley values show feature interactions and their impact on model predictions, providing a more nuanced perspective of feature importance. The final Shapley value ranking prioritises features for model training and interpretation. Choosing preliminary features involves comparing their utility to scrambled ones. This ensures a stable and impartial selection of significant and minor features. This combination outperforms permutation importance in speed and feature subset quality. Fig. 6.10 shows that this strategy may generate the most accurate and consistent global feature rankings for model inference and a superior subset of features.

Least Absolute Shrinkage and Selection Operator (Lasso)

Lasso is a regularization-based feature selection method that enhances model prediction accuracy and interpretability by performing both coefficient shrinkage and automatic feature elimination. It is an embedded method that incorporates feature selection as part of the learning algorithm. Lasso achieves this by introducing a penalty term to the linear regression cost function that is proportional to the absolute values of the coefficients (L1 regularization). The modified objective function is defined as follows in 6.4:

$$\min_{\beta_0,\beta}\left\{\frac{1}{2n}\sum_{i=1}^{n}\left(y_i-\beta_0-\sum_{j=1}^{p}\beta_j x_{ij}\right)^2+\lambda\sum_{j=1}^{p}|\beta_j|\right\} \tag{6.4}$$

Where: β_0: Intercept term. β_j: Coefficient of the jth feature.x_{ij}: Value of the jth feature for the ith sample. y_i: Target value of the ith sample. n: Number of training samples. p: Number of features. λ: Regularization parameter controlling the strength of the penalty. $\sum_{j=1}^{p}|\beta_j|$: L1 norm penalty to induce sparsity in coefficients.

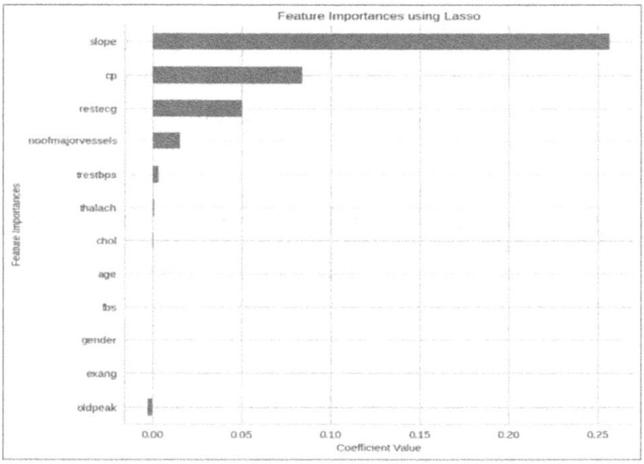

Figure 6.11: The feature importance with non-zero values of the Lasso method

When it λ is increased, Lasso shrinks some coefficients to exactly zero. Features with zero coefficients are effectively excluded from the model. Thus, only the most significant features with non-zero coefficients are retained. The best constant can be estimated via hyperparameter optimization. Some weights or coefficients can decrease to zero with Lasso regularization. This requires penalizing more sophisticated models to prevent overfitting and improve model generalization. It's then safe to remove those features from the data. Stronger regularization reduces dimensionality more. Penalization is optimized using 15-fold cross-validation to identify optimal alpha values that improved model performance and interpretability. Lasso is utilized to acquire the absolute values of coefficient magnitudes. Fig. 6.11 shows the *coef_* function for selecting essential features with non-zero values for the best feature subset.

The study uses these methods to find the best feature subsets for different selection procedures. Compare how each FS approach affects the final prediction of model performance. Explainable AI (XAI) techniques, such as SHAP and LIME, are applied to interpret model predictions using reduced feature sets, thereby enhancing transparency and clinical understanding. The integration of top-performing classifiers with selected feature subsets results in a more accurate, robust, and interpretable framework for heart disease decision support.

6.5 Experimental Evaluation and Comparative Results

This section provides a comprehensive assessment of the prediction models created utilising various feature selection methods and machine learning classifiers. The experimental study methodically evaluates the efficacy of models constructed using complete feature sets against those utilising reduced feature sets derived from several feature selection techniques, including Chi-square, Mutual Information Gain, Fisher Score, RFE, BorutaShap, and Lasso. So, to determine the optimal classification models, it initially evaluated the performance of each model independently, utilizing all available features. After that, it has evaluated the impact of the feature selection approach on classifier accuracy by assessing model performance using the selected features obtained from the designated procedures. The models are evaluated on a real-world heart disease dataset, utilising key measures like accuracy (Ac), precision (Pr), recall (Re), F1-score (Fs), ROC-AUC (Ra), and Cohen's Kappa score (Cks). K-fold cross-validation is employed to provide robustness, and the standard deviation is presented to assess model stability and address concerns of overfitting or underfitting.

6.5.1 Classification Results on Full Feature Set

The complete feature set is utilised to evaluate all machine learning models for predicting the binary disease outcome. After preprocessing and class balancing, all models are trained on the full dataset with an 80:20 train–test split. Each model is trained and evaluated using 10-fold cross-validation to compute the mean predictive accuracy. This strategy also helps reduce overfitting, particularly in scenarios with limited data instances. Initially, 15 machine learning models, including boosting-based classifiers (XGB, LGBM, HGB, GB, and AB) and traditional classifiers (SVM, DT, KNN, RF, LR, LDA, GNB, BNB, MLP, ETC), are deployed using all available features . Before applying the sampling method, the binary classification results of the machine learning model in predicting heart disease are presented in Table 6.3, incorporating performance metrics such as accuracy, precision, recall, and standard deviation.

Through the application of a sampling method to balance the target class, a hybrid method, SMOTETomek, helps mitigate the minority class biased prediction by removing the noise from the majority class. The performance accuracy of the selected models is increased due to the effect of class balancing, as represented in Table 6.4.

The corresponding confusion matrix is generated for each model to evaluate the classification outcomes concerning performance metrics and to compute the false negative (FN)

Model	Ac (%)	Ma (%)	Pr	Re	Fs	Cks	Sd	Ra
LGBM	97.00	97.75	0.97	0.98	0.97	0.94	0.94	0.97
HGB	97.00	98.00	0.97	0.98	0.97	0.94	1.39	0.97
XGB	97.00	96.88	0.97	0.98	0.97	0.94	1.70	0.97
ETC	97.00	97.75	0.97	0.97	0.97	0.94	1.56	0.97
GB	96.50	97.63	0.97	0.97	0.97	0.93	1.42	0.96
RF	96.00	97.13	0.97	0.96	0.97	0.92	1.59	0.96
DT	95.00	94.88	0.95	0.97	0.96	0.90	3.33	0.95
MLP	95.00	96.50	0.96	0.96	0.96	0.90	1.92	0.95
LR	94.50	95.75	0.96	0.95	0.95	0.89	1.27	0.94
AB	94.50	97.13	0.96	0.94	0.95	0.89	1.26	0.95
GNB	94.50	94.88	0.96	0.95	0.95	0.89	1.89	0.94
LDA	94.00	95.75	0.96	0.94	0.95	0.88	1.39	0.94
SVM	93.50	96.75	0.96	0.93	0.94	0.87	1.27	0.94
KNN	92.50	93.75	0.93	0.94	0.94	0.85	2.37	0.92
BNB	85.50	87.13	0.86	0.90	0.88	0.70	2.31	0.85

Table 6.3: The experimental results of all the deployed models concerning the full feature set before sampling

values for the HD prediction model. Furthermore, the ROC-AUC curve and the associated AUC probabilistic values are derived from the classification report to evaluate the efficacy of class differentiation. AUC measures the model's accuracy in predicting class 0 as 0 and class 1 as 1. Regarding the classification results in Table 6.3, LGBM, HGB, XGB, and ETC achieved the highest reported accuracy of 97% for the CVD dataset, accompanied by an ROC-AUC of 0.97 and a recall of 0.98. Several boosting classifiers, including XGB, HGB, and GB, alongside non-boosting classifiers such as RF and DT, exhibited commendable prediction accuracy when applied to the complete feature set, in addition to the LGBM model. LGBM excels at discerning complex patterns in datasets and the non-linear relationships inherent in medical characteristics, resulting in superior accuracy. Furthermore, recall values are elevated due to the boosting methods' capacity to address misclassified instances, enhancing the model's sensitivity to rare disease occurrences. Also, with the effect of SMOTETomek techniques, the higher accuracy is observed in the case of LGBM, HGB, and AB of 98.61% along with the recall and ROC values.

The confusion matrix (CM) and ROC-AUC curve of the best-performing model are represented in Figs. 6.12 and 6.13 concerning with and without SMOTETomek. The accuracy comparison of the deployed classifiers by considering all the features concerning the

Model	Ac (%)	Ma (%)	Pr	Re	Fs	Cks	Sd	Ra
LGBM	98.61	98.37	0.99	0.98	0.99	0.97	1.58	0.99
HGB	98.61	98.26	0.99	0.98	0.99	0.97	1.30	0.99
AB	98.61	97.21	0.98	0.99	0.99	0.97	1.74	0.99
GB	98.15	97.79	0.98	0.98	0.98	0.96	1.91	0.98
RF	97.69	97.56	0.97	0.98	0.98	0.95	1.51	0.98
ETC	97.69	98.49	0.97	0.98	0.98	0.95	1.17	0.98
XGB	97.69	97.91	0.99	0.96	0.98	0.95	1.01	0.98
DT	97.22	96.98	0.97	0.97	0.97	0.94	2.16	0.97
SVM	96.30	96.86	0.97	0.95	0.96	0.93	1.81	0.96
LDA	96.30	96.05	0.98	0.94	0.96	0.93	2.34	0.96
KNN	95.83	94.07	0.97	0.94	0.96	0.92	2.04	0.96
LR	95.83	96.28	0.97	0.94	0.96	0.92	1.86	0.96
MLP	95.83	97.33	0.96	0.95	0.96	0.92	1.38	0.96
GNB	95.37	95.47	0.95	0.95	0.95	0.91	2.04	0.95
BNB	81.02	83.37	0.83	0.79	0.81	0.62	2.60	0.81

Table 6.4: The experimental results of all the deployed models concerning the full feature set after SMOTETomek

datasets is depicted in Fig. 6.14.

6.5.2 Classification Results on Reduced Feature Sets

This part presents the experimental results based on the features selected using the approaches outlined in the previous section. Every feature selection technique identifies the most significant risk factor for predicting heart disease based on the respective dataset. A feature set (FS) is ultimately generated from each method to assess the influence of feature selection techniques on the classification accuracy of heart disease prediction. The highest-performing machine learning classifiers are selected based on the predictive accuracy of the default feature set. In both cases, LGBM, HGB, GB, XGB, AB, ETC, RF, and DT performed well; these models are also applied to the reduced feature set for accurate classification.

To assess feature importance from each selection method, the dataset is preprocessed only by removing missing values, without additional preprocessing or class balancing. The resulting feature sets from these approaches, shown in Table 6.5, are used for classification model implementation.

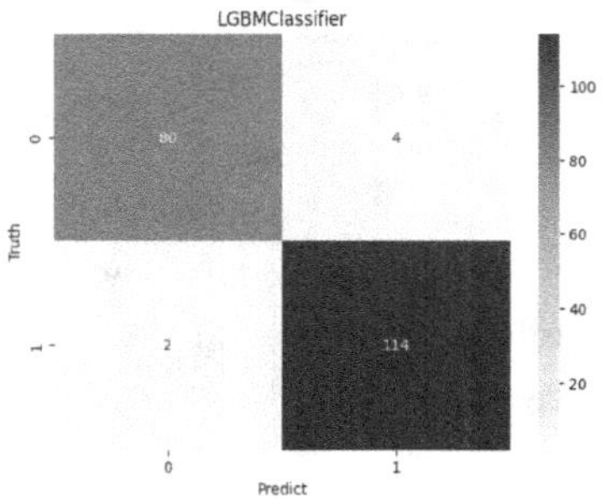

(a) The CM of the superior LGBM model

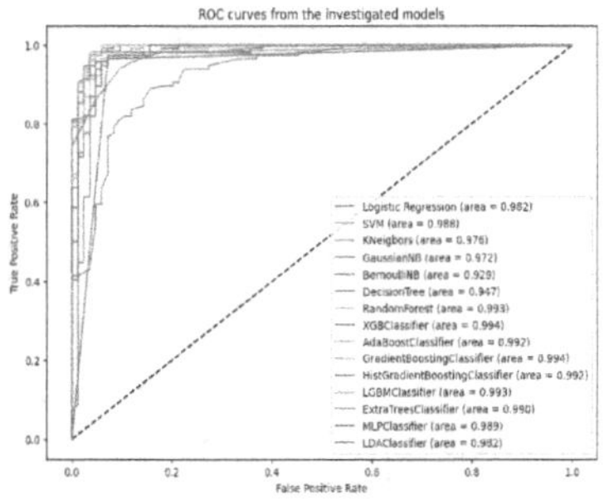

(b) The ROC-AUC curve of all models

Figure 6.12: The superior LGBM model's CM and the ROC-AUC curve of all deployed models without sampling

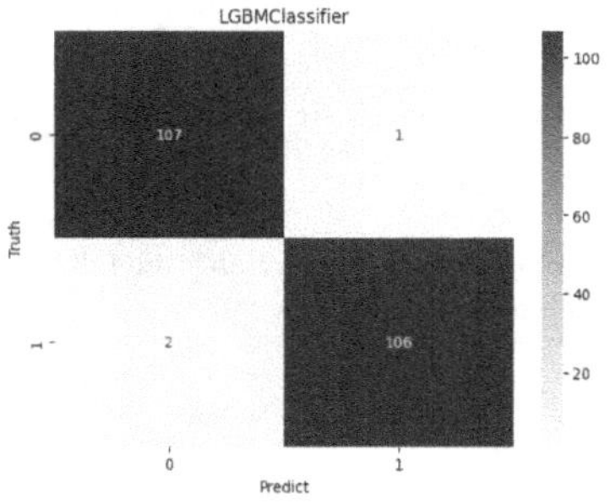

(a) The CM of the best LGBM model

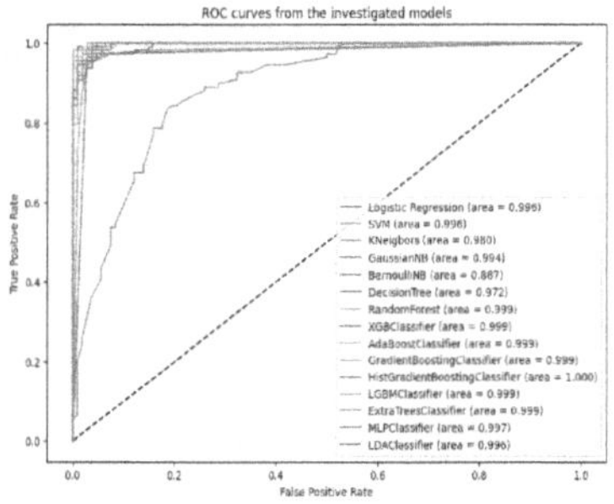

(b) The ROC-AUC curve of all models

Figure 6.13: The superior LGBM model's CM and the ROC-AUC curve of all deployed models with sampling

Subsequently, preprocessing strategies are employed to balance the target class data, applying the advanced oversampling method SMOTETomek. The selected eight classifiers are implemented on the chosen features, and the performance of the classification model is evaluated using the previously established metrics. The influence of feature selection techniques on model performance is assessed in terms of classification accuracy. Table 6.6 presents the results of each classification model alongside the diminished feature set associated with each feature selection procedure. All other metrics, including mean accuracy, recall, precision, F1 score, Cohen's kappa score, standard deviation, and ROC-AUC score, are also calculated. However, for simplicity, accuracy scores are shown to evaluate

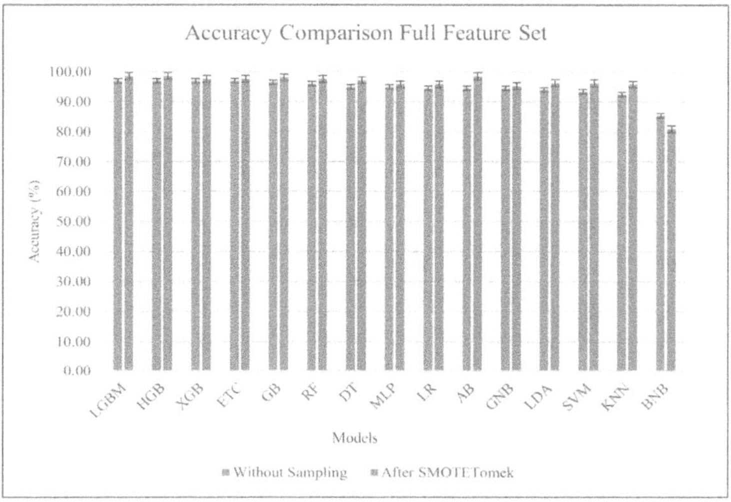

Figure 6.14: The model performance comparison on full FS concerning SMOTETomek

#	**Features**	$FS_{\textbf{Chi-2}}$	$FS_{\textbf{MIG}}$	$FS_{\textbf{Fisher}}$	$FS_{\textbf{RFE}}$	$FS_{\textbf{BorutaShap}}$	$FS_{\textbf{Lasso}}$
1	age						
2	gender			✓			
3	cp	✓	✓	✓	✓	✓	✓
4	trestbps	✓	✓	✓	✓	✓	✓
5	chol	✓	✓	✓	✓	✓	✓
6	fbs	✓	✓	✓		✓	
7	restecg	✓	✓	✓	✓	✓	✓
8	thalach	✓	✓		✓	✓	✓
9	exang						
10	oldpeak	✓		✓	✓	✓	✓
11	slope	✓	✓	✓	✓	✓	✓
12	noofmajorvessels	✓	✓		✓	✓	✓

Table 6.5: The derived feature set from each considered feature selection method

the effectiveness of each approach. Fig. 6.15 illustrates the performance comparison of each classifier's outcomes with the feature selection approaches.

ML Models	Full Feature Ac (%)	Filter Method			Wrapper Method		Embedded Method
		Chi-2	MIG	Fisher	RFE	BorutaShap	Lasso
		Accuracy (%)					
RF	96.00	98.57	98.58	99.54	99.54	98.57	99.05
LGBM	97.00	98.10	98.11	99.08	98.58	99.05	98.58
XGB	97.00	98.57	98.58	98.17	99.05	99.05	99.05
HGB	97.00	98.57	98.58	98.17	98.10	99.05	98.58
GB	96.50	98.57	99.06	98.62	98.58	98.57	98.58
DT	95.00	98.57	95.75	96.79	96.68	98.10	97.16
ETC	97.00	98.10	97.64	98.62	98.58	98.57	97.63
AB	94.50	97.62	97.17	97.71	98.58	98.10	98.58

Table 6.6: The experimental results of the reduced feature set concerning models

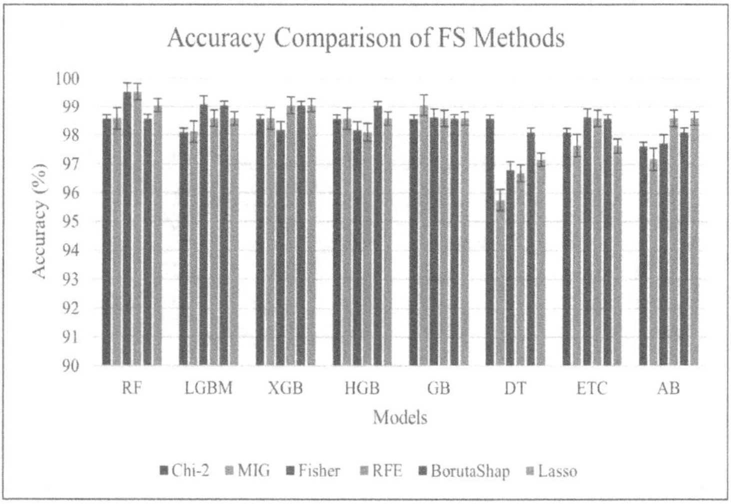

Figure 6.15: The model performance comparison on reduced FS corresponding to feature selection methods

It is observed that the RF models achieved the best results in both the wrapper (RFE) and filter method (Fisher score) with 99.54% accuracy. The LGBM model produces the highest accuracy of 99.08% with the filter method (Fisher Score) and 99.05% with the wrapper method.

6.5.3 Comparative Analysis

This subsection presents a comparative assessment of classification performance across the full feature set and various reduced feature sets generated through different feature selection techniques. A total of six feature selection methods are applied to reduce dimensionality and identify the most relevant risk factors. Each selected method generated a subset of features that are subsequently used to train and evaluate eight top-performing classifiers (XGB, LGBM, HGB, GB, AB, RF, ETC, and DT), chosen based on their baseline performance from earlier experiments. The objective is to evaluate the impact of dimensionality reduction on model accuracy, efficiency, and generalizability. The outcome comparison differences and the rate of changes on each best-performing classification model corresponding to feature selection methods are depicted in Table 6.7. Also, the performance changes comparison in terms of accuracy is graphically represented in Fig. 6.16 for a better understanding of the particular FS method effect.

Model	Performance differences (%)					
	Chi-2	MIG	Fisher	RFE	BorutaShap	Lasso
RF	2.57	2.58	3.54	3.54	2.57	3.05
LGBM	1.10	1.11	2.08	1.58	2.05	1.58
XGB	1.57	1.58	1.17	2.05	2.05	2.05
HGB	1.57	1.58	1.17	1.10	2.05	1.58
GB	2.07	2.56	2.12	2.08	2.07	2.08
DT	3.57	0.75	1.79	1.68	3.10	2.16
ETC	1.10	0.64	1.62	1.58	1.57	0.63
AB	3.12	2.67	3.21	4.08	3.60	4.08

Table 6.7: The performance change in accuracy for FS methods

A thorough side-by-side evaluation is conducted by comparing:

- **Full Feature Set vs Reduced Feature Sets:** All classifiers are initially trained using the complete feature set and then re-evaluated using features selected by each FS technique. The analysis highlighted how reduced feature subsets helped mitigate overfitting, improved training efficiency, and, in several cases, enhanced model accuracy.
- **Filter vs Wrapper vs Embedded Methods:** The study analyzed the classification

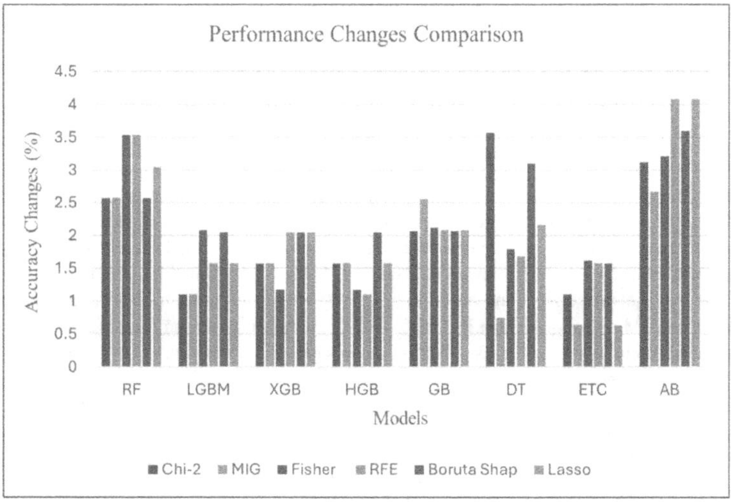

Figure 6.16: The model performance changes comparison on reduced FS corresponding to feature selection methods

outcomes using filter-based (Chi-Square, Mutual Information Gain, Fisher Score), wrapper-based (RFE, BorutaShap), and embedded-based (Lasso) feature selection strategies. The wrapper and embedded methods consistently demonstrated higher robustness and better classification metrics in each machine learning classifier.

- **Classifier-Wise Performance Comparison:** Certain classifiers, such as RF, LGBM, XGB, and HGB, maintained strong performance even after feature reduction. In contrast, other models showed significant improvements in mean accuracy and reduced standard deviation due to the lower-dimensional input space.

The few key observations include, after deployment, the following:

- BorutaShap emerged as one of the most effective methods, offering a strong balance between feature interpretability and predictive performance above 98%.
- Lasso Regression also performed competitively, reducing noise and improving model generalization.
- Wrapper methods like RFE provided the best results in the RF model with 99.54%, and also for other models but are relatively computationally intensive due to recursive elimination of non-significant features.
- Filter methods, while fast, occasionally missed complex feature interactions that embedded or wrapper methods captured better. Less computationally, and it produced

a good outcome for the RF model with 99.54%.

Overall, this comparative analysis emphasizes that feature selection not only enhances model performance but also plays a vital role in reducing model complexity. It also includes managing overfitting, enhancing generalization, and improving decision support reliability for HDP.

6.6 Explainability and Interpretation (SHAP & LIME)

In predictive modelling, particularly in important fields like healthcare, explainability is essential for validating model decisions and enhancing clinician trust. Despite the excellent accuracy exhibited by ML models, particularly ensemble and boosting classifiers, their decision-making processes may lack transparency. To address this, Explainable Artificial Intelligence (XAI) methods such as SHAP (SHapley Additive exPlanations) and LIME (Local Interpretable Model-Agnostic Explanations) are employed to further clarify the impact of input features on prediction results. This technique explains black-box models, identifies influential features, and enables multiple avenues for model optimization.

In this case, SHAP assigns each feature an importance value for a particular prediction based on Shapley values from cooperative game theory. It provides both global interpretation (feature importance across the entire dataset) and local interpretation (individual prediction analysis). In this study, SHAP is applied to the top-performing classifiers, RF, XGB, and LGBM, trained on the full feature set. The summary plots clearly illustrated the magnitude and direction (positive or negative) of each feature's influence on the prediction of heart disease. SHAP dependence plots further uncovered interaction effects between key features such as "cholesterol", "resting ECG results", and "exercise-induced angina". Fundamentally, the purpose of SHAP values is to give each feature a numerical value that illustrates the extent to which that feature affected the model's prediction for a given data point. SHAP values provide a thorough grasp of feature importance within the model by considering all potential feature combinations and their contributions.

Generally, the SHAP has a beeswarm plot and a waterfall plot, in which the beeswarm plot is used to interpret the features for the entire dataset (global explanation) and the waterfall plot is used to get explanations about rows in the data (local explanation), as depicted in Figs. 6.17 and 6.18. In the beeswarm plot, the **summary_plot()** function is used to rank the features according to their average SHAP values, placing the most significant features at the top and the least significant ones at the bottom. This facilitates comprehension of how each feature affects the predictions made by the model. Also, in the waterfall plot, using the *waterfall (explanation [188])* is used to explain instance 188 along with its importance corresponding to the target class. The decision plot can show how each feature affects a model's prediction step-by-step for an instance or numerous samples. It makes the cumulative impact of features from the model's base value (anticipated prediction) to the final output apparent and comprehensible, as depicted in Fig. 6.19.

LIME explains the model's prediction by perturbing the input and training an interpretable

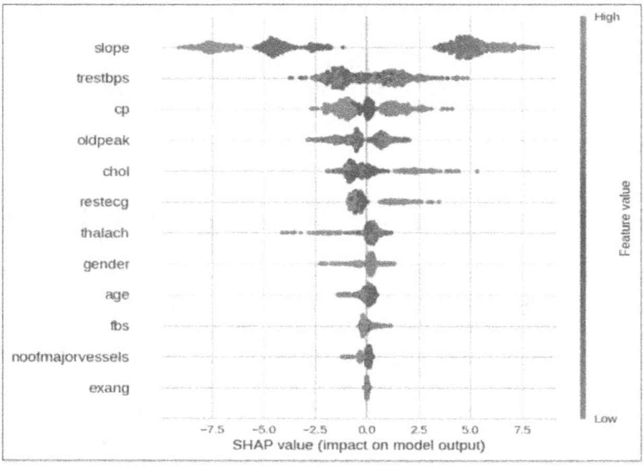

Figure 6.17: The features' global interpretation with the summary plot for global explanation of SHAP

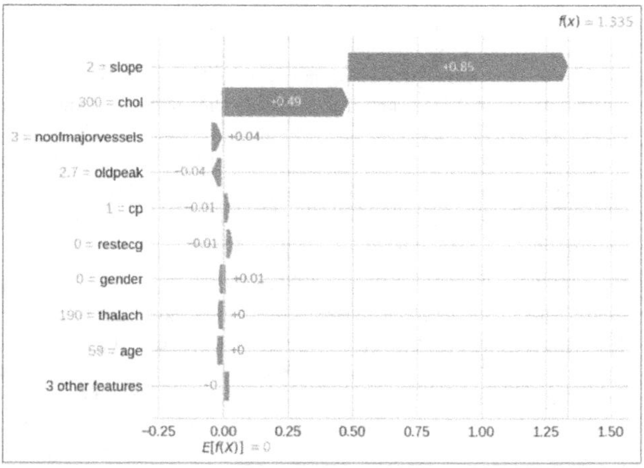

Figure 6.18: The waterfall feature interpretation for local explanation of SHAP

model locally around the prediction. It helps clinicians or decision-makers understand how a model came to a specific decision for a single patient instance. In this study, LIME is used to explain selected instances classified as heart disease positive (1) or negative

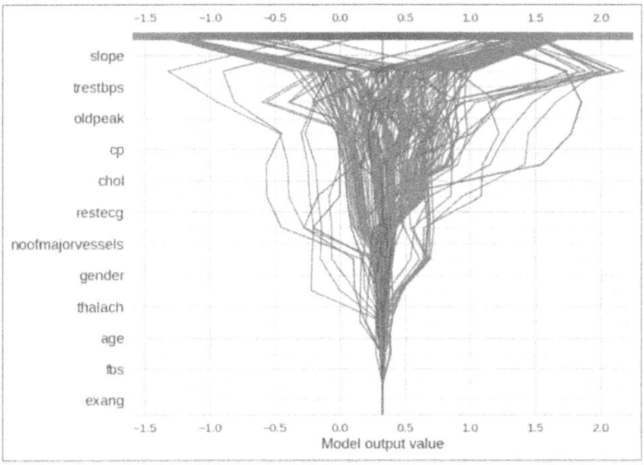

Figure 6.19: The SHAP decision plot of features

(0), confirming the reliability of features like "chest pain" type, "fasting blood sugar", and "maximum heart rate" in contributing to the predictions. LIME visualizations offered intuitive bar charts showing which features pushed the model towards or away from a certain class.

LIME emphasises clarifying the model's predictions for certain instances rather than providing an exhaustive understanding of the model over the whole dataset. Two steps are followed to establish the LIME explainer: importing the Lime module and adapting it with LimeTabularExplainer() using the target and training data. The mode is configured for classification during this phase, consistent with the tasks being performed. The LGBM classifier is used to build and display a LIME explanation for the 188 for "class 1" and 88 for "class 0" data instances of test data. It also presents the final feature contribution towards the target class. The three primary components of the result are the actual value for each feature, the contributions of the features, and the predictions made by the model. The 88th instance of "class 0" and the 188th instance of "class 1" in the text data are predicted with 100% confidence, represented in Figs. 6.20 and 6.21.

The insights and significance of both SHAP and LIME validated the effectiveness of the chosen features, as a result strengthening the feature selection technique. These tools not only confirmed the efficacy of the classifiers but also improved model interpretability and transparency. These are essential for medical professionals to embrace data-driven decision-support systems. The findings underscore the significance of domain-specific risk factors and offer therapeutic insight into the contribution of various features to the risk of heart disease.

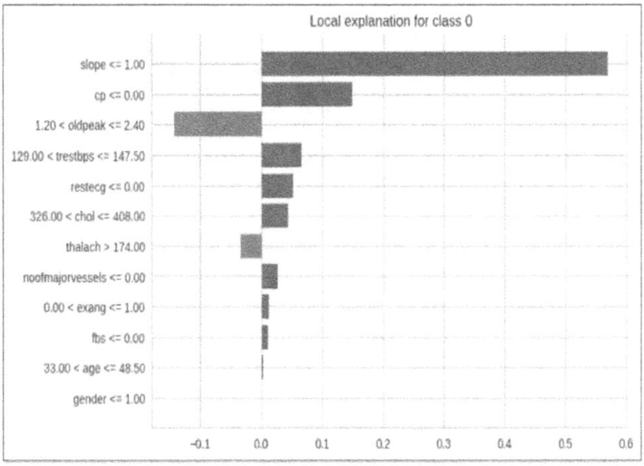

Figure 6.20: The features interpretation with the help of LIME for the class 0 of 88th instance

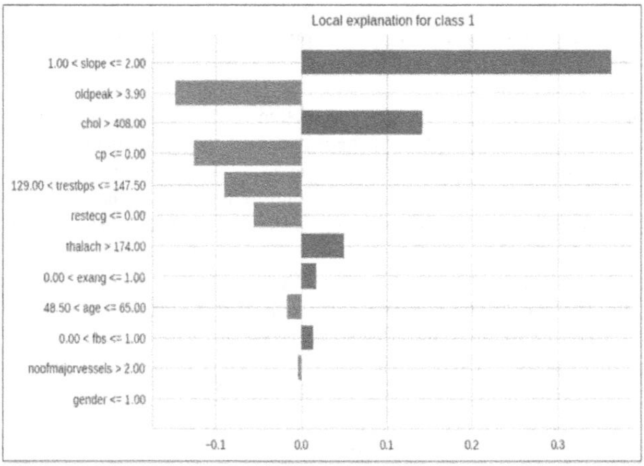

Figure 6.21: The features interpretation with the help of LIME for the class 1 of 188th instance

6.7 Addressing Feature Selection and XAI for Accurate and Interpretable HDP

The effectiveness of HDP models depends not only on predictive accuracy but also on their interpretability and clinical reliability. In this context, this subsection addresses three critical aspects: (i) the role of feature selection techniques in improving accuracy and interpretability, (ii) a comparative assessment of filter, wrapper, and embedded feature selection methods, and (iii) the integration of XAI techniques to enhance transparency and clinical usability of prediction models.

6.7.1 Impact of Feature Selection on Accuracy and Interpretability

Feature selection techniques such as LASSO, RFE, and tree-based importance methods play a vital role in enhancing the predictive accuracy of heart disease models. By removing irrelevant, redundant, or noisy features, these techniques reduce model complexity and mitigate overfitting, particularly in high-dimensional clinical datasets. LASSO performs embedded feature selection by shrinking less informative coefficients to zero, resulting in compact and interpretable feature subsets. RFE, a wrapper-based method, iteratively eliminates features based on classifier performance, preserving those with the highest predictive contribution. Tree-based models, including RF and GB classifiers, provide intrinsic feature importance measures based on impurity reduction. Experimental results in this study demonstrate that models trained on selected features achieve comparable or superior accuracy compared to full-feature models, while also exhibiting reduced variance and improved generalization across validation folds.

6.7.2 Comparative Analysis of Feature Selection Methods

A systematic comparison of filter, wrapper, and embedded feature selection methods reveals notable differences in performance, robustness, and interpretability. Filter methods such as chi-square, mutual information gain, and Fisher score are computationally efficient and dataset-independent, making them suitable for preliminary dimensionality reduction. However, they do not capture feature interactions and are less effective in optimizing predictive performance. Wrapper methods, particularly RFE and BorutaShap, directly optimize feature subsets for a given classifier and generally yield higher accuracy, albeit at increased computational cost. Embedded methods, including LASSO, integrate feature selection within the model training process, offering a balanced trade-off between performance and interpretability. In this study, embedded and wrapper-based approaches consistently outperformed filter methods, achieving higher accuracy and stability while identifying clinically meaningful risk factors. These findings highlight the importance of selecting appropriate feature selection strategies based on both predictive objectives and clinical interpretability requirements.

6.7.3 Integration of XAI for Clinical Transparency

To further enhance model transparency and trustworthiness, XAI techniques such as SHAP and LIME are integrated with feature-selected models. SHAP provides both global and local explanations by quantifying the contribution of each feature to the model's predictions, enabling an understanding of overall risk factor influence as well as patient-specific decision pathways. LIME complements this by generating local surrogate models that explain individual predictions, making the outputs more accessible to clinicians. The explainability analysis confirmed that the features selected through LASSO, RFE, and BorutaShap align with established clinical risk factors for heart disease, thereby reinforcing the validity of the predictive models. Although counterfactual explanations are not explicitly implemented, the framework supports their future inclusion to illustrate how minimal changes in patient attributes could alter risk outcomes. Overall, the integration of feature selection with XAI transforms black-box ML models into interpretable and clinically actionable decision-support systems.

In summary, this subsection demonstrates that the combined application of advanced feature selection techniques and XAI significantly improves the accuracy, interpretability, and clinical relevance of HDP models. Also, it provides a systematic comparison of feature selection paradigms and validates their outputs through XAI tools. This study addresses key challenges in predictive healthcare modelling and provides a transparent, reliable framework suitable for real-world clinical decision-making.

6.8 Key Findings and Summary

This final section summarizes the most important findings from the complete evaluation of feature selection methods and classification models for HDP. Advanced feature selection and XAI algorithms improve performance, interpretability, and comparative findings. This shows that data-driven selection techniques and interpretable ML can create reliable and accurate medical decision-support systems.

1. A total of 15 machine learning classifiers are methodically deployed to a real-world heart disease dataset to determine baseline prediction performance.

2. Sophisticated data preprocessing, incorporating normalization, categorical encoding, and SMOTETomek for addressing class imbalance, considerably enhanced model efficiency and predictive reliability.

3. An extensive evaluation of six feature selection methods, Chi-Square, Mutual Information, Fisher Score, Recursive Feature Elimination (RFE), BorutaShap, and Lasso Regression, exhibited significant enhancements in predicting accuracy and interpretability.

4. Among feature selection techniques, RFE and Fisher score are identified as the most effective in reducing dimensionality while maintaining essential predictive features with an accuracy of 99.54%.

5. Classifiers such as RF, XGB, LGBM, and HGB consistently outperformed others in performance across both comprehensive and reduced feature sets.
6. The integration of Explainable AI (XAI) tools, SHAP and LIME, facilitated transparent model interpretation, explaining the individual contributions of features and assisting informed clinical conclusions.
7. Feature selection mitigated overfitting, decreased computing expenses, and improved model generalization across the dataset.

In summary, the chapter introduced a comprehensive heart disease prediction framework using multiple ML classifiers and innovative feature selection methods. On a real-world dataset, the study compared filter, wrapper, and embedding feature selection approaches on predictive model performance. After deploying 15 classifiers on full and reduced feature sets, models trained on important features beat those using the complete feature space. RFE, Fisher score, and BorutaShap had the most powerful prediction features of the six methods tested. Further, SHAP and LIME explainability tools revealed how different features affected model predictions, improving interpretability and clinical applicability. The chapter concludes that a combination of effective feature selection, robust classification algorithms, and explainability techniques can substantially improve the performance and trustworthiness of predictive systems in heart disease risk assessment.

The thesis now transitions to its final chapter, having systematically addressed all defined research objectives across the preceding chapters. This includes a hyperparameter-tuned ensemble heart disease prediction framework in Chapter 3, as well as the risk prediction frameworks for coronary heart disease and advanced ensemble and deep learning techniques in Chapter 4. Moreover, an assessment of the risk factors of heart-failure patients' mortality prediction using automatic feature selection approaches in Chapter 5. Finally, a comprehensive feature selection and explainability approach in heart disease prediction is discussed in Chapter 6.

The forthcoming Conclusion Chapter 7 can capture the principal findings, summarize the overall contributions, and outline future research directions with limitations to enhance intelligent clinical decision-making systems in cardiovascular healthcare.

www.ingramcontent.com/pod-product-compliance
Lightning Source LLC
LaVergne TN
LVHW010720061126
851857LV00014B/1281
* 9 7 8 1 9 6 2 1 1 6 5 5 8 *